MODERN CATALOGUING
SYSTEMS AND PRACTICES

MODERN CATALOGUING
SYSTEMS AND PRACTICES

R. S. KHOCHAR

1999
DISCOVERY PUBLISHING HOUSE
New Delhi-110002

Reprinted - 2018

First Published - 1999

ISBN: 978-81-7141-460-4

Modern Cataloguing
(Systems and Practices)

Published by:
DISCOVERY PUBLISHING HOUSE PVT. LTD.
4383/4B, Ansari Road, Darya Ganj
New Delhi-110 002 (India)
Phone: +91-11-23279245, 43596064-65
Fax: +91-11-23253475
E-mail: discoverypublishinghouse@gmail.com
sales@discoverypublishinggroup.com
web: www.discoverypublishinggroup.com

Printed at:
Infinity Imaging Systems
Delhi

Preface

Libraries have long sought technological aids to facilitate and enhance their services. The introduction of the typewriter into libraries was a revolutionary concept in the late 1800s. Innovations ranging from printing presses to micro-computers have effected a wide spectrum of library operations, extending from how an item is described, to how it is circulated to the reader, and even to the format in which it is read. *Modern Cataloguing: Systems and Practices* text available to modern library. This book is a ready reference to the history of library information and gives practical, essential data on technical support systems, on-line public access catalogues, information retrieval systems, inter-library lending bibliographic utilities in reference and much more. *Modern Cataloguing: Systems and Practices* issues and aspects connected with library information. For readers of every level of involvement, *Modern Cataloguing: Systems and Practices* is a comprehensive treatment of expanding technology and human intervention. Modern Cataloguing: Systems and Practices is a process that will touch every library facility to one degree or another, so this book can aid every librarian and administrator in coming to terms with the issues that must be faced and decisions that must be made concerning for the library.

Editor

CONTENTS

1
Cataloguing Systems

The principal activity of cataloguing systems remains the production of catalogue cards, but the availability of high-speed printers driven by computers has sparked a remarkable revival of interest in an older way of presenting cataloguing information, the book catalogue. Other printed products, created usually as by products rather than as a primary goal, include spine labels, book plates, book pockets (or labels for placement on book pockets), and book cards for use in either manual or automated circulation systems. In recent years, there has also been a growing recognition that substantial economic benefits would result if cataloguing data could be provided to individuals libraries in a timely fashion from a centralised source, thus lowering the cost of the intellectual effort of cataloguing in the individual libraries; this in turn has resulted in an increased emphasis on the ability to search centralised cataloguing "data bass", usually via terminals linked to computers.

Other function performed by cataloguing systems include

1. Creation of worksheets for cataloguing, or for input of cataloguing data;

2. Prompting of system operators, typists or cataloguers by displaying possible input "tags" nothing misspellings and illogical combinations of data, and leading operators from one step to the next;

3. Maintenance of name and subject authority files, i.e., lists of terms used in the system, the sources of the terms, and the cross-references made to and from the terms;
4. Production of catalogue cross-reference cards;
5. Provision for editing of data for corrections and revisions;
6. Arrangement of entries in filling sequence, both for catalogue cards and book catalogues;
7. Controlling the movement or location of material, during cataloguing or physical preparation, or while in a cataloguing arrearage;
8. Ordering of catalogue cards from a central source;
9. Selective listing of catalogue records by specified criteria, such as subject, geographical area covered, data of publication, or combinations of such criteria.

The mechanical means used to perform these functions have generally followed the technological developments described, but with some important differences and additions. The following types are identifiable:

1. Systems based on unit record equipment;
2. Systems based on automatic typewriters and associated equipment driven by punches tape, magnetic tape, or punched cards;
3. Systems using card-actuated sequential cameras;
4. Off-line batch-processing systems using computers;
5. On-line systems using various types of terminals for searching for initiating catalogue card or book catalogue production (with the production itself

usually done off-line); and sometimes for reference by users to the catalogue data.

This chapter discusses the first three categories, as well as off-line systems implemented before the development of the MARC (Machine-Readable cataloguing) Project at the Library of congress.

Cataloguing systems based on unit record equipment

The earliest cataloguing applications used it record equipment to produce catalogues in book form. Typically, the catalogue information was keypunched, and the resulting punched cards were then sorted into filing sequence (either manually or with the assistance of mechanical sorters) and passed through a tabulator to produce printed pages. In many cases, these printed pages were photographed and then reproduced by offset printing to provide a large number of copies of the catalogue. The method is simple, and once created the machine record in be roused many times. There are marked disadvantages to this method, however:

1. Large files of punched cards must be kept in sequence and handled manually every time a catalogue is reduced, or when additional records are sorted into the file;
2. The typography available is primitive, without lowercase letters, diacritics, or special characters;
3. Only a limited amount of data can be placed on each card, so either extremely brief entries must be used, or multiple cards must be used for each entry, with the cards tied to-gether by a special number created for each entry and punched in each card;
4. Only the simplest filing arrangements can be handled mechanically; the rest must either be done by hand, or simplified filing rules must be adopted.

Despite these limitations, a large umber of book catalogues have been produced in this manner. The Library of Congress began experimenting with the process in 1946, and the catalogue of Serial Titles Newly Received (now called New Serial Titles), which the library began publishing in 1950, was probably the first successful, nonexperimental punched-card catalogue. Only a year later, in 1951, the King Country (Washington) Public Library system began a book catalogue system with separate catalogues for each individual library, supplemented by weekly lists. The punched cards were reproduced on an IBM 513 Reproducer for as many added entries as needed, arranged in the desired sequence, then run though an IBM 402 tabulator to produce the pages. Only one punched card was used for each book producing what later came to be called a "short-title" catalogue or "book list".

Similar catalogues were produced by the University of Rochester, the New York State Library, and a number of special libraries. In most cases, the book form was not intended as a replacement for the library's traditional more available to widely scattered patrons. At Rochester, for example, the "primary purpose" was to put an accurate list of all books and journals in the science libraries on the desk of each member of the faculty and research staff in the departments served by each library. Not every library keeps its card catalogue, however; since the 1960s, the Lake Country (Indiana) public Library has relied entirely on a brief-entry book catalogue produced on an IBM 403 with 15 part paper. The catalogue is in three sections author, title, and subject— which simplifies sorting and consultation. A closed-circuit teletype system connecting the 14 branches and their Technical Processing Center is used to provide additional information, as well as for other purposes.

Perhaps the earliest example of a machine-produced book catalogue with reasonably full entries was the Los Angeles Country Public Library catalogue produced in 1955. At that time, there were 114 branches and services outlets, only 25 of which had card catalogues, and even these were incomplete and softly to maintain. Meeting with the branch librarians resulted in decisions to include the full author, full title, edition (other than the first), data of publication, volumes if more than one, and a short annotation where appropriate for the subject catalogues were issued in eight parts: for adults, there were separate author, title, subject, fiction, and foreign language catalogues; and for children there were separate author, title, and subject catalogues. The subject catalogues were the most complete, as they included annotations as well as "see" and "see also" references, and analytic for anthologies. The author catalogues contained most of the bibliographic data except for annotations, and the title catalogues were even briefer—a straight alphabetic listing, with only the authors and class numbers given in addition to the titles.

A number of other public libraries adopted the Los Angeles Country system or one similar to it in the early 1960s, including the Montgomery Country (Mary land) Public Library, which (in a noteworthy example of library cooperation) was able to obtain from Los Angeles Country a full set of the latter's book catalogues, the subject heading code book, a detailed description of keypunching procedures, 220,000 subject heading cards, and even the wired control panels for the IBM 407 tabulator to be used! Studies indicated that the cost of the Montgomery Country catalogue was about the same as its card catalogues, with the added advantages of multiple copies for the branches (and incidentally for the country's secondary and elementary schools) and centralised control of error correction and filling.

A few unit record cataloguing systems produced catalogue cards instead of book catalogues. One example is the library processing center for the Albuquerque Public School system, which in 1964 began producing catalogue cards, book cards, and labels on a 407. Most unit record systems, however, concentrated on book catalogs.

Automatic typewriter systems

In contrast, automatic typewriter systems were used a almost exclusively for production of catalogue cards. In such systems, keying the data does not produce punched cards: instead, a spool of either punched paper tape or magnetic tape is produced, and printing is done not on a separate machine like the tabulator, but on the same machine that does the input—that is, on an automatic typewriter. The primary advantage of such systems is the improved typography: lower case as well as upper case is normally available, diacritical marks can be used, and some such systems subject headings in red, mimicking manually typed cards to such an extent that they are indistinguishable. Other advantages are the elimination of the need for great care in keeping sets of punched cards together, and the ability of most libraries to justify having the equipment housed in the library for its exclusive use, rather than having to depend on a centralised data processing facility for machine time and assistance.

Most of these early systems used Flexowriters (paper tape machines) and auxiliary devices that made it possible to program most of the operations involved in producing sets of catalogue cards. The U.S. Naval Postgraduate School in Monterey, California began using such a systems in the mid-1950s and the California State Library in 1958. In the latter system, the cataloguing data were type on the Flexowriters, which simultaneously prepared two tapes, one for the unit card data and a second one containing the added entry headings. The unit card tape was spliced it no a loop and placed on an auxiliary paper tap reader, the heading type was placed on a second reader. The unit card tape to reading the heading tape at the proper points in the operation. The heading tape contained similar codes for carriage returns and indentations, to that the headings as well as the rest of the data were located properly on continues catalogue card stock. Later, the continuous stock was separated into individual cards. The University of Missouri began a more extensive Flexowriter system in 1963, and developed a special cutter to separate individual cards from the continuous stock, thereby eliminating the objectionable serrated edges associated with pre-perforated stock. At one time as many as 250,000 cards per year were being produced with the system at an average cost of six cents per card. A similar system, based on Missouri's was developed at Washington University and began operation in 1964. All operation codes were inserted automatically by the machine itself from 'program' tapes, so that the operators were relived of the need to memorise codes and detailed procedures. Programs were also developed which automatically adjusted the spacing of the data for exceptional circumstances; if an added entry heading required three or more lines, for example, the rest of the catalogue card information was automatically lowered the required number of spaces. As the Flexowriters typed the main entry cards during the automatic production phase, they also produced yet another tape, which was used to create several by-products of the system. The tape was accumulated on a self-winding reel until cards, in punched-card format, for use in an automated circulation system. Next, the tape accompanied the book truck to the processing room, where it was placed on a specially built Flexowriter, equipped with a Se-Lin labeling device, which automatically produced the labels for the books. The by-product tape could also be passed through the 047 to produce decks of punched cards for processing by computer to produce accession lists and specialised bibliographies, although in actual practice this capacity was never used except for demonstration purposes. Other Flexowriter systems were installed at the University of Colorado, the University of British Columbia, Cleveland State University, and Georgia Institute of Technology, latter two based on the Washington University and Missouri systems. Another brand of automatic typewriter—the Dura Machine 10—formed the basis for similar systems at Boston University and UCLA. Virtually all of the automatic typewriter systems were later abandoned, how-ever, because of constant difficulties in keeping the machines running properly and because of their relatively slow speeds compared to computer-driven printers.

A closely related group of machines called the IBM 870 Document Writing System was used by a number of libraries in the early 1960s to produce catalogue cards. The machinery was operated by punched cards instead of paper tape, but in other respects similar to Flexowriter systems. The Los Angeles City Schools began using the 870 system in 1962, with the initial goal of reducing serious back-logs in catalogue card production. The backlogs were indeed eliminated, but for this type of application. The backlogs were indeed eliminated, but for this type of application the machines had many of the same drawbacks as tabulating equipment. Keeping sets of punched cards together as tabulating equipment. The librarian in charge saw this not only as an operational difficulty but also as an educational problem: "Since the cards are produced for teaching-learning situations as well as for finding purposes," she pointed out, "this is a serious drawback, especially since there is an increase in the study of foreign languages in the schools." The cost per set of catalogue cards for the new system was about the same as for the previous manual system.

Other 870 systems were implemented the following year, at the Anaheim (California) Public Library Yale University's Medical School, but by the mid-1960s the 870 was largely superseded by IBM's new 1050 system a similar set of equipment that could use either punched cards or paper tape (Or both), and could be operated independently or connected to a computer. It also used a ball-shaped printing mechanism like that of the IBM Selectric typewriters which permitted the substitution of interchangeable printing elements, and thus different type fonts; a special typing elements, and thus designed for library use. Early library users of the 1050 equipment were the Washington University School of Medicine and the University of Chicago; both of these later abandoned the equipment, however, because of frequent mechanical difficulties.

By the late 1960s, the 1050 system was itself superseded by another new IBM system, the MTST (for Magnetic Tape Selectric Type-Writer). As the name implies, it is also based on IBM's Selectric typewriter, and operates by means of magnetic tape rather that either punched cards or paper tape. The equipment has been widely used for the production of catalogue cards, using procedures similar to the earlier Flexowriter systems described above. The University of California at Irvine installed such a system in 1968, Cornell University in 1969, and the University of Houston in 1970. At Cornell and Houston, however, the MTSTs have since been replaced because of their cost, and Houston has installed a set of similar automatic typewriters called CPTs at about two thirds the cost of MTSTs. Tape oriented automatic typewriters are becoming increasingly popular for business office use, and several models competitive with the MTSTs have recently become available. On unique system of historical interest should also be mentioned here. In 1961 the Itek Corporation developed a system for the Air Force Cambridge Research Library in Bedford, Massachusetts, which used flexowriters for input of the catalogue data and for printing of the catalogue cards, but not for programming or arrangement of the cataloguing information. Instead, a special prototype machine called the "crossfiler" was used to expand and arrange the data after input and before printing it out on the Flexowriters. Input techniques were based on what its developers called a "machine-interpretable natural format," that is, the natural typing operations (carriage returns, tabulating shifts, and spaces) were used in a fixed sequence to format the data during processing as well. The technique was simple and effective, reducing greatly the amount of coding that had to be added to the record and in this respect presaging the development of "format recognition" by the MARC project at the Library of Congress some years later.

Sequential card camera systems

While the development of catalogue card systems was in a phase dominated by automatic typewriters, book catalogue systems passed from the unit record era to the use of another type of specialised equipment, the card-actuated sequential camera, some examples of which are still in use at this writing. There are several varieties, but in all such systems, the cataloguing data is typed directly onto cards, and lower-case chains and computer-driven photocomposition devices has lessened this problem. One of the earliest computerised catalogue card systems was developed in the early 1960s as a by-product of an information retrieval system called SHARP (Ships Analysis and Retrieval Project), a joint venture of the Navy's Bureau of Ship Technical Library and the Devia Taylor model Basin Applied Mathematics

Laboratory. In addition to subject searches and information retrieval, various printed products were generated, among them catalogue cards for all documents entered in the system by 1963, IBM had also begun to produce catalogue cards using computers. From the standpoint of its influence on later developments, however, the most influential of the early systems was without doubt the developed at Yale University. The Yale Medical Library had begun producing cards on an IBM 870 system as early as 1963. By 1964, the library was using an IBM 1401 computer to "expand" the catalogue data and create a full set of punched cards, with a "decklet" of cards representing all the information of each catalogue card in the set. These punched cards were then used to drive the 870 system described earlier. Later the same year, an IBM 709 computer was also incorporated into the system to sort the data into filling order before the cards were punched. By 1965, the library and abandoned the 870, and was using the computer printer with a special chain containing an expanded character set to print the cards. This system was used until 1971, when it was finally discontinued, for two reasons: maintaining the growing data base on magnetic tapes (as opposed to disks) had become increasingly cumbersome, and the computer center had brought in an IBM 360 computer to replace the 7094 for which the system was designed. By this time, personnel at Yale had come to feel that systems designed for one library along were rapidly becoming obsolete, and that the expense of reprogramming the system for the 360 could not therefore be justified.

Off-line book catalogue systems

Although the general procedures are the same, computerised book catalogue systems differ from card production systems in several important ways: storage of the bibliographic data between issues of the book catalogue is normally required; entries input between editing must be interfiled; and arrangement of individual entries in the desired filing sequence for book catalogs is complex, whereas most card systems arrange, if at all, only a relatively small number of cards in rough filing sequence before printing them out. Early book catalogue systems were characterised by the use of elaborate input coding forms, ruled into 80 columns like an IBM card. Catalogers or their assistants were required to print each letter carefully in a box, and to learn and assign a large number of codes identifying particular data elements. Later systems used worksheets with the codes (or "tags" as they same to be called) already pre-printed on the forms, and still later systems employed techniques which allowed conventional catalogue cards to be "edited," that is, to have the tags merely added to data already printed on catalogue cards or slips.

Processing of the catalogue entries after input normally involves not only duplication of the entries under each heading, but also a significant amount of computer editing (nothing missing data or illogical coding, for example) and several proofreading and error correction cycles. The computer must also sort entries into multiple sequences, since most book catalogs are divided catalog—that is, instead of being arranged with all entries in a single filling sequence, the entries are divided into an author catalog, a title catalog, and a subject catalog, or some similar combination.

When all of the data have been edited, proofread, corrected "expanded", sorted and arrange in the proper sequence, the final step-production—can begin. This may be on a conventional computer line printer (sometimes with a special uppercase and lower-case chain); with a computer-driven photocomposition device; or on a computer output microfilm (COM) device.

The earliest project to use computer line printers to produce full-scale book catalogue was also one of the most successful. In 1963, the University of Toronto was asked by the Ontario government to develop basic collections of approximately 35,000 volumes each, complete with the necessary catalogs, for five Ontario universities. In the ONULP (Ontario New Universities Library Project) that resulted, complete bibliographic information for the volumes purchased (including even the thickness of each volume) was keypunched; stored on magnetic tape by an IBM 1401 computer; edited, sorted and arranged on an IBM 7094 computer; and printed out in book catalogue form on the 1401. The computer printer was equipped with a specially designed chain which contained uppercase and lowercase letters and a large number of diacritical marks (100 character in all). The computer print-out was reduced to 60 per cent of the original before printing plates were produced so that more information would be contained on each page. Programs were written in COBOL (Common Business Oriented Language), so that the five new institutions could modify them more easily at a later data if they wished, and to make the initial programming task easier and more convenient, but the resulting programming task easier and more convenient, but the resulting programs were unusually lengthy in terms of processing time, a common problem with COBOL programs.

Another early computerised book catalogue project was especially significant in terms of the formation and programming techniques employed. The Boeing "SLIP" system was one of the first to provide a generalised set of programs which could produce a variety of printed products with only minor change in the specifications in -cooperated inn the input to the system, and it was also one of the earliest to use so-called "table-driven" programs for library automation purpose. A total of twelve different tables were constructed by the system's programs in the computer memory, and used to sort input data into varies categories, depending both on the nature of the data (whether it was author, title, subject or imprint data, for example) and the eventual use to be made of it. At the production stage, the programs then used the tables to rearrange the data by the broad group specified for the final product, and to arrange data within these groupings by filing sequence.

The book catalogue produced by the system was divided into an author catalogue and a title-subject catalog, the latter containing both conventional subject headings and "alternate title entries... generated by rotation of the complete titles about the normal indexing locus, the left margin these so-called "permuted" titles, which placed various significant words in the titles at the filing piston and thus used the titles themselves to construct a different sort of subject approach, were to become common features of later systems. A modified form of the Library of Congress filing rules was used for the book catalog. Titles and permuted titles were sorted full length, continuing on to the first six characters of the author's name if necessary; similarly authors were sorted on their full length, continuing into the first six characters of the title if necessary.

Friden Flexowriters were used for input, because the typewritten copy created at the same time made proofreading and correction easier, but the system was also designed to accept punched-card input. The paper tape from the Flexowriters was converted to magnetic tape using an IBM 1401 computer, the subsequent processing being done on an IBM 7094 computer as in the Toronto system.

In retrospect, one aspect of the Florida Atlantic system that seems especially curious is that despite its elaborate coding forms and input procedures, no proofing or editing procedures were established and no correction program was written. Not surprisingly, the first edition of the catalogue contained a remarkable number of errors; blind cross-references abounded, and William Shakespeare "appeared in at least four different places in the subject catalogue and at least four in the author catalogue due to variant spellings." More serious was the fact that although its automaton efforts were well publicised before implementation, no a attempt was made to inform the rest of the library community of its subsequent experiences.

By contrast, the difficulties encountered by the Washington University School of Medicine Library its book catalogue project have been frankly and fully publicised. The first WUSM catalogue was issued in 1965, and contained only entries cataloged between January and September of that year. The computer print-out used for production of the pages was not photographically reduced in size before the printing masters were made, so even for the relatively small number.

The staff, on the other hand, found dealing with the new system a serious difficulty. Part of the problem apparently arose from the fact that the system had been designed with the assumption that bibliographic information generated at the acquisitions step could be used for the. Catalogue step without rekeyboarding, but in the experience of this library idea did not work out. Series might be ordered under a series title, and cataloguing personnel were then faced with the necessity of expanding the single record into the necessary number of individual ones; on the other hand, acquisitions personnel might create separate records for volumes ordered separately, but considered by cataloguing as part of a set.

Another problem noted was the difficulty of changing printed records; once the catalogue had been produced, the records were there until the catalogue had been reprinted or superseded. The Nursing Schools Library was disbanded, but the records for it in the catalogue could not be readily deleted, so "it became necessary to paste a general statement on the cover of each that updating." 44 Problems also were attributed to the small size of the computer memory used; the Dental Library holding were to be added, for example, but only by inputting them little could this be accomplished. After four months or struggling, the library abandoned the book catalogue system entirely. Fortunately (and wisely in this case), the production of catalogue cards had been continued all along. By the mid-1960s, computer-produced book catalogs also became available from commercial firms. One of the first libraries to obtain a book catalogue in this way was the Baltimore Country Public Library, which contracted with Documentation, Inc., of Bethesda Mary land for one containing the 50,000 entries cataloged by the library since 1959. Input was done on Flexowriters, processing was done on the firm's IBM 1401 and 1410 computers, and the printing was done with the same "expanded character set" printing chain mentioned earlier. The first catalogue indicated which work were held by which branches, but these location indicators were later eliminated.

The time consumed and the cost involved in updating them were out of all proportion to their-use (and) in addition they were never accurate. If a book is not in one agency it can be reserved through intra-library loan and under ideal conditions, it can be in the hands of the borrower with two days. If a borrower has to have the book immediately he can call intra-library loan and get the names of the branches owning it. He can then call the branch and have it held for him to pick up.

Some 250 copies of the catalogue were produced, over half of them for the country's 125 public schools. By 1971, at least two other public library systems in the area using the BCPL data base for titles also in their libraries, thus avoiding the costs of converting these entries to machine-readable form.

The St. Louis Junior College District reported in 1965 that it had contracted with the Alanar division of Bro-Dart Industries sot produce a similar catalogue with brief entries. A code number was added to each entry, referring the user to fuller information on the same titles in a photographic reproduction of Library estimated that approximately $9, 000 per years was saved in salaries formerly required for clerical filing or cards, plus about $2, 250 per year through the elimination of catalogue card reproduction.

Although book catalogs were (and have continued to be) of interest primarily to public libraries, Toronto and Florida Atlantic were not the only universities to intimate book catalogue projects during this period. In 1964, Stanford University had commissioned one of the landmark studies in this field, 50 comparing the costs of various methods of book catalogue with the costs of a card catalog. 51 Based on these studies, a project was begun to produce a book catalogue for the Meyer Memorial Undergraduate Library, which was scheduled to open in 1966. The first edition was produced in time for the opening, and subsequent editions have been produced annually, supplemented on a quarterly basis. The first editing contained entries for 25,000 titles and by the fourth edition in 1969 the total had reached 60,000 a limit of 100,000 is planned.

Input is by punched cards, with an IBM 7090 used for the sorting and a 1401 to print, again employing the special printing chain mentioned earlier. A cost analysis based on the 41,000-title second edition issued in 1967 indicated total costs of $38,670, some percent more than original estimates but very close to the estimates made during the system design stage.

Photocomposed book catalogs

As an alternative to printing the final page copy on a computer printer, a computer-driven photocomposition device may also be used, Photocomposer of this type read information from tape and by projecting an electron beam on the surface of a cathode ray tube produce pictures of each character in turn, much like the images on a television screen. These images are copied on photosensitive paper at a very high rate of speed (several thousand characters per second) and at a very high resolution (hundreds of lines per inch). The legibility of the characters, combined with the fact that the resulting pages are much more attractive and readable that those produced by computer line-printer. The costs of this method prevented widespread use in the earlier days of book catalogues, but the cost per page has now been reduced to the point that the number of catalogs produced in this fashion is rapidly increasing.

A good example of the transition from computer print-out to photocomposition and an interesting use of the book catalogue technique are represented by the Harvard University shelflist project. The Widener Library of Harward College as late as 1964 still had its shelflist in the old sheaf form common in the nineteenth century—that is, had written in loose-leaf volumes rather than on cards. This form its size (some 1.6 million entries in 200 main classes) made it difficult to maintain and almost impossible for scholar to consult. Realising the potential value to libraries and scholars of a classified listing of Widener's holdings that would be more readily accessible, Harvard began in 1964 to convert Widener shelflist to a printed catalog, with indexes by another and publication date, and with each in a separate volume. The earliest volumes, published in 1965, used standard uppercase-only print-out typography; this was changed to printout using an upper case chain in 1968, and to photocomposition in 1970. All entries are brief, partly because the entries in the original sheet shelflist are brief and partly to reduce cost. An early cost analysis indicated a figure of cents per cent. An early cost analysis indicated a figure of cents per entry for conversion: cent for keypunching and cents of editing. Brief entries also take advantage of the space-saving feature of photocomposition: the print- out volumes averaged 70 entries per page, allowing substantial savings in printing and binding.

2
Retrieval in Online Catalogues

Online Public Acces Catalogues (OPACs) are IR systems used by end-users. Potential OPAC users from a very large population with extremely varied needs and backgrounds. As designers of computerised IR systems, and as specialists in information handling, processing and retrieval, we must be aware of the problems users encounter when interacting with our systems. We should shift our interests from catalogue use studies to catalogues as IR public systems: their usability and ease of use; HCL aspects; end-users; and, ultimately, user information-seeking behaviour.

OPACs and user interaction

There is now a well-known history of OPAC design developments and Hildreth has classified them into three generations. The initial OPAC generation was derived from circulation or cataloguing systems, and gives rather limited access to the bibliographic information. It is essentially based upon pre-coordinate IR principles. Their interfaces simulate traditional catalogues in their forms of access by providing mainly phrase access to separate indexes (subject headings, titles, authors). This is appropriate for known-items searching. The interfaces are usually menu driven. The second-generation OPAC systems are more similar to the commercial IR systems; they provide keyword or free-text access, corresponding to post-coordinate IR principles. Their interfaces are generally command driven, making use of Boolean logic which is well suited for subject searching. The indexes to be searched have to be specified by the user in the search formulation. The first kind of design improvement found in third-generation OPAC systems was to combine the features of the first two OPAC generations by providing both phrase searching and keyword searching in terms of interface this is often achieved by a simplified command language which facilitates user interaction. It leads users through menus and question/ answers as well as commands; the interface has improved help screens and instructions and operations are simplified. This is typified by recent developments of a few systems, such as MELVYL, LCS/WLN at the University of Illionis, and CARL, which now also provide access to other kinds of bibliographic information through their OPAC: accessing monographs as well as journal articles becomes more integrated. MELVYL gives access to the Medline files, CARL searches newspaper clippings, and LCS/WLN uses a PC front-end interface to traditional online systems.

This latter system assists users in the use of the command language; it helps them to build a search strategy offline, with a wealth of help screens and detailed instructions; it executes the resulting search strategy online; it downloads the retrieved references on the Pc and it offers to locate the journal titles in the Illinois University library catalogue. Obviously, offering command languages (and their powerful features, even if simplified) to OPAC users is a long-awaited and welcome trend. Nevertheless, it still presents problems with lack of ease and simplicity of use for a large proportion of users. Many endorsers would not necessarily want to plough through the lengthy text of LCS/WLN University of Illinois front-end's numerous screens. Other systems, either experimental or operational, are trying to overcome these problems using such means as retrieval, linguistic and semantic aids. Some of these improvements are also referred to by Hildreth. These will be reviewed briefly, starting with 'mechanical' devices and moving towards more 'semantically oriented' devices. Whilst the former try to improve the mechanical matching processes, their interface, design does not employ knowledge of the subject area. The latter, however, make use of subject knowledge actively to offer contextual and semantic support in order to assist user interaction.

Retrieval aids

There have been a few attempts at incorporating the knowledge learned from IR research and experimentation to improve conventional boolean retrieval systems. The most well-known systems are CITE and Okapi. They have implemented implicit Boolean searching on natural language input, weighting, and ranking techniques, and relevance feedback from the user. Thus, they enable the user to search without necessarily being knowledgeable about Boolean search formulation and reformulation.

Okapi also offers 'intelligent search sequencing'. This follows automatically various search 'trees', which combine phrase and keyword access and search various indexes simultaneously or consecutively, particularly for author/title searches. It therefore goes beyond an initial matching between the user input and the database indexes. Okapi attempts various further matches using all the information available from the system and the user. The system retrieves as many references as possible without the user having to reformulate his search. Depending on the result, it gives the user either short or full records, or indexes to browse.

Linguistic aids

More recent work done at the Polytechnic of Central London consisted of implementing automatic spelling correction and stemming. The automatic spelling is achieved using sound-matching algorithms and corrects miskeyings and other misspellings by mapping orthographically related words. The sound-matching most significant characters.

The automatic stemming links morphologically related words, hence providing a form of implicit truncation. The Okapi '86 team went some way into considering to what extent a word should be stemmed: keeping the longest possible suffix to start with, then stemming further. Both 'strong' and 'weak' stems are generated and a combinational method is used for term weighting so that the output is ranked. Weak stems get higher weights than strong stems. Spelling variations are incorporated into the weak stemming procedure. When a word does not stem to anything in the index it is then sound matched and looked up in the index for the nearest match.

These design features are basically mechanical devices to improve the system matching processes. They are intended to provide the users with as much and as good retrieval as possible, without them having to learn the search mechanics (e.g., truncation) to do it. The burden to the search interaction has therefore shifted from the user to the system. Some of these features have semantic implications; for example, the implicit truncation may bring in semantically related words, although the underlying mechanism uses morphological principle. Other design improvements are more definitely aimed at improving the semantic aspect of the searching process. They are describe below.

Navigational aids

LCS/WLN at the University of Illinois has implemented a way of leading users from retrieved information to related information that was not initially formulated by the user. It does this by linking relevant records retrieved with free-text words to other records, using their subject headings. It is an interesting attempt at relating free text to controlled vocabulary. This assists the user in navigating through the natural words and the subject authority entries of the database.

CITE, implemented at the National Library of Medicine, also has the same feature: from the user natural input it gives a list of the relevant medical subject headings (MeSH) to be 'weighted' by the user (rather than by the system, as in Okapi). However, the system assumes that the user will be familiar with the medical terminology and the structure of MeSH.

Semantic aids

Well-known suggestions by Pauline Cochrane Atherton and Irene Wormell are to add the back-of-the-book indexes, tables of contents and chapter headings to enrich the subject description of monographs. These have not yet been implemented.

Another area for subject access and semantic improvements is the use of classification schemes. A very interesting experiment was carried out by Karen Markey and Anh Demeyer at the Online Computer Library Center (OCLC). Using the Dewey Decimal Classification (DDC) Schedules and Relative Indexes machine-readable file provided by Forest Press, they tried: (a) to enrich the vocabulary of the database, and (b) to provide for systematic access through the DDC Schedules. by means of a rigorous experimental set-up they proved that the classification schemes and indexes did enrich the database vocabulary and retrieved records not found with the control OPAC system. With the DDC-based experimental OPAC, the user input is related to the class number(s) under which it appears; the system also displays the context of the search input within the classification scheme, emphasizing different 'perspectives' under which that topic is classified.

The class number of retrieved and relevant records could also be used for expanding and retrieving other records other records, as a search 'pivot' (in the same way, LCS/WLN at Illinois University uses subject headings). This design idea has not been implemented.

Work is also currently being done on the use of PRECIS (PREserved context Indexing System) as subject authority or online thesaurus by Juliet Congreve at the Middlesex Polytechnic.

Without actually implementing a full online thesaurus, it is possible to improve the semantics of the system. Okapi '86 does it in a simple way, using look-up tables which handle semantically-related words. A semantic tool can range from a simple stop-list of words to a full subject authority control list. Okapi '86 look-up tables contain three types of entries: stopwords; terms to be treated as equivalent ('child' and 'children'); and certain compound words to be treated as single terms (e.g., 'industrial relations' and 'Great Britain'). This was found to provide more precise and unique matching than stemming.

Other semantically oriented work has been done by Michael Lesk, using the eighteenth-century short title catalogue database at the British Library. He uses various dictionaries (e.g.) The Oxford English Dictionary (OED), Collins and specialised dictionaries) to expand the user query. An inverted file of dictionary definitions is kept, along with the number of overlapped words and their frequencies to enable a weighting procedure. The point of using and linking dictionary definitions is that it gives a large quantity of words which a thesaurus would not offer, and also a wide range of different meanings for the words. The dictionary definitions are called in if the user word(s) do not appear in the file, and bring in related words. If the user input retrieves only a few references, the system gets relevance feedback from the user and expands the query, using the dictionary definitions, to suggest other records to the user.

Summarising remarks

Hildreth states that, 'librarians should learn about (a) the potential of online retrieval, (b) catalogue access issues, and (c) user-system interface problems and promises'. The possible OPAC design developments presented above should help them visualize the various directions that future systems can take. It might also extend the debate beyond the traditional 'catalogue access issues' by introducing categories such as mechanical matching devices and semantic-oriented features.

Any attempt to avoid putting the burden on the user to reformulate and re-enter searches until satisfactory results are obtained is well worth pursuing. Most IR systems still do little to help the user transform in information need to the explicit descriptions understandable by the system. To optimize retrieval results in subject searching, more than one search approach may have to be employed to the over all search strategy. This quotation from Chan, referring to the use of various subject aids (e.g., DDC, keywords, Library of Congress Subject Headings, Library of Congress Classification) seems very appropriate: the process of seeking and identifying information to assist with a problem typically follows a more circuitous, cyclical and unstructured path than the one provided for by strictly matching devices.

The remaining research quotation is, 'How do we choose among all these numerous design features? A way of illustrating this problem is to refer to a recently designed operational OPAC system. This system features

Boolean searching on keywords, relevance feedback based on free text, mixed with Universal Decimal Classification (UDC) numbers. It seems that the design features mentioned above are now taken into account and being incorporated into operational systems. But which, or which combination, is the best and for what purpose?

User interaction

Any improvement is design must also be accompanied by an evaluation of its use and success or failure with the users. Furthermore, any design decision should stem from an understanding of user interaction problems. 'We have seen many information systems which a panel of experts would undoubtedly rate technical successes: however, upon talking to users in the organisations, we hear a different story...products should be more carefully matched to both users' skills and their psychological needs. Evaluation of OPACs has in the past chiefly concentrated on impact studies, public usage, technical and Ir performance and use patterns.

Impact and public usage studies

Impact studies look at how well react to and accept these new computer systems as compared with traditional catalogues, and if they prefer them or not. Public usage studies are concerned with which types of users or do not use the OPAC and the reasons why. These two types of studies are usually carried out using the traditional methods of data gathering, i.e. questionnaires, surveys and focus group interviews.

Performance and use pattern studies

Technical performance studies look at the computer workload, the response time or the required number of terminals. IR performance studies compare search keys versus keyword searching, title searches in OPACs and in card catalogues, or retrieval results using different features.

Use pattern studies monitor the number of known-item versus subject searches, the utilization and success of various search criteria by users, or the patterns of user's errors in searching the OPAC.

These studies use the transaction log analysis method and controlled experiments. The transaction log analysis enables us to monitor real usage and gives data on use patterns. Many case studies of individual systems can be found in the literature. Some cover several of these aspects; see Mitev and Efthimiadis, for example. However, on the whole, they tend to be specific to a system and to a library context. A few studies compare the use of two systems in an experimental manner, in order to support the choice of a system by a particular library.

Of special interest is a recent study which compares keyword subject searching on six operational British University OPACs available through JANET (Joint Academic Network). Two specimen subject searches were carried out on the six OPACs. The number of items retrieved on each were compared, together with whether they were retrieved using title keywords or Library of Congress Subject Headings (LCSH) keywords. The various searching features are surveyed and conclusions are drawn on their merits (e.g, nesting and truncation at Hull, LCSH indexing at Cambridge, phrase searching at Sussex, set creation and truncation at York, reverse chronological display and LCSH at Newcastle).

User interaction studies

In terms of evaluating the use interaction, several areas have been explored: ergonomics studies (screen displays, legibility, typing), ease-of-use studies (ease of searching, usability, search satisfaction), and studies of information seeking behaviour (cognitive aspects, mental processes, search strategies for subject searching and browsing in particular).

Work on the comparative ease of use of two types of user interface has been done. A menu-driven user interface giving access to a hierarchical classification scheme and a command-driven interface were compared in a natural setting. It was concluded that users would rather employ their own words than go through several screens of classified data to choose their topic.

This fast group of evaluation studies has made use of controlled experiments, protocol analysis and talk-around methods. This area is by far the least explored.

Human-computer interaction

First of all, it is worth pointing out that, 'we know that any system architecture has significant and widespread implications for user-friendliness, but we know very little about how to make fundamental architectural decisions differently as a result of an emphasis on human factors. On the whole, HCL research has only touched upon a few aspects of the user interface design. It has looked at hardware problems (keyboards and screen design) and at the very surface of software problems (e.g., command names and menu formats).

Beyond the description of these aspects, HCL is not so much concerned with artificial intelligence (AI) (the task of building a computer to reason as we imagine people do) as with what might be called artificial personality (how to make the computer behave the way we want it to). Ideally, the interface design should be dissociated from the rest of the system to allow for flexibility, adaptability and change.

The design of many interactive systems is often

influenced by our beliefs about the human mind as well as by the traditional (and still essential) criteria of functionality and efficiency.

Nature of HCL

The user interaction has been divided into four levels by Moran: a task level (the IR task in our case); a semantic level (how the objects and the operations on these objects are defined and represented); a syntactic level (what the things are called); and a physical interaction level (how the users can act upon these objects, operations, etc.).

These with which the user can interact with the system is also split according to these levels: how well the task is analysed and dealt with by the system and communicated to the user; how well chosen the objects and operations are in order to perform the task; how well expressed this choice is; and how easy it is to manipulate them.

It is important here to stress the existence of the first two levels (task and semantic). These are often neglected. The last two levels (syntactic and physical) are more often dealt with, perhaps because they can be seen. They are also more easily modified; one can experiment with them and compare them. Although less obvious, the other two levels (task and semantic levels) are just as crucial for a good interface, perhaps even more crucial than the syntactic and physical operation levels.

Direct manipulation

'The interface should be unobtrusive, not interfering or intruding. If the interface itself is noticed, then it stands in a third-person relationship to the objects of interest, and detracts from the directness of engagement.' This idea of 'direct engagement' or 'direct manipulation' is related to (if not issued from) the recent WIMPS developments. Users interact directly with objects represented graphically on the screen, instead of having a conversation about these objects in order to act upon them. The interface is itself a world in which the user can act, and which changes state in response to user actions. The world of interest is explicitly represented. The interface is not an implied intermediary between the user and the world about which things are said. Although this feeling of direct engagement is of critical importance, the actual requirements for producing it are little known.

The purpose of the system is to serve the user, not to use a specific technology and not to be an elegant of programming. The use of icons that look like waste-paper baskets is of questionable value if associated concepts are not supported.

'Metaphor crucially depends on knowing enough about the attributes of the objects in both the central domain and the domain to which it is being likened, to determine what it could possibly make sense to import. The computer is capable of using many arbitrarily complex mappings between symbols— including those displayed on the screen—and the objects, situations and events they refer to. The relationship between what appears on the screen and, for example, a file being edited, is non-retrieval: it is a copy that is being manipulated (although this is not apparent). Failing to save it, a common mistake, may result in the loss of many hours' work. Such relationships become more sophisticated with the use of icons and customized direct manipulation workbenches. There is potential for confusion between actions performed on the object itself and its manifestation in one of several displays. The relationship between what happens to an object and what happens to its screen manifestation has to be accepted by a novice user as arbitrary.

Icons and OPACs

One example of the use of icons in the context of OPACs is the system designed by Benest et al. at York University Department of Computer Science. In it, the user is first offered a picture of the indexes the user can search (Subject, Author, KWIC, Classmark, personal indexes). Each index is represented as a book on a shelf, and the user can select one with a mouse. The chosen index is then displayed on the screen as an open book, two pages at a time, and the use can flick through these pages of index entries alphabetically.

There is a way of skipping to a particular letter if required, by selecting a letter among an A to Z sequence on the side. Once an index entry is selected, the book is located on a physically simulated bookshelf. The physical sizes of the books are related to the actual number of pages, format, etc. The authors envisage that the spine could be used for giving further information in the future. The user can browse through the classified items on the shelf. If a book is selected, there is a book emulator, and pushing buttons will flick and jump through its pages. Pages may be annotated with a highlighting pen and book-markers can be inserted. References within the main text may be selected, causing the full reference to be displayed in a nearby window. Selecting a reference within the list of references causes the display of those page numbers on which the reference occurs.

The use of icons in this system is based on the idea that the physical presence of a book, particularly its front cover design, provides the reader with an overall impression of its contents. Spatial awareness is seen as providing recognition clues. A first remark one can make about this system is that its form of access is phrase searching. Even if it offers sophisticated graphics, it is at heart a first-generation OPAC. It does not make use of the potential power of computer retrieval capabilities. Furthermore, one can question the use of these pictorial representations. Is it pertinent to the user to have books physically displayed on the screen? Is the traditional way of searching bookshelves in any way related to searching a computer? Is it a relevant way of representing and referring to the process of searching monographs online? It could be seen as a diversion from the primary aim of an IR system. One could comment that it may be over-simplifying the issue of ease of interaction, as if ergonomists decided to paint telephone sets pink to make them more user-friendly. Users of such a system might very quickly get frustrated with its apparently simple representation of the IR ask, and with the poverty of its retrieval features.

This kind of approach is only tackling the representation of objects and operations on these subjects, i.e., Moran's semantic, syntactic and physical interaction levels mentioned above under the heading 'Nature of HCL.' Moran's task level is not really addressed. To put it differently, the task is assumed to be a certain nature. The designers have a preconceived model of what the task should be (the traditional task of searching books in a library, reproduced exactly on the screen). This might not be necessarily related to the computerized IR task.

Nevertheless, this system offers an unusual approach to reading full text and physically annotating pages. It also provides for browsing a classified sequence of books, whichever selection criterion was used to retrieve them.

Direct manipulation and IR objects

With user interfaces and their quality of HCL, one has to be aware of the fact that the feeling of directness can depend on how much practice the particular user has. Users may adjust themselves to the interface and, with sufficient practice, may view it as directly supporting their intentions. This gives credit for the work the user has done. Nevertheless, this notion of direct engagement is of interest. One can see that for IR, the use of command language is like having an intermediate layer between the user and the actual task. Command languages force the user to think about the mechanics of how to ask for something; they are noticed, distract from the task itself, render the interface 'visible' and suppress this sensation of directness.

What would be a feeling of directness for an IR task? The IR task is not a straightforward execution task, but a search/find/explore task. What could be manipulated, interacted with directly; and not just talked about, asked for, ordered or executed? Users often cannot formulate precisely what they are looking for. They should not have to get involved with specific retrieval mechanics (boolean operators, field specifiers, adjacency, limiters, truncation, etc.). Similarly they should not have to understand fully record structures, search keys, indexes, thesauri, controlled vocabularies, etc. One could envisage a direct manipulation of words and/or documents on the screen via joysticks, highlighters, touch-screen, etc., to negotiate a search formulation. Some interesting questions immediately arise. Should users have to go through a thesaurus or a subject authority file? Should they access and manipulate documents directly? Or should they be given both forms of access and manipulation? How should it be implemented? A list of subject headings, a classification scheme or a thesaurus could be seen as surrogates of the real objects (the documents). They introduce an extra layer between the desire outcome and the user.

Another interesting notion found in the direct manipulation literature is the following: 'the expression of a direct manipulation output language must be such that the user can assume that it, in some sense, is the things it refers to. Furthermore, the nature of the relationship between input and output languages must be such that an output expression can serve as a component of an input expression. Input and output languages of the interface should be interreferential, allowing an input expression to incorporate or make use of a previous output expression...This is crucial to create the illusion that one is directly manipulating the objects of concern.

This seems to apply immediately to retrieval systems. Parts of document(s), individual word(s), sentences or groups of word(s) displayed could be used directly as something to be input for another search. This could be done, for example, by pointing and 'picking' them on the screen and carrying them across another area of the screen. The user would not have to input them again.

We can conclude here that although WIMPS do obviously offer considerable advantages, their automatic use should not go unquestioned. Nevertheless, it is important to recognize that the direction manipulation concepts and features do address some of the problems of HCL design, in particular its semantic level. This approach should be considered when designing online public access catalogues and therefore a few ideas were explored.

Expert systems

The possible contributions of AI to the design of online IR systems have already been examined for some time. AI first, then expert systems or intelligent knowledge-based system, attempt to overcome barriers to database access by casual users; the AI approach tries to build a better database system with understanding of the user, his requirements and natural language communication. It tries to put all the load on the computer and make it clever enough to deal with the casual user. The HCL approach, in contrast, attempts to remove as much of the load as possible from both human and computer and share what is left between them, through user-computer interaction or 'negotiation.'

AI has been extremely concerned with HCL and ease-of-use problems (natural language interfaces are often assumed to solve that problem). Rather it has concentrated on the issue of computer understanding of users' general reasoning processes, especially knowledge representation and inference mechanisms, in order to simulate them in the machine.

Expert systems have a more pragmatic approach. They concentrate on limited domains as opposed to general problem-solving mechanisms. They build specialized knowledge bases and inference engines; this knowledge is generally acquired from human domain experts using knowledge elicitation techniques. It is formalized using knowledge engineering methods, so that it can be implemented on a machine, often using an expert system 'shell.'

However, the sometimes excellent decision-making performance provided by expert systems does not necessarily guarantee user acceptability. Expert system users still have HCL needs. Moreover, 'for some major practical applications the interface should be developed ahead of the reasoning part of the system; Berry and Broadbent even predict that, 'there will soon be more power associated with the interface of an expert system than with the knowledge base and inference engine.

IR and expert systems techniques

There have been various attempts at incorporating expert system techniques in IR systems, such as CANsearch,

EXPERT, Expert System Assistant, etc. A recent book by Brooks reviews the current developments in this area. There was a special issue of Information processing and management on expert systems in 1987. The reader is also referred to Belkin and Vickery for a through theoretical review of research into document retrieval and knowledge-based systems, within the conceptual framework of 'interaction in information systems.'

Expert front-end IR systems

The first category of intelligent IR systems might be more appropriate classified as 'front-ends.' These systems' interfaces assist users with search strategy formulation. They use improved retrieval techniques, i.e., term weighting, document ranking and relevance feedback, techniques already mentioned above under the heading 'Retrieval aids.' These techniques are now being incorporated in OPACs. In other systems (e.g., EXPERT) searches are carried out using a common command language which the system translates into the appropriate query language command. EXPERT embodies a number of rules for deciding which database to search, how to select synonyms and how to combine terms. It enables users to represent their search topic; it assists users with selecting a database to search; it automatically constructs a search strategy from the topic representation and executes it; and it uses relevance feedback to reformulate the search strategy.

So far, these interfaces are concerned with mapping the user's input into appropriate search terms, constructing a search strategy and carrying out the search automatically. This deals with the automatic query formulation. The task of assisting with the online search itself, where the role of the interface is to monitor and advise the use rather than to do the search, has been neglected. For example the problems with EXPERT are: it is unable to formulate database-dependent strategical it is unable to suggest search terms; and, perhaps more importantly, it lacks sufficient user involvement in search strategy reformulation. Apart from its use of production rule techniques, EXPERT seems to be little more than a gateway plus relevance feedback retrieval system. With the exception of the construction of search statements and assistance with database selection, the intellectual effort is still largely on the user's side. An exception is IIDA (Individualised Instruction for Database Access) developed within a training/teaching context. IIDA examines commands and responses, looking for errors or indications of problems and detecting 'faulty' search patterns. However, it is more of an intelligent tutoring system, which trains inexperienced searches in the use of Boolean command languages.

These systems still envisage the IR task as a strict matching process, and the underlying dominant searching model is the Boolean retrieve model. The designers have a limited preconceived idea of Moran's task level.

Expert IR systems

A second category of projects is trying to develop intelligent interfaces for online IR systems, based on expert system techniques. Expert systems try to embody and use some of the knowledge and skills of a human expert in such a form that the system can offer intelligent advice or take on intelligent decision about a processing function. The system, on demand, should be able to justify its own line of reasoning in a manner directly intelligible to the enquire. The domains to which expert system techniques have been successfully applied, though, are areas such as medical diagnosis and geological prospecting. These areas are of a very different nature from that of an interface to an IR system. Another critical difference is the very wide subject domain covered by most document retrieval systems. Little work has been done on expert systems which can cope with domains which are broad and not very detailed, and which involve large numbers of concepts and relations. Also, IR systems depend heavily on language. 'Information conveyed by a document is conveyed by the specific linguistic expressions of that document.

The successful use of expert system techniques in our field may not be possible until such techniques have been further advanced. Still, it might be useful to look into it, as we can gain insight into possible design developments. This could be helpful for several reasons: the interactive nature of OPACs, the complex nature of the IR task, and the fact that it is impossible to train the large population of OPAC potential users to the through understanding and manipulation of command languages.

An interesting example is described in Shoval: this system is designed to assist users with the selection of terms. It employs a knowledge base which contains the knowledge available to the human expert —a thesaurus and additional knowledge of terms, meanings and associations. This knowledge is represented as semantic networks. The usual hierarchical and synonymity relations found in thesauri are enhanced by the addition of two others types of relation, generator and modal. Generator relations link the components of multiwordphrases (e.g., 'industrial' and 'relations', see under 'Semantic aids' above); modal links are used to express more general relations (e.g., the relation between 'business' and 'organizational structure'), The user decides which terms represent his query and enters them one by one. The system then conducts a search of its knowledge base and additional terms of probable relevance are selected. An evaluation process is applied to distinguish terms which are most representative of the user's request. This system employs more powerful term selection heuristics than EXPERT, and does so as a co-operative effort with the user. Whilst the system 'knows' about the vocabulary of particularly subject domains and some of the relationships between the concepts, it does not appear to embody knowledge about how these terms are applied by the indexers to documents in the database. Thus, however well the final set of terms may express the user's request, it is no indication as to whether useful documents will be retrieved using these terms.

CANsearch enables medical practitioners to access directly the online databases which cover the cancer literature. The MeSH thesaurus is not easy to use and indexing policies are complicated (CITE also tries to help the user with this problem. CANsearch helps further, by assuming that a cancer therapy search topic involves certain facets. It uses these facets as a framework, guiding the user through relevant sections of the MeSH thesaurus. The user touches the screen to select the appropriate facets. The facet structure also guides the combination of terms with Boolean operators to form a sophisticated search strategy. CANsearch incorporates subject knowledge (including facet metastructure), indexing knowledge of the query language and knowledge about searching.

In terms of IR for both these systems (Shoval and CANsearch), the domain is narrow enough to be well represented and structured. These systems go a long way in terms of semantic or contextual assistance. Obviously that would be much more difficult with an OPAC and its large subject domain. In terms of HCL, Moran's task level is taken a step further than a straight matching process; the IR task is seen as involving semantic/contextual help as well. It is pleasant to use (touch-screen hardware), but users have to go through the same long sequence of facets to choose their topic from, every time they use the system. And, as we have seen under 'User interaction studies' above, users tend to like to use their own words rather than go through screens of facets or classification headings. Moran's semantic level (how objects and operations are represented) and syntactic level (what are the things called) are only touched upon.

The last IR system considered using expert system techniques is PLEXUS, designed under a British Library Research & Development Department grant at the Central Information Service of the University of London. PLEXUS was designed to help librarians to deal with referral queries about a particular domain, gardening'. It has a dictionary of terms, a database of referral resources and a hierarchical classification of the subject domain (by facets using the Broad System of Ordering (BSO). The user is asked to describe what the gardening problem is about; the input is stemmed; and semantic categories, synonyms and pointers to the BSO classification are found. The system then displays concepts in the domain (a section of the BSO classification) from which the user can browse and select term. If the model is incomplete, rules direct what questions should be passed in order to elicit the missing information (e.g., 'Is it a plant?). The search employs knowledge of search strategies and tactics to broaden and narrow the search if necessary (enter broader descriptors, exclude concepts, add synonyms). The results is a Boolean search strategy, which is modified automatically if the user wants more or less information.

Perhaps the most interesting aspect of PLEXUS is the fact that it constructs a user a model: by a series of questions it assesses the level of experience of the user, his gardening experience, geographical location, previous searching habits, etc. It will use this information when giving results, for example, by giving introductory manuals if the user is non-expert at gardening.

Again, this system deals with a vary narrow knowledge area, and user queries are maybe more of a problem-solving nature than of a strict reference retrieval nature. Nevertheless, it provides an interesting semantic/contextual approach to IR. The underlying task model is complex. Perhaps more interestingly, the task interaction/negotiation with the user is fairly sophisticated. The designers had not foreseen that the interface design would assume so much importance when they started off, and they did pay a lot of attention to it: their system offers much more of a search 'conversation' about the task with its users than most systems.

OPACs and expert systems

As has already been shown, OPACs have started incorporating some intelligent IR devices, classified above as 'expert front-ends.' Maybe OPAC design should gain from the experience of providing a semantic/contextual intelligent approach, as illustrated in other IR expert systems in the previous section. This semantic/contextual approach should not merely aim at improving the retrieval process (recall and/or precision). It should be envisaged as a means of assisting the user in his negotiation of a search, or task dialogue, with the system.

In contrast to traditional IR systems, OPACs' coverage is very broad. Perhaps this contextual approach could be of prime importance. Our having borrowed design concepts from traditional IR systems (Boolean post-coordinate matching) shouldn't make us lose sight of the contextual nature of our systems. Broad subject IR systems such as OPACs, full text and mixed media databases are characterized by the fact that the structure of the information is not known a priori, unlike expert systems domains. This prevents advance knowledge of the types of questions that will be asked, unlike the situation found in hierarchical and relational database management systems, or in narrow domain expert systems. It is much more difficult to explore and design expert systems for reasoning on open-ended domains. Nevertheless, current efforts at using expert systems techniques for retrieving information, even on small domains, have shown that the semantic/contextual approach is vital. This should be borne in mind when examining OPAC designs.

Eastman's recent chapter examines similar issues, although from the evaluation viewpoint (recall and precision). More specifically, she mentions the classificatory nature of online catalogues as opposed to other IR systems; how expert system techniques have been used for classification problem solving; and she even considers the problem structure of classification systems for catalogue selection to be a subclass of expert systems, and more so than traditional IR systems. The general architecture of the operation of a classification system is broken down into three major steps: abstraction of the problem data, heuristic matching of the abstraction in a specialization network and refinement into specific solutions....The architecture of a number of expert systems can be viewed in this way.

Another interesting design effort, although unfinished, is reported by Micco and Smith. Their goal was, 'to explore the possibility of building an expert system that would serve as an assistant to the reference liberation by helping end-users to refine their search strategies before going online in the databases. This was to be accomplished by means of a sophisticated user interface. It would use a windowing process to build a user profile and negotiate an appropriate search strategy. It would include faceting and various other techniques for improving search precision. They also planned to experiment with a graphed display of appropriate subject headings showing how the literature was distributed over the subject area.

This chapter describes the problems and issues involved in such an ambitious project. They soon realized that, to be effective at all, their system needed to be fully integrated: it had to provide access to all library databases and other tolls such as the name authority list and a greatly modernized LCSH.

They produced a limited system (in terms of the size and possibly the coverage of its database). It offers dictionaries, reference works and Books in Print as 'pop-up' reference tools, and the display of subject headings and simulated databases, including the online catalogue. They developed a knowledge base and sets of rules, rather than producing an operational system.

They looked into author and title searches, fiction/ recreational reading, periodical literature and subject searches. The search strategy negotiation screen' allows users to flip through two thesaurus windows: the first one is a series of concentric circles and permits the user to scan for broader and related terms; the second one permits the user to scroll across the hierarchy. The underlying classification system can also be superimposed. One problem the authors do point out is the integration of all these subsystems from a system design point of view.

Although we wondered if the user's viewpoint was at all present in the authors' mind when producing all these pop-up screens, windows, etc., and these variously integrated retrieval tools, an interesting point is made: in order to design a system which assists a reference librarian, they analysed the task of the reference librarian. They found out that, 'the librarian obtains a great deal of information about the clients, their background, interests, reading skills, knowledge of the library and the nature of their information need, before beginning to determine the most appropriate source of information.' They also state that their original expert system, which was intended simply to focus on the use of online databases, went back to the drawing-broad. It was decided to focus on capturing and encoding the analytical techniques used by experienced reference librarians. This aspect will be covered further in the next section.

Ease of use, users, mental models, HCL modelling

There has been a fair amount of work on the applications of psychological theory to the study of computer users in general; on the study of usability and ease of use; and on the study of users of IR systems and/or OPACs in particular.

Psychological models of HCL

Fundamental work has been carried out by psychologists and HCL researchers on psychological models and theories of human-computer interaction, in order to make predictions about aspects of the behaviour of the users of a device. There is a collection of complex and unrelated modelling approaches to be found in the literature. Each deals in some depth with some aspect of user behaviour. It is useful to try to draw some distinctions which may help to differentiate between different types of models.

The first distinction is competence models versus performance models. Competence models, such as the task action Grammars, are concerned with what the user needs to know and needs to be able to do in order to carry out the task. There is no performance element, so the dynamic aspects of the interaction are not covered.

Performance models take into account the user competence, plus how the user carries out the task. There are many performance models, covering different behaviours to varying degrees of depth and breadth.

Performance models can also be process models, in that they cover mental/cognitive operations. An example of a performance non-process model is the keystroke level model. An example of a performance process model is ICS (interactive computer system) developed at the MRC Applied Psychology Unit, Cambridge. Interesting results regarding this latter work relate no to what the users didn't know, but to what they wrongly thought they did know; this type of error appears to be related to the number of opportunities for false inferences that the system provided. Users evidently do not patiently collect a bundle of facts, waiting for them to gel into a complete whole. They use inferences and actively build knowledge structures which combine observation, guesswork and inference. If we knew more about how knowledge is built, we could design systems to support the natural processes instead of misleading them.

A further distinction to be made is whether the models deal with routine skills or problem solving. A routine skills model deals with methods within a well-known task domain. The main characteristics of user behaviour involve selecting between these methods. A typical task investigated with these models is text editing. This leads to building models of expert users' behaviour. A problem-solving model pays more attention to figuring out the user's next actions, based on user's knowledge.

A psychology of OPAC users

Some of the sources of problems on the users' side have been identified as being: (a) individual differences and demographic characteristics; (b) usage patterns and error behaviour; and (c) content of training and searching abilities. Individual differences and demographic characteristics refer to age, spatial memory ability, educational background, personality types, achievement tests, academic status, etc. Usage patterns and error behaviour correspond to the number of descriptors searched and of commands used, the connect time, the number of retrieved references, recall and precision, etc.

This type of data is often gathered using transaction log monitoring. Training and searching abilities mean experience with OPACs and other computers, learning styles, symbolic reasoning, logical deductive skills, etc. Researchers have tried to correlate these users' characteristics to their searching attributes affected the search process but not the search results. They found that under laboratory conditions none of these measures explained much of the variance in any significant manner. This type of research, 'has done more to identify the range of performance and satisfaction than it has in identifying the variables responsible.' Furthermore, 'the degree of variance is perhaps the strongest user behaviour finding in Information Retrieval to date.'

One could possibly argue that this direction of research is only substantiating the (probably previously held) insight that users search in extremely varied and different ways, even when they have to do pre-determined searches under experimental laboratory conditions. However, this should be seen as a reassuring fact! Maybe one of the problems with this approach to HCL aspects of OPACs, and of IR systems at large, is that the modelling technique used is definitely of a 'competence model' type (see above, under' psychological models of HCL'). It might be linked with how users and their task are envisaged. Borgman and Bellardo are focusing on users' levels of competence and how these related to a performance defined as retrieving a previously known document or not. There is no emphasis on how the search process takes place.

Non-ease of use of OPACs

Borgman classifies the problems users encounter when

using IR systems as 'mechanical' and 'conceptual' problems. The mechanical problems encompass things like typographical errors, command errors, term errors, quitting the system, no matches for wrong author names, etc. She concludes that users face more mechanical problems with OPACs than with other IR systems. 'The mechanical aspects of searching appear to be a problem in other retrieval systems only for infrequent and inexperienced users. Mechanical aspects are therefore the very first hurdle users have to overcome. Intermediaries, being frequent users, do not have this problem.

Users are then faced with conceptual problems. Even intermediaries do not use the full potential of search capabilities: they do not use obvious synonyms; they have difficulty in assessing relevance; they fail to consider the inverse relationship between recall and precision. 'Only when the conceptual aspects are understood can the user exploit the system fully.

However, many people have noted that Boolean logic appears to be one of the most difficult aspects of IR for users, experienced or not, to grasp. It is an inherently difficult task and one that is not 'common sense' for most people. This is even more pronounced for OPACs since many online catalogue users probably remain permanent novices. Designing menu-driven systems for 'naive' users and command-driven systems for 'sophisticated' users might not be appropriate. Similarly, wanting to train all users might not be the answer. The belief underlying these approaches is that the IR task is a strict matching process (a routine skills task?), and that good searching is equivalent to mastering a Boolean command language.

OPAC users' mental models

Borgman focused on users' mental models through an experimental study of the use of a prototype Boolean logic-based OPAC. Her research is based on the mental model is theory which proposes that people can be trained to develop a 'mental model.' This mental model.' This mental model will aid users in generating methods of interacting with the system, debugging errors and keeping track of their place in the system.

A laboratory condition was set up in which users were subjected to two different modes of training, a procedural one (based on the mechanics of the system) and a conceptual one (based on an explanation of the system). The conceptually based training was based on an analogy with the card catalogue. The results seem inconclusive in that, although the training effects were not as strong as predicted, we did find the hypothesized interaction effect between training method and task complexity, indicating that model-based training is not always superior. Other conclusions are drawn about the individual differences (especially educational background) and their related performance.

It seems that this particular work is mainly concerned with teaching IR by giving a conceptual model to the subjects (assuming that their mental model of this particular task is inadequate or non-existent and checking how well they perform with/without that model. It may not be surprising that the results are rather inconclusive, since this work is not exploring how users conceptualize actively while interacting. It is not concerned with users' activities and understandings. This is highlighted by the choice of methodology: the subjects are given some pre-determined retrieval questions, hence maybe suppressing some aspects of the IR task and only examining a straight matching process. The task is equalled to a straight computing match routine. The result of this matching process is evaluated. The fact that the system's complexity might interfere wit it by triggering some inadequate representations is not taken into account.

It could be argued that the model provided by the conceptually based training is also inadequate since it refers to card catalogue searching which is very different from online searching. We could reflect that we were never totally able to teach our users to use traditional catalogues 'properly' anyway, and they coped with the catalogue's inadequacies by browsing through the shelves.

Maybe the most interesting results are:

(a) the fact that one-third of the subjects were unable to achieve a minimal level of competency; and

(b) that few of the subjects could apply Boolean logic effectively to the search tasks.

This should make us question OPAC designers who carry on implementing command languages. But, as Gould and Lewis put it, 'designers underestimate user diversity, don't appreciate the role of cognitive processes in system interaction...and don't put their faith in empirical data.

Borgmen focuses on how to give the 'right' conceptual model for users to search with. The IR task is seen within a Booklean logic model to be taught to users, and it being the unique model for searching. The fact that, 'users seem to have a difficult time defining search strategies and executing them in an optimal manner' may be more of an argument for stopping to impose Boolean logic upon them than for trying to find such factors as individual differences to explain those difficulties.

OPAC users' behaviour research

Another area of investigation is illustrated by the work of Janosky et al. They used a think-aloud' data gathering technique on subjects having to perform standard searches (for example, difficult author searches, author/ title searches with stopwords, subject searches for words in titles and journals searches). A detailed analysis of errors and associated verbal protocols provided insights into the design features and mental processes contributing to the commission of errors.

The main conclusions were:

(a) the profound influence that incorrect mental representations have on the viewing and interpretation of online/offline help and instructions; and

(b) the snowballing effect of a misconception as a user tries to seek and interpret additional information in attempts to recover from an error.

This analysis also served to 'illustrate the often severe problems that can occur when the mental representations developed and/or activated by a computer system user are inconsistent with the actual system design.'

They mainly looked at manipulation of syntax and the use of commands. Not only could users not get the commands right, but there was also confusion about bibliographic elements. This work concentrates on Moran's syntactic and physical interaction levels, and does not include the task level. Nevertheless, its approach to HCL modelling is very much a user's performance and process model in that it covers mental/cognitive operations, applied to mainly manipulation and syntactic problems. They rightly conclude that the designer's goal should be to be consistent with those mental representations that the users will activate/develop and use as a result of interacting with the system. This requires a great deal more understanding of cognitive processes in general than does simply designing to be consistent with the system designer's personal representation. It is unlikely that the system designer will predict all of the information processing sequences, errors and misconceptions that users are likely to generate. Empirical evaluations can be very effective in identifying the existence and causes of unanticipated behaviour.

User modelling and IR

A related area of research is user modelling. That is the ability of the system to tailor its behaviour to the specific needs of an individual user, especially when used by people with substantially differing backgrounds. The eventual aim of building a user model in the machine is for personalized interfaces where the machine either knows about the user from past experience, or learns about the user as the interaction progresses. In either case, the system adapts its behaviour to suit the user. There are several ways in which user models can be built, and there is a classic book by Elaine Rich which thoroughly describes them.

To summarise user models can be based on stereotypes or prototypes (Rich has built such a system, called GRUNDY, which advises a user on the choice of a novel from a library fiction catalogue using stored stereotypes and feedback from the user), or they can be based on individual users. The information can be gained:

(a) through explicit interaction with the user through a short series of questions and answers about his level of expertise, preferences, interests, goals, etc. (PLEXUS, mentioned earlier, does this); or

(b) by implicitly inferring or abstracting characteristics through the actual user's interaction with the system.

The user models held by the machine can contain short-term and/or long-term information. The area in which user models have been applied most successfully is intelligent teaching/tutoring machines, where the user model generally feeds into the teaching strategy so that the system adapts itself as the student progresses. User models are beginning to be implemented in expert systems. 'Although the nature and purpose of user models have not been critically enough investigated...we should look at the extent to which user models contribute towards a system's effectiveness, efficiency and acceptability.

For IR systems, there are some current attempts at exploring this user modelling, approach. For a review on this see Daniels and Brajnik et al. More specifically, Brooks's and Daniels's PhD studies at the City University Department of Information Science investigate this method.

Their basic assumption is that IR systems do not have any understanding of the individual user or his problem. In order to gain some of this understanding, they start from the premises that the elicitation and use of information about users, their status, goals intentions, beliefs and so on, during the reference/pre-search interview is something that reference librarians and human intermediaries do as a matter of course.

Inquirers may not be able to define what they want, but they are usually able to explain why they need it. With the exception of GRUNDY and PLEXUS, these aspects of the intermediary's task in the reference pre-search interview and their effect on the outcome have not been taken into account in intelligent interface designs. The large amount of backtracking, reiteration and side sequencing taking place during human-human pre-search interviews has been ignored by system designers, who have produced highly linear sequential systems.

They therefore state that, 'the development of an intelligent interface which approaches human functional behaviour requires an understanding not only of what tasks are carried out by human intermediaries but also a model of functional interaction which will around for the complex patterns observed and which can be then incorporated into the design of the system.

Their raw data consisted of audio-recorded pre-search interviews between intermediaries and end-users, which they subjected to a functional discourse analysis. This was found to produce a wealth of detailed information about each interview, both with respect to the tasks of the intermediary and the knowledge he employs and also with respect to the process of negotiation between user and intermediary. From this they derived a set of functions, such as 'problem description,' 'retrieval strategy,' 'user model,' etc. They analysed and described them in depth; they formalized them in terms of tasks, subtasks, plan building and knowledge resources used; they suggested how to implement each function in a 'distributed expert problem treatment system', using expert system techniques and a 'blackboard' architecture. One function (the user model) was partially implemented but the results are not yet available. One very strong point about this current work is its extremely detailed analysis. It is going very far in the understanding and modelling of the actual task carried out by intermediaries in order to elicit knowledge from the user. It offers ways of incorporating this in system design, possibly including OPAC design.

One possible objection, with respect to its usefulness for the understanding of HCL problems which end-users encounter when searching IR systems, is that intermediaries are highly trained, specialized and experienced at searching online. One can wonder if untrained end-users would behave in the same way and if they should. Brooks concentrates on the performance and process aspects of intermediaries' behaviour;

focusing on intermediaries' tasks might entail an analysis of a more routine expect skills task as opposed to looking at end-users' behaviour. This may lead to modelling expert users' interaction (see under 'psychological models of HCL above). The outcome of a pre-search interview is a search strategy executed by an intermediary. This might not allow specifically for perhaps more interactive, negotiated, reformulated exploratory, general browsing, serendipity and discovery types of searches which end-users may need.

Nevertheless, where systems are to be used by more than one class of users, some degree of tunability of obviously desirable. 'In many cases presenting users with a few simple questions at the start of an interaction would be sufficient to ascertain the necessary critical information,' as illustrated in PLEXUS.

We have seen that OPAC design developments are beginning to offer:

(a) improved retrieval and linguistic features which may help users overcome their difficulties with the use of Boolean command languages and the complexities of computerized matching; and

(b) various semantic/contextual devices which may support them in finding contextual information, orienting themselves and browsing through files, hence enhancing the nature of the IR computerized task.

Recent interface features and expert systems developments also highlight this trend of offering various knowledge devices to help the user formulate and negotiate his information need. Psychological research work which investigates users' interaction with IR systems from various viewpoints was also presented. This work is still fairly limited in that:

- It examines the human-computer interaction largely under its physical interaction' ad 'syntactic levels and often does not tackle its 'semantic' and 'task' levels.
- The HCL modelling techniques used are based on:

(a) A 'competence' model focusing on individual differences.

(b) A 'performance non-process' model which does not examine how the user carries out the task.

(c) A 'performance process' model. This latter modelling approach can be further subdivided into: (i) a model which examines the syntactic and operational aspects of the interaction only; and (ii) a model which, by focusing on intermediaries' expertise, treats the interaction as an expert skills task rather than an end-user problem-solving task (see under psychological models of HCL' for further explanations of these models).

If we want to discover which design features are the best to suit our users' needs, we have to start investigating end-users' problem-solving behaviour while doing computerized IR. It was shown that confronting users with the use of a Boolean command language is probably forcing a model of IR upon them. Also, it might well 'load' users in a cognitive sense: they are busy enough thinking about their search topic and should not have to think about complex computational IR principles. Owen suggests that we should try to understand better what 'naive' theories of computation users hold (they do have some kind of pre-existing conceptual models and actively build and modify them), so that we can try to, 'resolve the tradeoff between confusing users by swamping them with information and confusing them by concealing it'.

This is even more crucial if we are to opt for interfaces using windows mice, icons and the like, in order to provide for graphical/contextual IR features, as a recent project using hypertext software illustrates. These interfaces might be easy to use but one often 'needs four legs and three arms to press all the buttons' and probably five eyes and two brains too! We know that people tend to use fairly simple classification structures and that elaborate systems are not maintained.

We must pay more attention to the understanding of human processes involved in comprehending and manipulating a complex system. Exploring users' conceptual models, cognitive resources and activities should be a starting-point for the choice of interface design features.

3
Library Automation

The automation of library operations can very readily be regarded as a way of escape from the pressing problems of everyday life in a library; ordering and cataloguing books, answering awkward reference questions, tracing lost books. Automation will certainly simplify many of these tasks, but it must be built upon a sure foundation of good library practice which, as far as possible, prevents problems from arising. Librarians best know what the problems are in cataloguing, acquisitions work, reader service, and circulation control, and it is important that their knowledge be brought fully to hear on the job of designing automated systems in the first place. Librarians must understand fully what automation can do in all areas from book ordering to natural-language text processing. Then this knowledge and experience will enable the goals of automation to be defined rightly and attained more readily. Library automation calls for a close working relationship between two disciplines and the men who practise them. The purpose of this chapter is to give some indication of the extent to which automated library systems are actually being used by libraries in their everyday operations. It is based on the author's personal knowledge of the state of automation in libraries in Britain and also, to a greater extent, on the published literature describing particular projects in Britain and in other countries. This is not a comprehensive survey: a process of selection has been applied so as to draw attention to the more important individual projects, and it is felt that it will be more valuable because of this.

One major problem which arises when reliance is placed on the published literature in this way is the twofold difficulty of distinguishing between projects that are planned for some unspecified future date and those which are actually operational at the time of writing and of learning about automated projects which have ceased to function. It is only natural that projects should be widely publicised at their inception and that their demise should be concealed from the public gaze. But librarians a body will learn as much from honest reports of failures and the reasons for them as they will from reports about automated systems that are planned newly-implemented. The lack of such a literature about failures is keenly felt, especially in the present context. A second major purpose of this chapter is that it should provide for comment on the systems outlined in previous chapters. These systems are "ideal" and do not necessarily represent any particular real-life operational system. Although they are naturally based on real life, their purpose is to illustrate the principles embodied in real systems. The system design discussed is based closely on one being developed as a co-operative venture by a number of British university libraries. All have access to ICT computers and this has led them to attempt to reduce development costs and to speed the introduction of appropriate automated routines by working together to produce common systems. The fullest statement of the order system specification was given at a conference organised by the group. It is designed to include the majority of outputs that libraries are likely to require from such a system and in order to make it more widely usable it is being programmed in COBOL.

The University Library in Newcastle-upon-Tyne has been operating a computer-aided ordering system. The introduction of this system was facilitated in that it makes use of a number of programs already in existence as part of the Newcastle file-handling system. This is a suite of programs written for the English Electric KDF9 computer to facilitate the handling of structured data of the kind found in bibliographical applications. It is interesting to note that Newcastle University library report a small saving in staff time compared with the previous order system which used edge-notched cards. If computer time were charged to the library, however, the automated system would be considerably more expensive. For new books which are included in the Virginia Kirkus Service pre-punched cards are distributed, one for each title, giving the usual bibliographical information. To order one of these books all that a library has to do is to return the appropriate punched card to the data-processing centre indicating the number of copies needed. This is an interesting example of one way in which cooperation between libraries can make for simpler automated systems, save time, and reduce costs.

At the University of Maryland an acquisitions system is in operation utilising punched-card equip-ment only. Orders and auxiliary listings of outstanding orders, receipts, and fund reports are made using an IBM 407 accounting machine. "On order" cards are filed manually in the public card catalogue and pre-cataloguing is carried out whenever complete Library of Congress cataloguing data is available. Shaw has recently described an application of data processing techniques to the accounting side of library acquisitions at the University of Hawaii. He shows that accounting costs are reduced to one thirteenth of their previous level by this very simple system which just uses the computer as a calculating machine. In libraries where funds are limited it is important to remember that modest automation programmers can result in significant savings which can be directed to improving conventional services. A unique computer-aided system for ordering replacement copies of standard books is now operating in Toronto. Public librarians there have selected a standard list of about 2500 titles, all of which are available in paperback editions. Given information on the quality rating of publishers' editions, the computer prepares monthly lists of replacement orders which enable each branch library to have in stock a determined number of copies of all the standard titles, all in good condition. A number of library systems in the Toronto area are cooperating in this scheme which, because of its size enables substantial discounts to be obtained.

A number of other libraries have reported automated acquisitions systems to be in operation. At the library of the University of Michigan a disc memory store is used in the computer processing of order records, while at the Redstone Scientific Information Center a system christened ALPHA (Automatic Literature, Processing, Handling, and Analysis) utilises an IBM 632 electronic typing calculator for key punching the original order records.

A typical computer-aided circulation control system is now operational at the University of Southampton. It is being implemented in four stages of increasing sophistication the first of which commenced in operation. The first stage, as a by-product of its operation, produces a book card for each book that is circulated, thus building up an "active" collection of books with books cards ready for automatic input of charging data during the second stage of the system. The final two stages provide for on-line interrogation and updating of the loans file. The price which has to be paid for this gradual method of building up an active collection is the heavy work load involved with the first stage. Borrowers fill in slips for each book they borrow and reserve and data-processing staff keypunch one card for each of these transactions and also one card for each book that is returned. The advantage of a crash programme is that the circulation system can employ automatic collection of charging data right from the very beginning, and that there will be no need to cater for books being circulated without cards.

Although cards will be made for many books which will in fact never be circulated again, it will not be necessary to punch cards for books that are returned as at Southampton. Trueswell has shown that for a university technical library where it is the newest books that circulate most, it is more economical to prepare book cards for books on loan during the loan period than to carry out a crash programme for the entire collection. And if all new acquisitions are supplied with book cards at the technical processing stage, possibly as a by-product of an automated order system, then in time only a small percentage of books will be presented for circulation without book cards. However, in a public lending library where a high percentage of the stock is circulated and books have a long "half-life", a crash programme may be appropriate. Ruecking has made a mathematical analysis of future circulation growth at Rice University in order to make a more accurate comparison between different methods of circulation control. As circulation increases and as filed grow, linear relationships do not necessarily hold, so that it is necessary to include the cumulative costs of a system when evaluating it. His calculations show that over a 6-year period the total cumulative cost of a computerised system would be about half the cumulative cost of any other system.

A number of libraries in the United States have now adopted circulation control systems based on either the IBM 357 or 1030 data-collection units, accepting data from eighty-column punched book cards and readers' plastic badge cards. Among these are Southern Illinois University, Florida Atlantic University, Lehigh University, Oak Ridge National Laboratory, and the University of Missouri. An unusual system operates at Johns Hopkins University which represents one solution to the slow charging speeds which are associated with computer-aided circulation control. The price paid is an extra operation in the circulation procedure. Charge and discharge data is captured on microfilm by photographing the reader's identification card and the spines of up to twelve or fifteen books being borrowed. After developing the film the data is keypunched and processed by the computer in the normal way.

In Germany, two university libraries, Bochum and the Technical University of Berlin, have implemented automated circulation control systems using book cards edge-punched with paper-tape codes for automatic collection of charging data.

Circulation control systems using punched-card machines have not yet been displaced by computer-based systems. One has recently been installed in the Atomic Weapons Research Establishment at Aldermaston. It makes use of the card duplicating facility of an IBM 026 printing card punch to create three transaction cards for each loan from punched book and reader cards. One card is filed manually in the issues file and the other two are used by a computer to apply various controls to the system; to test for overdue books, for example. Eighty-column cards are filled in by borrowers and then keypunched for processing. A computer is used only for printing letters recalling overdue books. Judging from the experience of the University of Hawaii it would be foolish to assume that computer-based circulation systems are the only ones worth introducing in this modern age. The best system for each individual library can only be arrived at after rigorous systems work and careful costing.

Periodicals listing and accessioning

Many libraries have produced lists of their periodicals holdings by computer punched-card methods and taken advantage of the opportunities thus afforded for distributing the list widely and updating it easily and frequently. A union list of periodicals held in Institute of Education libraries in Britain was also published in 1966. It was produced with the aid of some programs of the Newcastle file handling system. Experiments are in hand to print new editions of this union list by computer typesetting techniques being developed by the University of Newcastle-upon-Tyne computer typesetting project. The Atomic Energy Research Establishment at Harwell produced a printed list of its periodicals holdings by punched-card techniques in 1960. The main library at Harwell is responsible for purchasing periodicals for its own collections as well as for those of twenty-two divisional libraries. The use of mechanised methods for compiling the list made it a comparatively simple job to supply each library within the system with a frequently updated union list of periodicals.

The most important British union list of serials produced by mechanical means is, of course, the new BUCOP. Input is from punched cards and processing is done by IBM 1401 computer. In the case of a widely used list such as this it becomes important that computer typesetting techniques should be introduced quickly, even though the present frequently updated list is an immense improvement on the older ones. An interesting holdings list in the United States is that of the Francis A. Countway Library of Medicine, formed by the merger of the Boston Medical Library and Harvard Medical Library. The incentive to mechanise was the immediate need to merge the records of the two libraries. An impressive number of different outputs have been produced including a KWIC index of current titles.

Semi-automated serials check-in systems have a number of attractive features and have been adopted by several libraries. They can be regarded as an intermediate stage between systems producing a list of holdings and fully automated systems embracing accounting, checking in, and binding routines for periodicals. For libraries which cannot afford to develop a fully automated system directly they are a useful stepping-stone whereby the final goal can be approached by degrees. In Britain a computer-produced checking-in list has been developed at the City University. Periodical parts expected to arrive during the coming month are listed on a line printer. As the parts are received in the library they are ticked off on this list, making it a simple matter to inform library users about the arrival or non-arrival of a particular journal issue. This printed checking-in list gives full titles of journals, unlike systems which punch an eighty-column card for each expected part, where title have to be abbreviated. The system is capable of conversion to a fully automated one, which would require only a minimum amount of keypunching to cater for parts which do not behave as expected. Another semi-automated system has been installed at the Louisville School of Medicine, Louisville, Kentucky. Using only punched-card equipment, check-in cards are prepared for each expected title. These require the manual addition of volume number, part number, and date of receipt to complete the full bibliographical data for each part. A number of libraries in the United States have reported the installation of fully automated computerised systems.

Bibliographies and catalogues

The very simplest level at which entries for

bibliographies and catalogues can be prepared by automated methods is that involving the use of a paper-tape typewriter or the IBM Document Writer. These machines are used widely in libraries nowadays and their routine application is seldom reported in the literature. Two useful articles which explain how they have been used in particular libraries are those by Wilson and Bernstein. Conflicting reports have been published on the relative costs of producing catalogue cards by tape typewriter and by other techniques. Mackenzie shows the tape typewriter to be about 75 per cent as costly as either a stencil duplicator or a small offset litho machine. Moore, on the other hand, finds the reverse to be true-duplicating methods works out to be approximately 75 per cent as costly as tape typewriters. The cause of these divergent results is to be found in the relative amounts of clerical time stated to be required by the two methods.

An interesting variation on these methods has been reported by Fasana *et al.* Catalogue records are prepared in machine-readable form and in a special machine-interpretable natural format using a tape typewriter. Working from the tape punched by the tape typewriter, a special digital machine-the Itek Crossfiler-prepares a catalogue entries. Running this second tape through a tape typewriter produces the required card set directly. Briefly, this technique obviates the need to use a program tape when added entries are being typed and makes for greater flexibility in the production of added entries of different kinds. There is a large literature dealing with various aspects of the production of card and book catalogues by means of punched cards and computer methods. In the following paragraphs only the more important contributions to this literature are mentioned. Dewey gives a brief historical survey of the earliest catalogues produced by punched-card methods and records that the first non experimental catalogue of books was made in 1951 for the branch libraries of King County (Washington) Public Library System. More widely known are the book catalogues of Los Angeles Country Public Library, first introduced in 1953. Before that date only 26 of the system's 114 service outlets had card catalogues, while the introduction of book catalogue enabled each branch to have a union catalogue of the whole library system. A book catalogue produced by punched-card methods was introduced to the science and engineering libraries of the University of Rochester in 1962. This short-title catalogue, now made using an IBM 7094 computer, is designed as a supplement to the libraries' regular card catalogues and each entry is accordingly limited to one line only. In the latest editions of this catalogue refinements have been made to the sort programs.

Among the North American libraries that have made book catalogues by computer are Stanford University Library, where the decision to automate was based on a thorough comparative cost analysis, Florida Atlantic University, where the original intention was that the catalogue should also be searchable by machine and Toronto University Library, which prepared a book catalogue of the combined holdings of five new university libraries in the province of Ontario—the ONULP project.

At Harvard University Library a project is under way to convert the entire shelf list to machine-readable form. In that a shelf list is a classified sequence of bibliographic records, the whole job can conveniently be split into small units and one main class keypunched at a time. The first Harvard class, the Crusades, was completed in May 1965. As with the short title catalogue at the University of Rochester, these printed shelf lists, invaluable as they are, can only be regarded as supplements to the main card catalogue where full bibliographic details are available. De Gennaro has recently developed this classwise conversion technique into a proposal for creating a national union catalogue in machineable form for the United States. Each class of the Library of Congress shelf list would be converted and machine printout compared with the holdings of other large research libraries. They would add to the machineable records their own locational symbols and titles held only by them, and could print their own book catalogues by selective listing of the master tapes.

The medical libraries of Yale University and Columbia University are co-operating in a project which will eventually provide them with a common pool of books and journals the catalogue of which will be in machineable form and accessible through remote on-line consoles. Kilgour has described programs to produce printed catalogue cards as the first stage in this ambitious project. The programs were written in a symbolic-assembly language to take fullest advantage of the potential of a small computer-a two tape 4K IBM 1401. In another paper Kilgour outlines the advantages to be gained from writing programs in such a machine-oriented language as compared with a higher-level language such as COBOL, which is proposed by Culbertson as a standard language to be used for library data processing.

An unusual computer-produced catalogue on microfilm has been operational in the Technical Information Center of Lockheed Missiles and Space Company since July 1966. Using a machine to compose directly from the computer onto microfilm is stated to reduce costs considerably. Access to the catalogue must be by means of a microfilm reader, but film kept in cartridge makes for simple handling and a Xerox Copyflo can be used to produce hard copy quickly and cheaply if this is wanted.

The Library of Congress project MARC has had a marked influence on libraries' plans for catalogue automation both in North America and Britain. The MARC pilot project, in which cataloguing copy was distributed on an experimental basis to sixteen libraries, began in October 1966 and is still continuing. At the time of writing, the Library of Congress is developing an improved format for the catalogue records on MARC tapes, designed to facilitate the communication of bibliographic data in machineable form. Coward describes this new format and discusses the United Kingdom MARC service, which is hoped to be made available within the next few years. It will be firmly based on co-operation with the next few years. It will be firmly based on co-operation has already been established in regard to the actual data going into catalogue records as part of the Library of Congress Shared Cataloging Program. The introduction of standard book numbering to the British book trade has provided a convenient tag for identifying the records on the British MARC tapes and should reduce greatly the problems associated with matching catalogue records by computer. A possible file structure for the weekly magnetic tapes produced by the U.K. MARC service might be as follows: firstly, a main file consisting of a series of catalogue records in standard book number order; and secondly, a title index to the first part of the file. The index might also be produced in printed form along with a listing of the SBN's of records in the first part of the file. The public library systems of the London Boroughs of Barnet, Camden, and Greenwich have had computer-produced book catalogues for nearly 3 years now. Using the services of a computer bureau and accepting severe limitations on the format and layout of entries, these libraries have been able, nevertheless, to improve their public services by supplying all branches with union catalogues, a virtual impossibility with a manual system.

Tait and Anderson, of the Department of Librarianship at the University of Strathclyde, Glasgow, have recently described an experiment to test the effectiveness of an ICT package program for library indexing and cataloguing-NIC. They are using citations from Library Science Abstracts as inputs data to the system. It will be interesting to compare the effectiveness of the indexes produced by NIC (Nineteen hundred Indexing and Cataloguing) with the conventional indexes published for Library Science Abstracts. At the Cambridge Philosophical Library project has commenced to produce by computer a union catalogue of books in the many departmental libraries with in the University of Cambridge. The entire shelf lists of a sample of these libraries are being converted into machineable form and a thorough investigation will be made into the problems of merging the separate catalogues at the University of Rochester. Unless entries referring to identical books really are truly identical the computer will include them both in the updated catalogue.

At the University of Newcastle-upon-Tyne, Hunt is working on a computerised catalogue for the two special collections in the University library. Using programs from the New Castle file-handling system, this catalogue will be indexed by author, binder, provenance, etc. Particularly interesting techniques being developed by the computer typesetting project at the University. In Germany, book-form catalogues are being produced by computer at the University of Bochum. This is a new university and in fact has no card catalogue at all. Germany has also made an important contribution to computer-aided cataloguing methods by being the first country to produce its national bibliography by computer. Type-setting is by means of a Linoquick machine, a norma data-processing system became apparent with the first half-yearly cumulation, the Halbjahres-Verzeichnis. Normally this job takes from 12 to 15 months, but it has now been reduced to 2¼ months.

Future developments

The pattern of automated library service in the future can only be predicted by educated extrapolation of the developments that are taking place in libraries today, bearing in mind other factors which will have an important bearing on libraries. Included among these will be an expected continuing exponential growth in population and the increasing the importance of libraries in the developing countries. The expansion of knowledge shows no signs of abating, and libraries will also be faced with a continuing proliferation of disciplines, coupled with a trend towards inter-disciplinary study. The volume of publications will continue to grow but there should be an increasing recognition by central governments of the importance of libraries and their functions of bibliographic control and information dissemination. The consequence of this recognition will be greater financial support for library programmes. The key requirement in such an age is that libraries should be flexible. This will be manifested in all facets of librarianship; library buildings, systems for subject representation, forms of publications and the reader services provided for the library's clientele. Co-operation between libraries at local, national, and international levels will increase in importance, but it must be flexible so as to ensure that individual, importance, but it must be flexible so as to ensure that individual, seemingly more important goals. Most important of all, perhaps, is the recognition that libraries serve as an intermediary in process of communication between human beings. They are not ends in themselves and the fact that libraries must deal ultimately with people, not merely with inanimate documents and machines, obliges us to design systems which treat both readers and library staff with understanding and respect for their personal feelings and needs.

The computer has a central role to play in such future library systems. As a reliable, competent, accurate, and cheap manipulator or library infor-mation it can bring to fruition many idealistic concepts about flexible library services. In that it has the capacity to free human beings from much of the repetitive labour that is a necessary concomitant to library work, it can also give us the opportunity to provide personal service to real people. The necessary prerequisite to the wise and proper use of computing machinery in libraries in the future is a body of wise and informed library managers now. It is possible to distinguish two general directions in which computer aided services will develop. Printed lists prepared by computer processing of a basic corpus of bibliographic records will increase in number and in diversity, and facilities for on-lie interrogation of files held in machine memories will become more widely available.

At the present moment computer-aided library systems almost invariably produce as their end product some sort of printed list for human consultation or scanning. In the future, then, we can expect to see more such lists prepared in circumstances where they can be justified either by reducing costs or increasing services. At present, too, a number of experimental on-line library projects are either operational or under development. It is reasonable to suppose that these will be successful and will eventually find application in certain circumstances.

It is possible to divide present-day on-line projects into two broad categories; those involving the automation of one or more library housekeeping functions, and those concerned with information retrieval and the processing of natural language text. The major area of library housekeeping which librarians tend to regard as being suitable for on-line methods is circulation control.

Although no system is operational yet, work is either in progress or under consideration at the University of California, San Diego and Los Angeles, and at Harwell and Belfast. A proposal for on-line accessioning of periodicals has come from the University of Lancaster, and a number of libraries are considering systems for on-line manipulation and cataloguing data. Assuming that it remains essential to make non-programmable alterations either to ordering data or catalogue data from a central agency before it can be added to a library's own catalogue file, then an on-line visual display console equipped with a keyboard and light pen would appear to be an attractive piece of hardware for doing this. All of these on-line systems, however, involve only minor modifications to existing patterns of library activity.

More far-reaching changes to present-day methods of library use appear to be implied in on-line systems for information retrieval and text processing. Those that come closest to everyday library operations involve the on-line interrogation of a file of bibliographic records. This enables a search to be directed in the first place to the names of authors, editors, etc., titles, class numbers, or coden. Secondary search of a body of records retrieved by one of the above terms can be by means of a subject term; publisher's name, date of publication, place of publication, language, or location. The details of the system have yet to be worked out, including the bibliographic record format to be used, but the body of records will be indexed in four ways corresponding to the four data categories by which primary access to the file may be obtained. Presumably, search statements can combine more than one term in logical relationship. A project is also under way to create an on-line union-catalogue for the public libraries of metropolitan Toronto. Here, in addition to the design of the machine system, difficulties have to be overcome in respect of the machine system, difficulties have to be overcome in respect of differences of cataloguing practice between co-operating libraries. It is likely that this project will provide for only limited degrees of search complexity, and will handle only abbreviated bibliographic records in order to minimise the size of file required.

Kessler is conducting an interesting experimental project at Massachusetts Institute of Technology which permits on-line searching of bibliographical records by various novel search strategies. Articles from twenty-one specially chosen physics journals are "indexed" for the system, but conventional subject indexing is not employed except in so far as it is made available in Physics Abstracts. Search strategies can be defined on the basis of journal titles, author's names and—words in titles. Citation-orientated searching is also possible, for example, one can search for all papers which cite a chosen article or alternatively, all papers that have a stated number of references in common with the chosen article. Kessler has introduced the concept of bibliographic coupling to describe the linkage formed between papers which have references in common. Two papers are said to be bibliographically coupled with coupling strength of one (two, three etc.) when they have one (two, three etc.) references in common. Kessler has found that groups of papers coupled in this way are quite similar to the groups of papers coupled in this way are quite similar to the groups made by a conventional subject index.

Indexing by means of bibliographic coupling is likely to become more common in future than it has been in the past. Relying on the authors of papers for the intellectual efforts which is required for a good index, it demands the use of new search strategies on the part of library users. The technique is particularly suitable for machine applications in that no intellectual effort is required to construct the index. The printed volumes of Science Citation Index are compiled on these principles and make it possible to experiment now with search strategies which will be appropriate with some future on-line information retrieval systems.

A detailed description of an imaginary on-line library system has been given by Licklider. Termed a "procognitive system" in that it exists for, or to serve, knowledge and learning, it replaces the codex and the card index of present-day libraries by direct-access computer memories containing the same information. Computer processors in the procognitive system are able, in an unspecified way, to organise and mull over the data in store, and also to search it. An experimental approach to such a system has been described by Bobrow *et al.* A program named SYMBIONT enables a number of basic operations to be performed on textual matter. Once a document has been input to the system, 150-word "pages" of it can be displayed on the face of a console. Pages can be turned forwards and backwards, and selected passages of text can be named and stored for future reference. Searches can then be made using these names.

Project INTREX is another experiment in the same general direction. Begun in late 1965 it is a research programme whose main aim is to provide, a solution to the problems of large libraries by means of on-line computing techniques similar to those of SYMBIONT and the procognitive system. There is, of course, a dual problem here. Not only must some very sophisticated computer programs be developed, but they must be related to an understanding of language and of the way human beings interact with the body of knowledge which these systems plan to hold in computer memory. The fact is that we are woe—ignorant of the ways in which scholars approach the literature of their subject, or the reason why readers come into a library. To design on-line computer systems which perform limited file-searching functions may be to miss the real needs of most library users.

4
Library Systems

The university education of librarians derives significance from encouraging inquiry that goes deeper than uncritical explanations of this kind. The thesis advanced in this chapter is that the connection between modern librarianship and modern civilization is close enough to make educated librarians more or less indispensable. The object of the discussion to follow is to show what the interconnection is. Writings on library history tend to describe individual libraries or the libraries of a country or period. These account can be expected to cover such topic as: the growth of collections, acquisitions, classification and cataloging, housing, financing, regulations and personnel. All of this information is good as far as it goes, but too often it leaves the reader to search in vain among assorted facts for some internal order—some mosaic—which will give the several fragments range of meaning. It is of course plain to all that libraries are among the thins that are products of human effort, so if some larger configuration of meaning is to be found in their history, it is better to relate them to the whole stream of social evolution than to separate them as it were from human strivings. What has man been striving to do which accounts for his having history of libraries at all? While there is too much backwardness in library development for the present generation in any country to feel complacent about it, modern library achievements in the aggregate are undoubtedly beyond anything that could have been imagined back when it all began. To get from there to here, man had no lodestar to guide him along a predetermined countless footsteps gradually beat into shape a few giant strides forwards. It is these achievements, not a chronicling of activities internal to some library system or period, which form the more significant chapters of the epic. The first long stride was the act of developing an instrument which empower one mind to reach across all barriers of space and time and communicate a message to other minds.

The feat involved inventing writing, experimenting with different kinds of writing material and testing the merits of the tablet and scroll against the merits of the codex. Ancient bookmen of Bergama contributed a writing material, parchment, whose superiority over clay tablets and papyrus hastened the forming of the book as we know it. It was a step that centuries, but the work was done so well that the physical from of the book has in essential respects remained the same ever since. In range of influence, none of man' other achievements surpasses the invention of writing and the book. All those who live in the crescent which bounds the Eastern Mediterranean are entitled undying pride in it.

But we are getting ached of the story. To speak of the influence of the new instrument is to go long way past the invention of letters per se, on past the triumph of the codex to the social effects of the revolution they brought about. To picture the second step something needs to be said about evolution of the use of letters. Writing found a variety of uses ranging from keeping accounts to publishing official news or transmitting short messages of lesser importance. Early thinkers however turned the use of the new medium away from simple recording or publicizing events and names to the presentation of sustained sequences of thought. It was writing in this from that men took to their hearts enough to make them start building collections. When in the dim past this practice of collecting the writings of others began, the library idea was born. Library collections to start with were private. "Private libraries" will be used here to include not only those libraries which are owned by the serve a person or family but also those organization libraries which are administered along lines similar to personal libraries, whether their doors are ajar to outsiders or not.

The creation of the private library was the second step forward. It has an institutional pattern which is characteristic, influential, yet not commonly noticed since it shades so imperceptibly into a later pattern—that of the library which is organized to further the interest of the public. To start with, the sponsor of the private library was and normally still is the source of financial support, the governing authority, clientele ("public" served) and library staff all rolled into one. In this characterization, nothing is said of the purpose of the private library. The subject is a complex one, for books have a many-sides appeal. What for example did Willibald Perkheimer of Nuremberg mean by announcing on his bookplate that his superb collection of 2000 volumes was for himself and his friends. The answer in part is suggested by Nicholas V when he speaks of a certain inexplicable thirst for books which drove him on to notable success in building the Vatican collection. How any private collectors, like him, have built their libraries because of a love for books and a desire to be near them! Great calligraphers, scribes and typographers have all shared this devotion with great collectors. Caesar helped to popularize motives of another sort by bringing home captive libraries as trophies of war. Roman patricians, aided by a flourishing booktrade, started building collections of their own. It become so fashionable that

Seneca once wryly observed that things had got to the point where a library was considered, along with hot and cold baths, as necessary adornment for a home: "Iam enim inter balnearia et thermas bibliotheca quoque ut necessarium domus ornamentum expolitur." Time passed, and ass wealth increased merchant princes adopted the habits of collecting books as symbols of status, while the example of those rulers who were genuinely interested in learning was followed by other who collected with equal zeal mainly to add luster to their courts. The ultimate benefit to civilization from collecting books shows no consistent relation to the motives of collectors, but it has been pointed out time and again from Seneca and made of books for purpose other than reading and study are all derivative ones.

Man started building libraries in order to hold concourse with other thinkers and something happened to him in the process. He grew in stature; his life was enriched; and in some ways he was made over into a new man. The private library is here identified as the second step in the advance towards the twentieth century because of this influence which it has exerted in the making of civilized man. In the heyday of its influence, it had an effectiveness which has in some particulars never been matched by its institutional successor, the library organized to serve the general public: until as late as the eighteenth century, a man was able to surround himself in one room with the total record of learning, or at least all of it he had need for. The specialization of knowledge since then, coupled with other changes, has gradually forced the library built around the interests of one man into a subordinate place, and the intellectual worker in consequence finds himself dependent on libraries which are larger, more complex and farther away from his own study. It leaves a feeling of nostalgia. Who does not long at times for a recovery of this older standard of service which puts within arm's reach all the books a man ever needs?

Rise of Society Based on Letters and Learning

This is the step that lies between dependence on private libraries and the rise of libraries organized to serve needs of a different magnitude. There is precedent for using "preliterate" or "non-literate" to refer to a culture where little or no use is made of letter. "Literate society" will be used in a similar manner here to refer to a culture with a built-in need for letters—or, to be more technical, to refer to a culture which depends so heavily on books, reading and writing for recording and communicating ideas that letters may be deemed indispensable to its good health and indeed its very survival. Societies still exist that are predominately non-literate while, on the other hand, islands of non-literates semi-literates are to be found in all literate societies. This however should not be allowed to obscure the fact that Western man has since the Renaissance developed societies where the use of letters is inseparable from matters which are essential to keeping people who are now the most advanced from sliding back to a lower state of civilization. Common speech takes this for granted and makes the use of letters a rough equivalent of the sort of learning which is indicative of the highest civilization.

The organization of formal schooling, the curbing of labor practices which interfere with prolonged, systematic education of children, the spread of required attendance at school as a means of preparing youth for their adult responsibilities. The rise of universities, the rise of enlightened patronage of letters and learning by individuals, private organizations and the state, the growth of public support for systematic pursuit and dissemination of knowledge. The invention of printing, organization of prosperous trade in books, maintenance of high professional standards among publishers and booksellers. Displacement of guild-control over "useful knowledge", recognition of copyright and other rights of patent. Acceptance of the rule of law and the attendant growth of parliamentary systems, a step which made written codes essential to the processes of government. Spread of universal suffrage, which hinged the future of self-government on the enlightenment of the individual citizen. Development of the newspaper, popular magazine and other media to aid in the diffusion of knowledge and informed opinion.

Decline of the monastic ideal of scholarship, progressive acceptance by men of letters and learning of responsibility for imparting knowledge and information through written channels, the rise of entirely new professions such as journalists and librarians to aid in closing the gap between rapid advances in knowledge and the application of knowledge in social practice.

Recognition of the dignity of work, decline of the concept of learning as the prerogative of a ruling class separate from the workers, reconstruction of higher education as a deliberate aid to developing leaders in all those fields having an intellectual base which are required for the good of a society of workers. The last named item, it is worth adding, was an answer given by liberal people years before international communism rose to make its own peculiar challenge to education based on class distinctions. The list of civilized advances enumerated above do not of themselves prove that habitual exercise of freedom of expression or reliance on written codes of behavior, etc., builds dependence on letters into the fundamental processes of modern civilization. The proposition can be presented with more cogency by taking a particular advance such as the industrial revolution and showing what the inter-connection is. Any relation which the industrial revolution may have to twentieth century needs for library service may not be as transparent as other examples that might be chosen, but it is of course fitting to use just such an example in searching for proof. In a narrow sense, the industrial revolution was an episode that is now entirely past—a switch to the factory system following the introduction of power-driven machinery to replace hand-labor, after 1760. It enabled England to forge ahead in all lines where the new source of power could be put to work. In an effort to keep pace, other nations struck back in what Bismarck called a new kind of war which was to pit the technical competence of one nation against that of another. France concentrated on products requiring good taste and superior craftsmanship. the results shown in the early international expositions, which began with the one in the Crystal Palace in London in 1851, were considered by a good many observers as proof of inborn superiority of French workmen. A German study however brought out the fact that the superiority lay rather in the type of training the craftsmen were receiving. To skip over absorbing details in order to bring the story down to date, the rivalry shifted from public expositions to training establishments, scientific laboratories, libraries of information, and there it remains. The lesson is now commonplace knowledge: the economic capability of a nation depends on access to raw materials, access to better knowledge than one's competitor, and well-qualified manpower.

In other words, while the application of power-driven machinery to production was one episode in one country, it was at the same time a spectacular inauguration of a process that has spread to many countries and is still spreading. It is the habit, both social and personal, of applying to the business of everyday life the best ideas—or to use another phrase, the best intelligence—available for the recorded experience of the race as a whole.

The significance of this habit in revolutionizing industry and in devising other ways of doing things can best be seen by contrasting it with the habit of depending on tradition. The dependence on handed-down ways is not met so often in countries where habits of thought engendered by the industrial revolution have made themselves felt, nut no country is free from it.

For example, at the southern tip of Andrews, North Carolina. Years ago, Andrews prospered from making tannic acid out of the bark of the chestnut tree. Then somewhere beyond this secluded valley improvements in producing tannic acid were introduced. Andrews failed to keep up. Hard times fell in the people, and the prosperity they lost has not been regained. The lesson is the same for men everywhere: ways handed down from the past are not always the best, yet they often hold people back from free application of new-found knowledge in daily life. Those who would make such application, wherever they are, find it imperative to have at hand the books, journals and other sources through which knowledge is disseminated. The foregoing focuses attention on the organized practice of using the best available information to promote material progress. To give balance to the treatment, it should be stressed that modern society showed be stressed that modern society shows even greater organized dependence on letter in intellectual and spiritual matters. The point can be illustrated by referring briefly to the rise of the university, one of the most original institutions to be perfected by literate society. It is impossible to point to a data and say, "This is when the university originated"; but in terms of the sociology of learning, the essential pre-condition of its rise was an accumulated intellectual heritage voluminous enough to justify splitting off a new division of labor and turning it over to specialists called processors who were ready to devote their energies to its transmission and further development. Not enough is known about the steps which led up to this departure. One of the extraordinary things about it is that while the university movement has been predominantly secular, the adherents of no less than three great religions figured in originating it. Further search of manuscripts scattered around the southerly crescent extending from the Bosphorus to Gibraltar will undoubtedly throw further light on these contacts. Already however enough is known to say that between the fifth and the twelfth century Western man was finding it increasingly difficult to educate youth by continuing to rely on the preliterate methods of live university arose to cultivate youth and higher learning in a society, the university arose to cultivate youth and higher learning in a society which was making ever wider use of letters, and in time it obviously further widened the gap between the two worlds.

The superior achievements which set the two worlds apart—the world created by literate peoples and the world created by non-literate peoples—has now and then been attributed to differences of native intelligence. Anthropologists find no support for this idea that one race or people has innate intellectual capabilities denied others. Their findings however do establish a close connection between superiority in civilized arts on one hand and skill in accumulating and using man's intellectual heritage on the other. The library is the chief instrument so far perfected for the performance of this latter function, and its claim to indispensability in literate society can be indicated by elaborating briefly the idea just stated. By learning to depend on letters instead of depending merely on live memory and the spoken word, man vastly increased his effectiveness in preparing youth for adulthood. Since the library has been perfected as the principal vehicle for carrying forward and making available the means for one thing that formal education at all levels can be conducted more effectively with well-equipped libraries. There are few left today who would dispute this: community after community the world over is struggling to adopt and maintain high libraries. The central point, however, goes far beyond what this community or that may or may not to do. Assume two cultures where native ability is the same but one is literate and the other is preliterate. The educational capabilities of the two people in such a case will necessarily differ, regardless of what the community is innately capable of, or wishes to do. One will be capable of prolonged, systematic education of youth in subjects of great erudition except as normal capability is spliced by the social facility which has come to be known as the library.

The remaking of Librarianship

Collecting the though to others had to wait as was seen till the use of letters to convey though was perfected. Similarly, modern librarianship had to wait on the creation of a society where man's need for intellectual sources was so great that private libraries could no longer meet the demands by themselves. The fourth and last step to be noted was the movement to develop library service on a scale commensurate with there demands, and the rest of the book shows how representative nations demands, and the rest of the book shows how representative nations have gone about it. National programs differ, as one might expect of separate creations of energetic peoples faced each with its own peculiar conditions. Major library systems of the world nevertheless have enough in common to set modern librarianship off as a stage noticeably different from the past.

Librarianship as portrayed in the chapters to follow is not very old. Ernst Cassirer describes Leibniz as the last man of learning to master the total sum of recorded though. Limits were being reached beyond which the mind could not keep up with or fully utilize the learning that was accumulating without relying upon the specialty which the library profession was to rise to handle. It is plan in retrospect to see what librarians of new type were needed for. It was up to somebody to assemble, organize and make available this expanding record of the mind. It could no longer be done by private individuals who took on the responsibility as a side job while doing other things. To develop this emerging specially in scale with the times, library service would have to be organized and supported along the lines of other public responsibilities like police protection, formal schooling, and public health. High standards of service would be required for all classes of people, of all ages, and steady financing in terms of program needs would be called for.

Librarians as last as the eighteenth century, at the time of Leibniz, were clearly not ready for this responsibility. The chaotic state then of library organization and service is described in Zachrias K. von Uffenbach's Merkwiirdige Reisen durch Niedersachsen. Uffenbach shows a clear grasp of the way any undertaking depends for success on the calibre of people who are in charge of it, but blames library personnel to a degree that suggests insensitiveness to the role other besides the specialists play in the launching of a profession. What Uffenbach overlooks is that the act of instituting any new division of labor is a social act; it is not taken till the people who form the society will it. The social climate affects the rate at which the new movement advances, indeed whether it gets under way at all. Once under way, it is again the attitude of people outside the specialty that determines the social status, the economic incentives and other perquisites held out to those who choose to invest their lives in the work. The over-all social worth thus attached to the calling in turn has a reflex effect on whether superior or mediocre people are recruited. If leaders of the eighteenth century society cannot be absolved from their shares of responsibility fro the mediocre library talent recruited, neither can they be excused for the state of moral among library workers. The people of an emergent calling, just as other, rise to the full height of their powers with greater heart when the work they pour their lives into is treated with respect. Library work had by the eighteenth century risen in dignity in some ways since the days when educated Greek slaves served the best Roman families in luxurious surroundings, but the disheartening conditions pictured by Uffenbach leave so little ground for professional pride that the librarians he criticizes may have wondered at times whether the advantages were all on their side.

The transition to the transition to the twentieth century owes much to enriched material and bibliographical resources, but even more to leaders inside and outside libraries who promoted a new concept of Librarianship. One of these was Leibniz, who served for a while as librarian of Wolfbuttel. If he came toward the end of the line of men of universal learning, he was at the same time among the first to see that a world which was enlarging the record of the mind so rapidly was, in the process, developing built-in requirements for a library program well beyond the capabilities of the private library. His proposals for developing research libraries included: establishing a basis of support firm enough to assure continuous development of collections; regular appropriations; systematic acquisition of all major works of outstanding contributors to learning; classification of the entire collection; an alphabetical catalog, with subject index; the entire administration to be aimed at giving the library a role in the life of the state and society comparable in importance to that of the school and the church. The remarkable progress of the Gottingen library in the eighteenth century, other advances in and out of Germany inspired by its example, even the spur to library development given by Althoff late in the nineteenth century, all felt the influence of Leibniz' ideas. He was however ahead of his time. In France, the Royal Library, already of leading rank in his time, was undoubtedly the most princely library in the would when the Revolution struck, yet it was more a national treasure than an institution designed to serve the intellectual needs of the public. Across the channel, the British Museum, with its library, opened in 1759. It was to provide "free access to all studious and curious persons" but the era of public service for which it become world famous could hardly be sail to have begun before the reforms which occurred toward the middle of the nineteenth century. Hansard's Debates quotes William Cobbett as saying of it in 1833: "Why should tradesmen and formers be called upon to pay for the support of a place which was intended only for the amusement of the curious and rich, and not for the benefit or the instruction of the poor? If the aristocracy wanted the Museum as a lounging place, let them pay for it."

The Education of Librarians

From all this emerges a simple conclusion about what man, the architect of twentieth century librarianship, has been striving to do. He has been learning how to use letters more nearly to achieve his full potential in the realms of mind and heart; learning how to build a civilization in which he and these things he so highly prizes will be at home; and in so doing, learning how to apply to the practical problems that beset him the best fruits of the mind regardless of time or place of origin. These past advances suggest asking what the next advance will be, but this is a question which cannot be answered any more than one could tell at the other end of library history what the future held. Present-day uses of the image, the recapture through radio of the power of the spoken word, recent break-through to mechanical storage and retrieval of information, will undoubtedly affect the future of libraries: they are already affecting the society to which libraries have become indigenous. Whether the influence of the printed page, relative to these, is waxing or waning is hardly the central point about the epic of literate society and its libraries. Writing is only the first, in the course of developments which have given man power to retain, organize and use the accumulated heritage of all generations of all mankind. If it is possible to single out one thing among many as a special preoccupation of modern librarianship, it would be fair to say its chief concern is to assure continuance and full use of this power. The future of a particular means of doing it, such as the printed page, is secondary to this larger purpose. One hastens to add that the newer media of mass communication, mechanical storage and retrieval of information, etc., appear so far to be rather supplements than substitutes for the book. To date, the latter has found no match as a means of communicating sustained sequences of though across barriers of space and time.

This is the perspective which gives the tide of interest in educated librarians which is rising around the world its special meaning. Pushing from below are new forces and demands which make trained manpower in this field more important in more nations than ever before.

It may be asked why the responsibility for providing qualified library personnel is gravitating to universities.

The answer falls into four parts. First, the library task of the race has grown to a magnitude where it challenges and rewards the best minds. This alone is enough to enkindle the interest of university men.

Over hundreds of years, universities have steadily broadened their usefulness to the public. They have one so by making it their special task to develop leaders in all division of human endeavor which involve a high degree of intellectual cultivation. Second, universities are concerned about the future of their own libraries, and would be slow to accept librarians who are not university trained. Third, all leading nations have experimented with the use of apprenticeship in training librarians, only to find that this ancient method of instruction, while it has its uses in manual trades and occupations, is in the field of librarianship wasteful in money and time—wasteful about all of priceless assets of youth which are never regained once lost. It is on this account that recent library history in all major countries shows a slow but unmistakable drift away from apprenticeship towards methods of instruction which have been pioneered and perfected in centers of formal education.

Fourth, experience in educating librarian is still limited when compared with professions were curricula have been in operation for hundreds of years, nut library science is rapidly gaining recognition as a field of study and research which not only commands the respect of university men but requires for the solution of its problems the same standards of scholarship applied in other fields. There is a rapidly-growing library literature which represents scholarship of a high order. Research in librarianship however is not yet highly developed, and it is important to understand that the reason lies in the way most nations start out. When thinkers in the practicing arts have the freedom to do so, they normally set to work to develop through research a scientific base, a substructure of theory from which evolve changes in the arts themselves. the tendency is illustrated by the history of the emergence of medical research, research in jurisprudence, etc. The same tendency can be seen in those library schools were the teaching of beginners has cased to be an all-consuming task. A case can be made for developing the research potential of a new field from the outset, but the characteristic procedure in most countries has been to begin the other way around and to concentrate at first on instructing young librarians to go out and take charge of practical library operations.

University sponsorship of the education of librarians has yielded two principal benefits. It has raised the level of scholarship, introduced research and research programs in as field where nothing of the sort had existed before. Second, it has broadened the education of the operating personnel, balancing instruction in the technology of the subject with supporting instruction in other fields. Libraries are concerned with the entire spectrum of knowledge: balanced instruction thus becomes of necessity an interdepartmental task. In this respect, educating librarians is something like educating writers. Each speciality, writing just as librarianship, presupposes a certain technical competence as well as a special language and some knowledge of a particular literature, all of which can be taught by a single department. But the great librarian, just as the great writer, needs the well-rounded intellectual development which normally is the contribution of several sister disciplines working together in unison. The prevailing philosophy of education for librarianship is quite specific in assuming, first, that the prime requisite of the well-qualified librarian is a university education and, second, that the function with that more specialized preparation which is essential to intelligent practice of this profession.

Is the library the creature or the creator of this literate world in which we live and move and have our being? It is both at once. Librarianship stands for the accumulated power over the works of the mind, and out type of civilization depends on the works of the mind as the mammal depends on the heart-beat. Any civilization is always in process of change and ours in some ways magnifies change; but the changes we sanction are those sanctioned by reason, intelligence. Till such time therefore as man turns back the clock towards dependence, once again, on blind passion or unquestioning tradition, the functions now served by libraries will continue to remain at the heart of our society, and so long as this is true we shall need men and women of superior ability and superior training to see that these services are well performed.

Comparative Study of Library

"BASES" as used in the general title may refer either to separate geographical locations or to the fundamental principles of a subject. The two meanings correspond to two purposes of the present work. One is to introduce beginning students to librarianship as practised in selected countries whose work has attracted the attention of librarians elsewhere. The second is to illuminate problems of theory by examining librarianship in different social settings.

The problems involve in adapting libraries to the needs of readers are similar the world over. Different people solve them differently, but sooner or later the library procedures of a country begin to settle into a pattern. Accordingly the three resident lecturers, from Britain, Germany and the United States, were asked to describe characteristic procedures in their countries—methods of governing, organizing and financing libraries; methods of cataloging and classification; methods of giving good service to readers, etc. But of course modern librarianship is a more complex phenomenon than local-library methodology, important as that is. Therefore, each lecturer was also asked to describe his country's library program considered as a whole. "Program" as used here suggests the presence of system, of orderly planning, the over-all library policy that a nation s following. The task accordingly was one of articulating the goals and standards consciously or unconsciously used by the architects of the system as well as one of assessing national accomplishments in terms of these goals and standards.

Using these specifications, the following chapters tell what Librarianship is like country by country, and this is all that can be expected of papers prepared independently of one other. Comparative librarianship is a subject which deals with material on theory and practice found in different geographical and political areas, but it is a method of study as well as a subject. The purpose of this chapter is to use this method to identify some of the common characteristic is sufficient, especially in the light of later chapters, little discussion is added. Other common features can be found besides those mentioned. The object is not so much to exhaust the subject as to illustrate the use of the comparative method and thus suggest the fruitfulness of applying it in further study of library problems. These problems, instead of remaining, as once they were, the province of a few nations, are taking on global proportions. At any rate, here are common characteristics worth noting:

Trend away from Personal Libraries and Imitations of them

The story of man's early reliance on libraries which the individual owned and administered as he saw fit, need not be further elaborated except to stress the fact that as learning expanded, privately operated libraries become too costly to keep up to data. German universities developed the seminal library as an aid to academic work and it helped bridge the transition to dependence on public-supported libraries for professional purposes. The innovation gained popularity in the nineteenth century when America and other younger nations were relying heavily on these pioneering universities for advanced training in scholarship. Returning students planted libraries of a similar nature in their own countries, and they took deep root.

The seminar library resembles, in convenience, organization, use of space and how it is controlled, a personal library, and some scholars remain strongly attached to it for precisely this reason. It is the model they are accustomed to and like. But while the seminar library, along with libraries which are organized and administered along similar lines, still survives and flourishes, no major country accepts it any longer as the best model to use when planning further library advance. there are several reasons why it is being superseded, but they add up to saying that it is giving around to the same forces which pushed aside the once all-sufficient personal library. Since the nineteenth century, intellectual materials have continued to increase at a prodigious rate. There are more fields, with more overlapping interests, as well as more publications in each one. In all important fields, there are also more scholars and students. And on top of all this, the practice of drawing heavily on the literature, which the seminar library was created to foster has become so commonplace that it is now standard practice throughout this vastly enlarged community of learned people. The seminar library is designed best to serve the private interests of a small group, whereas we now live in a day when library service must, in fairness to all scholars and all taxpayers, be planned to serve the greatest good of the greatest number at minimum cost.

When the popularity of the seminar library was at its crest, one American university, the University of Chicago, projected a library system which would give each department its own library. The very thoroughness and fairness with which the system wás planned helped to make it vividly apparent how poorly adapted it is to the needs of a new day in scholarship, and how expensive it would be to maintain a system which ate up so much space, demanded such expensive duplication of books and personnel, and made such inefficient use of suitable hours of opening. This demonstrated inability to serve justly, efficiently and economically the twentieth century's greatly enlarged community of serious readers has forced a search for some design or model better adapted to the needs of the times.

Provision of library service at public expense is now the established policy of the three nations whose experience is being drawn on most in this review. The total financial cost each year amounts to sums hardly dreamed of in the nineteenth century.

The procedure for carrying out this policy is by no means uniform, but the prevailing tendency is: to recognize library service as a new social responsibility to be delegated, in the same way as other work requiring high personal and academic qualifications, to professionally trained personnel; to place the work on an economic footing, to enable those who make it a full-time career to live in dignity and self-respect; and to create a hierarchy of positions in the field by which the most able rise to top positions of leadership. In sociological terms, modern society has reached the stage where a new division of specialized labor concerned with books and people has arisen, and responsibility for this new work is being institutionalized, with all that this means in organization, recruiting and training or personnel, professional status, and responsibility for social leadership.

As already intimated, however, there are being built up at public expense many collections for which the library profession has no responsibility what so ever. The best examples are in universities, where a professor may exercise a degree of personal control over university-owned books which differs little, if at all, from the sort of control he would exercise if they belonged to him. Of course a scholar must have books. Furthermore, special subsidies are required to get certain types of work done. The combination of these two things has produced confusion, even heated debate, as to whether the purpose of public support of book purchase for universities is to subsidize the work of the individual scholar or to help finance a public service which may benefit him but which he is not empowered to control to the disadvantage of others.

Each nation must decide for itself which activities it will subsidize and which it will institutionalize. Meanwhile those communities, where library systems of the highest quality are developing appear to be those which institute library service as a bona fide public responsibility. By this term is meant acceptance by the state, or by some philanthropic body, of responsibility not only for financing, but at the same time for regulating and controlling the service independent of the individuals thus served. An analogous process is the organization of a public school system to relieve families of some of the responsibility of educating their children—or the organization of hospital to aid in caring for the sick. The private citizen benefits from the new service, but good citizenship calls on him in return to comply cheerfully with regulations designed to serve the common good. If any regulation is found detrimental to the common good, democratic government provides orderly ways of making changes.

Libraries of Four Major Types

Certain countries have national libraries. The Library of Congress and the British Museum Library function as such in a general way, but Britain, Germany and the United States are alike in having no national library in any formal sense of the term.

They are alike also in having well-developed system of libraries comprising four major types. The terminology used to describe them varies, even in one country, while the extent to which librarians treat these several types as branches of a single profession differs from country to country even more. Terminology aside, the literature shows substantial agreement on what might be called the social basis of the four types. One type has risen to serve the needs of higher learning and research and is often referred to as the academic and research library. Academic instruction and research are of course not the same thing, but the clienteles of those libraries which fall in this general category overlap so much that separating them into two classes is considered artificial.

A second type provides library service for student in lower schools. It originated, as did the academic and research library, as a result of literate society's growing dependence on letters as the main source of contact with accumulated thought, but it exists to serve a younger clientele. School librarianship came late. As an organized movement, it can hardly be said to go further than World War I and most librarians would put the date later than that. Once members of the younger generation are equipped through lower and higher schools for adult life, they enter their chosen callings and there they find people across the whole spectrum of practical affairs making constant and necessary use of information and information sources in their daily work. These demands for information to be applied to the business of everyday living began to be felt in the nineteenth century, and an organized movement to create appropriate service got under way early in the twentieth. It gave birth to organizations variously referred to as special libraries, information bureaux, and documentation centres. Librarians less sensitive to the undercurrents forcing these services into being greeted efforts to organize them with inertia and ever opposition. It was unfortunate, for the new movement became in part as a result a protest movement, introducing confusion and disunity where mutual understanding and harmony would have been, and still is, more fitting. This stress on the importance of the third type of library links up with the treatment in the last chapter of the ways that a civilized man's deepening dependence on accumulating intelligence found expression in institutional form. Seen in this perspective, modern information services are part of an institution which could go by any name but which for lack of a better is called the modern library movement. Indeed these services mark a sort of culmination of this movement—the step where the use of letters or organized intelligence or information leaves the cloister to be taken out into the office, workshop, market-place.

The special library thus resembles the keystone in the arch which some builders at first rejected. Its peculiarities grow out of deliberate effort and skill exerted to satisfy the information requirements of a specific clientele, often limited to members of some organization or other. As a rule, this type of library concentrates less on procedures which are common in libraries of other types and specializes on getting published or unpublished information for specific, carefully anticipated uses. It also goes beyond the normal standard of library service in getting the information in the shape to be put to work at once with a minimum effort on the part of a clientele which may not consider themselves "readers" in the accepted sense at all.

The fourth class, the public library, stands at the other extreme as a sort of beacon for the community as a whole. Sometimes it is overshadowed by the academic and research library and may venture but casually if at all into information services or into serving readers of school or pre-school age. When its usefulness is thus circumscribed, it is fittingly called the "popular library", meaning a library which specializes in providing leisure reading and entertainment. As is recognized, however, the public library at its best is a more virile force than that. Public librarians make a point of cooperating with and helping out library service available elsewhere in the community, and this fact at first has a negative suggestion bout its role; but is another way of describing a range of interest, a flexibility which enable it to respond to the demands of scholars or school children or businessmen whenever the good of the community requires it. One of the later chapters speaks of the foundations of the public library. The treatment there and elsewhere suggests that, in those countries where literacy and literate habits are deepening and where the academic and research library has not branched out to bear the responsibility, the public library has been in process of becoming the broad base or foundation of the entire national library system. Its clientele consists of common people who, with the specialities, many of which require the use of intellectual resources of one kind or another.

Similar National Library Objectives

Libraries provide services which are so numerous that it would take several pages to detail them. While they vary a great deal from one library to another, they have a certain family resemblance the world over, so it is not surprising to find attempts made to classify them. A sample classification is to be found in Library Trends volume where it is suggested that most of the hundreds of services available in libraries of various type can be grouped under the following headings: free lending of library materials for use, personal assistance by a trained staff in helping the reader get what he wants, counseling and teaching which go beyond ordinary reference service, preparation and publication of library tools, information services which save the inquirer the trouble of doing the necessary research for himself, building library collections, and other technical services which take place behind the scenes but which are important in procuring, conserving and organizing library materials for present or future use.

Notwithstanding the fact that the use of letters and learning, and therefore of libraries, has slowly been built into the structure of literate society, any attempt to isolate library service to society from services to individual readers runs into the same kind of difficulty that troubled Browning's Fra Lippo Lippi who, enjoined to paint spirit, found himself everlastingly painting the flesh. Comparative study of library systems reveals that the social functions they perform do in fact differ from one another. The difference is radical, for example, between West Germany and Germany under the Nazis. The library programs of the countries on which this survey is based are much alike. Essentially, their library objective are as follows:

To accumulate and make available now and in the future the best work of the mind, regardless of when or where the work was done. This is the task of conserving those intellectual resources which may be said to document in any significant respect the experience of the race. Man stands to benefit in very practical ways from having at hand the best of his cultural heritage, but some obligation is felt to retain it not merely for practical benefit but for its own sake. Opinion varies, however, on just what material should be conserved strictly for its own sake.

To afford access to all responsible intellectual work without interference from political or religious authority. These countries adhere to a policy of making the results of serious intellectual work freely accessible. The following statement made by a public official of high rank in one country expresses a tolerance found in all three of them. "If this nation is to be wise as well as strong, if we are to achieve our destiny, then we need more new ideas for more wise men reading more good books in more public libraries. These libraries should be open to all—except the censor. We must know all the facts and hear all the alternatives and listen to all the criticisms. Let us welcome controversial authors."

To further research. Some subjects can be studied with little or no reference to the literature, but nearly all important research nowadays depends on knowing what has been done, and is being done, by other workers. It is impossible to keep abreast of the status of knowledge in rapidly advancing fields without having at hand a well-equipped library of sources for reference. Provision of suitable materials and services is costly, nut usually cheaper than trying to get along without knowing what else has been done.

To aid formal instruction. Textbooks and lectures have their place, but all three countries rely less on these in most subjects than formerly and rely proportionately more on the use of the library as an aid to instruction. A good many progressive thinkers have come to treat the library as the heart of instruction; more is said on this subject in later chapters. The central role it now plays comes about as a result of three influences. First is the greatly increased and rapidly increasing number of well-written books which will facilitate and broaden the student's comprehension of the subject. Second is a gradual reform in methods of instruction, brought about by research on the learning process. The evidence established that learning is more effective when the learner's work is so planned as to stimulate him to master the subject he studies through at least some independent work in a library instead or depending on lectures alone or combining them with required readings. Third, re-examination of the purposes of formal education has led many to conclude that one objective should be to encourage people while they are still young to form a life-time habit of reading. Habits of course are formed only through exercise. It follows that students at all levels of instruction should first of all have access to libraries which are well-stoked with good books to read. They should moreover have a chance to live in an atmosphere, complete with good library service, which stimulates the forming of this habit. An inescapable obligation thus falls on teachers and librarians to work together to help young people learn for themselves the enjoyment of reading and this includes the supplying of sympathetic guidance which young people require in these matters. Experience has shown that required readings can create distaste for reading, rather than pleasure, but this outcome is usual. Meanwhile it is widely agreed that a student may graduate from some universities without learning how to work independently, perhaps even without ever knowing the tingle of excitement which good reading can bring; but it is also agreed that no such graduate can be called literate or cultivated in the higher meaning of the term.

To supply information in the management of practical affairs. For a long time, the advancement of knowledge was an enterprise which was considered separate, indeed aloof, from the business of the man in the street. Literate society, it has been observed, is quite as much a process as a static condition—a process of permeating all phases of life with the practice of obtaining and using the best available information in deciding and doing things of all kinds. The very success of the advancement of knowledge in the erudite sense of the term taught the man in the street how to improve on the older techniques which relied on tradition or on snap judgment wherever tradition failed to show the way. It has also been observed that the rise of a branch of library activity specially concerned with procuring reliable information and putting it to work marks the breakdown of the older idea that knowledge belongs in the cloister apart from the bustling world outside. A literate society makes use of the scientific process and the results of careful inquiry in any and every sphere of human effort.

To promote popular enlightenment and enrich human life. Every free man has an inalienable right to remain as ignorant as he pleases once he meets compulsory school-attendance requirements; ut the attitude of these three nations, and others, is that when any citizen choose to exercise this right others suffer. For self-government is an empty, retreating ideal unless citizens resolutely qualify themselves to decide intelligently the various issues which determine how the people are to be governed. The level of popular enlightenment thus becomes a barometer of self-government to which a people can rise: it is a sobering fact that is general we get the quality of government which we first qualify ourselves to demand.

The free library has come to be prized as a special aid to popular enlightenment, but its role in deciding issues of state is incidental to a more basic purpose of democracy which is often overlooked. It is a sacred tenet of free men's faith that nobody is to be considered merely as a tool of the state. It is rather the other way around. The state is a tool to aid in the highest cultural and spiritual development of all the people. Libraries are prized for many services, but self-governing communities prize them for nothing more than in helping each person rise to and live at the full height of his powers. By putting such things first, the population better enables itself as a matter of course to handle its political affairs.

The characteristics of the literature in these three countries are not the same, nut in general the birth of an organized profession has been accompanied by publication of journals to use in exchanging ideas, and by production of library tools including labor-saving manuals, guides to good library practice, and aids of all kinds for the use of readers. The sharing of experience and improving of tools to work with are tasks that are never finished: the publishing activities of major library organizations give these things high priority now as they did to start with. Critics of the literature, if they complain that too much writing is didactic and shallow, wisely refrain from objecting to these purposes.

The gradual acceptance of library science as a university responsibility has been accompanied on one side by rising standards for the education of librarians and on the other by more competent critical analysis of library problems. If a particular data is singled out to mark the banning of an attendant change in the literature, perhaps the most appropriate one would be the launching of the Library Quarterly by the Graduate Library School of the University of Chicago in 1931. During the interval numerous monographs reporting results of careful scholarship have taken their place on library science shelves alongside work reported by the Quarterly, but the change is more pervasive than outstanding individual contributions by Joeckel, Wilson, Tauber, Bryan, Shaw, Shera, or others. Better educated librarians are doing more substantial work, and this is subtly influencing the literature.

To these three branches of literature, others can be added. The "survey" has been perfected as an administrative tool of the first importance. It is sometimes described as an application of the methods of objective research to a particular library situation. This is good as far as it goes, but the survey dose not stop with reporting the results of research. in the technical sense in which it has come to be employed the term survey also involves the application of expert judgment in proposing what should be done about the situation. This clearly is something that goes beyond research as ordinarily understood. Second, considerable source material is being produced by systematically gathering and publishing data on various subjects ranging from library salaries to the rate at which book collections are growing and how much they cost. Third are systematic treatises on school libraries, university libraries, technical libraries, or other aspects of librarianship such as reference work and "technical services". General texts of this kind are not yet available in all field. For example, a comprehensive treatise on the modern public library, for the use of the beginning student, is not to be found. Fourth, there is a voluminous amount of library legislation, badly scattered. Even a cursory account should not omit the vast amount of writing, referred to as "promotional", which interprets the meaning of librarianship. Much of this writing has no permanent value, but here the librarian customarily makes his bid for public understanding of his mission.

Bibliographical Access to Library Holdings

Access to books and related materials may be provided by removing all barriers and permitting readers to go directly to the shelves. This is called physical access, or more often "open access". The litter phrase was coined when the idea was new a librarians were experimenting with methods by which they could successfully break away from the practice of keeping books behind closed doors or behind other barriers to ready access. Although open access is spreading with the growth of influence of the public library, the practice is be no means universal.

Bibliographical access refers to any method of gaining access to books through bibliographies, published or unpublished. Thus when the reader goes to a library and finds a printed catalog or a card catalog where all of its holdings are listed, we say he has bibliographical access to the holdings of the library.

All three countries have invested thousands of hours of time in listing the contents of their libraries. Long experience has shown that the material needed by a reader can most conveniently be located if he is able to approach it either by author, subject or title. In general, the libraries of these countries have each a carefully prepared catalog which provides all three approaches. The service does not stop there. Normally a reader may in a few days' time ascertain whether a book he cannot obtain through his own library can be obtained from some other library; for libraries in each country cooperate to obtain material wherever it is located, and books may also be borrowed from other countries. The three plans to facilitate bibliographical access thus have similar objectives and, up to a point, use similar methods. Examples of similarities include: spread in the practice of depending of card catalogs instead of printed catalogs, the use of author and title entries, and the listing of all the holdings of a library and its branches is in subject approach. The issue is whether to have a classified catalog or an alphabetical catalog with cross references.

It is a complex problem. Arguments for the classified catalog start from the value of thorough systematization of knowledge. This method brings all related material together and, moreover, shows what the relationship is. The inquirer in locating a particular work thus funds beside it works on the same subject and works on all cognate branches as well. It is a service of such usefulness in much academic work that studies have shown scholars of different nations to prefer good classified catalogs. The problem of locating specific subjects in the classification scheme is usually facilitated by the availability of a separate alphabetical list of subjects.

The dictionary catalog arose during the early days of the modern library movement as part of a revolutionary movement to make of books, libraries and reading a force more significant than they were at the time. The pioneers of the movement agreed on a general strategy aimed at bringing more readers and more good books together. It was a many-sided effort which involved developing better librarians, more attractive libraries and methods of attracting readers to the libraries; but it also involved breaking down the then-existing barriers to books. One decision made was that readers would be served best if the books were arranged on the shelves in classified order and if ways could be found to open the shelves so readers could go directly to the books. Open access, it was argued, is better than any kind of intermediary—whether a classified catalog, a dictionary catalog, a reference librarian or reader's adviser.

The classified catalog was widely in use then and was, as now, in great favor among the more sophisticated readers especially those who were familiar with the scheme in use. However, the reader who was not familiar with the library found it a barrier and it took time to educate him on how to use it. The dictionary catalog was found to be easier to learn.

Theories of subject cataloging thus impinge on other questions. One is whether bibliographical access is to be used as a supplement to direct access to the books on the shelves or as the only means of access. A related question is whether the primary purpose of the library catalog is to be a tool for locating some work in a particular library or whether it is as more ambitious bibliographical tool designed to show the organization of the universe of knowledge. There is no disagreement as to the importance, agreement that the best, most economical way to render this service, is to construct independent catalogs based on the holdings of individual libraries. The difference in approach is thus seen to go beyond the respective merits of the classified catalog and the dictionary catalog. The two forms are each part of a larger strategy which an energetic, library-minded nation has worked out for the service of its people; so they must be evaluated in terms of what they contribute to the success of the total system within which they are constructed. Meanwhile the objectives of both systems are similar and if members of the international fraternity of librarians find improvements they can make by borrowing from their neighbors, these adaptations we may be sure will be made as soon as they can be fitted into the system they work with.

Active Professional Organizations

A library movement is made of people. Till far into the nineteenth century, this was not realized; Librarianship was considered more a matter of physical things which a clerk could care for—books, rooms, tables, etc. The library movement in each of these countries has been furthered, specially at the beginning, by scholars and public-spirited citizens who recognized the worth of libraries and who aided in creating full-time positions of rank where the gifts of capable librarians could find full scope. Higher education for librarians was inaugurated in

America and Germany in the early 1880's, and from this point leadership began to pass over to specially trained full-time workers. But earlier, in 1876, the American Library Association was founded and the next year, inn Britain, the Library Association. No date can be set for the beginning of the modern library movement, but the spiral of achievements associated with it begins in the fourth quarter of the nineteenth century which followed these first steps. Professional organizations have served as effective forums for the discussion of national library problems. They have given librarians a channel for making themselves heard; and through contacts with other organizations, government agencies and the general public have greatly influenced public sentiment and action on libraries. They have been particularly helpful in developing and promoting adoption of national standards affecting personnel as well as major aspects of library organizations and service.

Development of Human Resources

If one digs into the organization on libraries in these countries, few things stand out more plainly then the hardly surprising fact that librarians of stature are not found in little libraries. It is not that the smallest library cannot benefit from the finest talents: It is a matter of applying the idea that an individual library program, the same as the library movement as a whole, is made more of people than of than of things. The administration of libraries still shows traces of an older idea when the human element was not wisely utilized. The neglect is apparent in perpetuating seminar all small departmental libraries in poorly coordinated university library systems, in the number of weak public libraries which operate independently of libraries elsewhere in the same region, in indifference to separating clerical and professional responsibilities so as to make better use of different levels of ability in the same library. It is instructive to observe by way of contrast how uniformly international experience shows that good library service to a community cannot be given without an annual expenditure of several thousand marks, pounds of dollars. There is of course no magic in fixed sums of money, for the thing at stake is not of a material nature. It is rather a tangible manifestation of the fact that an effective program of service entails, over and above everything else, a program of effort involving a sizable pyramid of human energies. At the base are jobs for manual workers and clerks while at the top are jobs capable of attracting and holding professional talents of a high order. this explains the tendency to develop larger units of service in all these countries. A library too small to provide scope for a hierarchy of well-organized human talent kills the whole possibility of library service of high quality.

Well-Designed Library Buildings

The history of library housing falls roughly into three periods: (1) when space was used that was not specially planned for library purposes; (2) the era of the monument to letters and learning when beauty and magnificence were stressed but criteria of excellence for library service were not well understood; and (3) the era since professional librarians and a new generation of architects began to learn how to work together. Their combined efforts have radically changed the whole planning process and produced a new conception of what a library building should be and do. The best building have been erected since Would War II in the United States and Germany. By today's criteria, few buildings before that date would rate very high.

As soon as one stops to reflect, it is apparent that much of the difference between the attainable and the unattainable depends on space—on distance, geographical relationships. It is this simple insight that accounts mainly for the revolution in the planning of library buildings. As an example, one of the objectives of the modern library is to attract people to the library—not to wait for people to take the initiative themselves. Experience has shown that one of the ways to bring people and books together is to select a site close to where two main arteries of pedestrian traffic interest, then plan an exterior as well as an interior which generously exhibits attractive books, thus arresting the attention of passers-by. One college faculty decided at the suggestion of the librarian to do all it could with a new building to encourage student to read books related to the ones on the regular reading lists provided them by professors. The solution was to place shelving in the middle of the first floor where required readings in a subject—say history—could be surrounded by a generous selection of related works among which students would be free to browse at will. It is one of many imaginative departures from tradition that have been made in the newer library buildings which has proved very successful and is now being copied elsewhere. When the student leaves this building, he is forced by physical arrangements to pass close to an attendant who checks to see that all books are properly charged, but aside from this control, he is free to move at will among thousands of books and recordings, newspapers and magazines, all on open shelves with good lighting and comfortable chairs similar to those one might expect to find in other well-appointed "living" rooms.

5
Research Methods in Librarianship

Empirical scientists in the modern world have traditionally relied upon carefully structured experiments. At times, scientists have conducted experimental studies in which phenomena were not directly observed in an actual situation but in which prototypes of existing processes or events were closely examined. Nonetheless, some investigative tasks do not lend themselves readily to randomized experimental designs: therefore, other methods of inquiry must be selected. For examples, the following kinds of inquiries would not be particularly amenable to ex-perimental designs because these studies would require either extensive direct observation or descriptive/historical methods.

1. An evaluation of the research and screening procedures used last year by a large research library to select new professional employees.
2. A study of the impact of automation on a group of special libraries in the field of textiles over a 3-year period
3. A project designed to assess the effect of the attainment of faculty status among a group of academic librarians
4. An inquiry to determine factors related to the

selection of library building consultants for a group of newly constructed metropolitan libraries in the South

5. An assessment of losses and thefts of college library book in a 5-years period.
6. An examination of the administrative practices of a research library's serials department
7 An analysis of the role state library consultants in the development of rural library programs during the early years of the Library Services Act
8 A study of the utilization of a computer-produced book catalog in a group of special libraries within the chemical industry
9. An evaluation of the use of student assistants in New York City school media centers
10. A project designed to trace the development of bookmobile library service in South Carolina between 1930 and 1960.

This list should demonstrate that experiments are not always appropriate in some settings or areas in which librarians seek new information. There-fore, in such situations, research workers can sometimes rely upon the direct inspection of "real-world" phenomena. Furthermore, several-often quite different-methods can be used to obtain optimal data in the course of conducting a single study. Sometimes, the use of multiple data gathering techniques in a study enhances research precision. For example, two or more research processes can be used to minimize error. More-over when research data are collected by means of several strategies, scientists can often be more certain and can draw more reliable conclusion. Even though several methods without definitude or distinction might be employed in a single inquiry, investigators may use the data obtained, provided that weaknesses are taken into consideration as the new information and its sources are evaluated and analyzed. Therefore, our concern in this chapter is with supplemental research techniques, many of which contain direct observational and/or descriptive elements.

Observation and Description

Libraries are formal organizations that encompass a group of people resources, services, facilities, and activities, all presumably directed to-ward common objectives. In addition to the research data-gathering methods outlined in previous chapters, origins of new research information about libraries as organizations and information systems include data obtained from the following sources: (a) institutional and agency records and collected statistic; (b) experiences of librarians as a result of "trial and error"; and (c) several observational and descriptive techniques, in-cluding the user study, evaluative study, library survey, community survey, content analysis and comparative study among others. To provide a logical discussion of these studies, methods associated with them will be approached separately in this chapter; however, the reader should be aware that difference are not always so clear-cut in actual research settings. In this approach to descriptive research, emphasis will be placed on several, well-fined observational strategies, some of which might be used to complement other useful research methods. Indeed, many descriptive procedures are based upon an amalgamation of methodological approaches. Generalized procedures of scientific method provide leeway for the use of numerous research techniques, many of which cannot be classed as experimental, survey, or historical methods, but which are based upon direct to indicate that the object or subject of an investigation is being subjected to close-usually visual-surveillance and that the information obtained will then be related to more general propositions or theories. Therefore, the term observation implies that some type of surveillance is undertaken for the purpose of satisfying an investigator's interest or curiosity about a distinct research task. Observation is widely recognized as a prime requisite of research in general and of descriptive research in particular. Although observation is a relatively primitive procedure, it is frequently very valuable in research and is often described aptly as a technique for securing "measurements" without and aid of instruments. W.I.B. Beveridge points out in *The Art of Scientific* "observation involves noticing something and giving it significance by relating it to something else noticed or already known." Research subjects are commonly observed by scholars who intend to identify and delineate situations which the objects behave in the situations. When an investigator engages in the observed entity or activity, participant observation occurs. Investigators who use direct observation may employ either obtrusive or unobtrusive techniques. Obtrusive observation is forward and open; unobtrusive observation, however, is clandestine and discreet. Both methods can be employed by investigators without direct interaction with research subjects. For example, in a study of library services to migrant farm laborers, a research worker might observe the process as an outsider-watching but not participating in the service. On the other hand, the investigator might even pose as a migrant worker to gain a discreet position from which to examine the service from the recipient's viewpoint.

When research workers take special vantage positions to unobtrusively observe phenomena in a direct manner, controlled observation can be accomplished. For example, observers in a large university library might pose as students or other library users and station themselves in the reference department to discreetly observe activities of librarians and to record selected behavior of both the clientele and the reference personnel. By observing the interactions of librarians with their clients in an actual service setting, samples of selected events can be procured. In turn, these observations may lead to valid conclusion about the observed phenomenon. The primary advantage of such observational strategies is the access they yield to a variety of perhaps unanticipated research data. However, clandestine observation does pose an ethical problem, and investigators must be sure that the privacy of research subjects is protected and the confidentiality of collected data is maintained.

In field studies, direct observation and the ensuing description of phenomena are used to better understand situations, processes, development, events, or some other phenomenon. The act of describing also involves the preparation of factual reports about observed phenomena, including-insofar as possible-an account of relationships noticed among variables. Research data for many descriptive studies are comprised of newly generated information, rather than prerecorded data. In historical research projects, however, information contained in sources such as archives, journals, reference sources, government publication, or other media or agencies is often valuable. Studies in which a phenomenon will be characterized over a lengthy time period usually rely upon historical records or documents. In both descriptive and purely historical studies, however, investigators do not manipulate variables. Moreover, controlled conditions are not used to initiate the occurrence of a desired event. The direct observation of library phenomena-as distinguished from a contrived and contrived and controlled research situation-offers excellent opportunities for investigators to acquire new data. As events occur in natural settings, observational methods allow their documentation: thus, validity of the procured data can be very high. If research problems have been conceptualized clearly and productive investigative methods have been formulated so that observational data can be very high. If research problems have been conceptualized clearly and productive investigative methods have been formulated so that observational data can be recorded systematically, validity and reliability checks high be made in the form of supplemental modes of inquiry. Under such conditions, direct observation becomes an effective and cogent research tool, and investigations can benefit from its high degree of reliability. Herbert Goldhor wrote that direct observation "is a good method by which to verify data secured by other methods."

In descriptive studies based upon direct observation, capable investigators are prudent to avoid the mere accumulation of facts. To be meaningful and fruitful, and observation undertaken in descriptive research must be followed by a synthesis, analysis, or interpretation of the collected data. Assume, for example, that an investigator will conduct a comparative study to determine how planned decentralization was accomplished in several academic libraries as opposed to expedient decentralization in a similar group of libraries. Research workers would probably interpret and compare data from the two groups in relation to factors such as user access to needed materials; supervision of staff and staff efficiency; problems related to the inefficiency of the duplication of library resources; faculty interest and input in library operations; sharing of materials; ordering, classifying, and cataloging materials; and many other pertinent variables. In descriptive studies, the process of observation normally takes precedence over that of evaluation. Moreover, generalizations are not made unless representative observations have been selected from samples of defined populations. Historical studies assess past events-their incidences, distribution and relationships. But to determine present conditions investigators must seek contemporary data about ongoing phenomena. Structured observation can produce contemporary or current data about the actions of persons, or information about how phenomena occur in particular environments and under certain conditions. Structured observation is carefully planned; it commonly involves the deliberate, systematic viewing of critical aspects of an operational process or the behavior off particular group of subjects. When the observer is well aware of the numerous activities and interactions pertaining to a phenomenon, structured observation can be most effective in gaining access to original information. For example, in examinations of the roles of groups such as boards of trustees, friends of the library, or library committees, investigators could carefully schedule and plan periods of direct observation of pertinent activities so that needed data about the functions and actions of group members might be obtained. Structured observation is also more conducive to examinations of hypotheses than unstructured observation, because the investigator is keenly aware of the kinds of data needed to test an unproven proposition and is in a favorable position to gather them. Interviews with subject are sometimes conducted as concomitants to structured observational methods of descriptive studies.

Bias is a major problem related to observation and description. Thus, research workers must subdue their natural tendency to selectively view phenomena that tend to support personal conceptions, presumptions, and prejudices. When observations are not unduly distorted by biases and subjective interpretations more objective and reliable data are collected. Objectivity has been defined as "the capacity of a scientific observer to see the empirical world as it 'actually' is and the resultant quality of the body of knowledge." Therefore, objective research data are relatively free from personal bias and are not based upon value judgments.

Objectivity is not so much a virtue of the data as it is an attitude of the investigator toward research evidence. In their attempts to eliminate biased distortions, scientists tend to explain phenomena more accurately, rather than to suppress information, criticize the object of the observation, or offer prejudicial explanations. For example, assume that a research workers has been engaged by a state library to examine and make a report on procedures whereby large municipal libraries submit their budgets to city officials. Although the investigator favors the practice of allowing the librarian to recommend a budget directly to the chief city administrators, data collected in the study support the tailoring or budgetary procedures to local practices of other public institutions, insofar as possible. Thus in the collection, analysis, and reporting of the data, the research worker should objectively indicate the various advantages and disadvantages of different procedures for the submission of budgets, including the following practices; (a) the librarian's recommendation of the library budget directly to the chief administrator; (b) the adoption of the budget by the library board and the approval of tax monies only by the city council; (c) the submission of the budget by the library board to the city council through the chief city administrator; (d) the direct submission of the budget to the city council by the library board; and (e) other observed miscellaneous procedures. Thus the investigator's report budgetary procedures should reflect what was actually observed rather than what any one concerned individual, including the research worker, believes to the best practice.

Recorded descriptions obtained as a result of inquiry are truly objective when they reflect what was observed, rather than who did the observing. But when investigators become personally and emotionally involved in an observed phenomenon, objective descriptions are difficult to obtain-if not impossible. Thus observers who strive for objectivity will rely primarily upon physical inspection, rather than intuition or common sense. Many problems of bias can be reduced appreciably when investigators realize that the act of describing a phenomenon is not synonymous with theorizing or contriving appraisals and evaluations of it.

In numerous, studies, comparisons are made among several entities or among many phenomena; however, some investigators are interested in a single research object and attempt to gather extensive data about it so that relationships among variables associated with the observed phenomenon can be identified. The case study is particularly appropriate for the latter type of inquiry; this approach allows a concentrated focus on a single phenomenon and the utilization of a wide array of data-gathering methods. The overall purpose of a case study is to obtain comprehensive information about the research object. Data-gathering methods used in case studies are based primarily upon direct observation; both participant and nonparticipant observation can be used. When necessary, these methods are supplemented by structured techniques such as interviews and questionnaires. In librarianship, the objects or subjects of a case study are typically one or more of the following entities: (a) organization such as libraries, media centers, information centers, or library schools-or significant aspects of them (b) librarians, library assistants, clerical workers in libraries, or groups of library users; (c) programs or processes such as information systems and various library projects or techniques.

Case studies conducted in librarianship have focused on many group of library clientele, including the following: persons in institutions; disadvantaged or culturally de-prived citizens; children and high school students; college or university faculty members and students; professional workers such as doctors, law years, engineers, or professors; persons employed in business or industry; and other groups of library and information users and nonusers. Case studies allow close examinations of unique problems of individual groups or situations-something that many other methodologies do not readily permit. In view of concern about the social utility and responsibility of libraries as institutions, the case study approach to inquiry appears to be particularly appropriate in studying relationships between library services and a variety of social problems. Indeed, the case approach is particularly applicable in inquiries concerned with the role of libraries as social institutions-that, is their social control, performance, and impact on society in general and special groups in particular.

The primary advantage of case studies is the opportunity they afford for through and detailed examinations and analyses of a research problem so that findings can be applied directly to the object of an inquiry. On occasion, the case method has also been used in Librarianship between variables. In some cases, these exploratory studies have been used to clarify vague concepts or to challenge assumptions sot that more penetrating investigations could be undertaken in which hypotheses were tested. But case studies have disadvantages that should also be recognized; they tend to be time consuming and expensive. In addition, a single case study does not generally yield definitive results; therefore, collected data must be supplemented by information from other research modes, especially when research workers attempt to make generalizations about observed phenomena. When the objects of case studies are large groups of people or complex entities, several research workers might be needed to serve as observers. Because most observations generated by case studies result from nominal techniques of measurement and could be considered as "soft" rather than "hard" data, sophisticated statistical analysis of this collected information is difficult to accomplish, perhaps impossible in some instances. However, findings of case studies can be strengthened by utilizing whatever means of quantification are amenable in a given project.

The following steps are generalizable procedures for the conduct of case studies:

1. The research object is explicitly identified and described at a level of explanation commensurate with whatever pertinent knowledge has already been produced about it.

2. Information about the research object and investigative task are then assembled and analyzed, and relevant terms and variables are defined and described.

3. The research question is stated or hypotheses are formulated-if appropriate-based upon available information and the body of theory related to the topic of the study.

4 An entity is chosen as the specific object to be studied with reference to the research problem.

5. The object of the study is then carefully observed, and if necessary, causal factors associated with the observed phenomenon are identified.

6. If sufficient research data are collected, the hypothesis may be tested with some degree of certainty; however, investigators can be more certain when they select and examine similar cases.

Should collected evidence fail to allow the hypothesis to be tested or to solve the research problem, propositions of the inquiry may need to be reformulated, or the examined phenomenon may need to be conceptually refined. An answer to the question of whether the collected data provided insights relating to the research question or whether they sustained the hypothesis might provoke adjunct studies that could lead to the identification of definite relationship between pertinent variables off the selected case.

Upon completion of some case studies, observers have elected to take an additional step-that is to apply specific remedial procedures to the objects or research. When suggested operations or measures are applied, research workers normally follow through and attempt to observe whether these are effective. It should be apparent in the final analysis, however, that the case study method is a technique tasks. But this primary purpose does not necessarily preclude the testing of hypotheses in case studies, particularly in situations that allow collection of sufficient quantitative data. Descriptions obtained by conducting numerous, similar case studies of the observed phenomenon may be incorporated into the body of existing theory, In turn, these phenomena may also be associate with whatever theory is relevant to the specific topic of the inquiry.

The case study approach has been employed in librarianship by a number of investigators, including some doctoral students who have achieved varying degree of success. One case study was conducted to determine the role of a large public library as an agency of social reform. Other case studies have been directed toward the identification of library goals in terms of milieu requirements; the effectiveness of the New York State Reference and Research Resources Program; and the determination of whether four libraries in Kentucky had responded adequately to changes in the status of their parent institutions from that of state teachers colleges to universities. Venable Lawson employed the case study method to investigate reference services provided by two academic libraries. The primary purposes of the inquiry were to determine the following; (a) whether reference services offered by the two institutions; (b) whether reference objectives were determined by the reference function itself, and (c) whether changes in services were dictated by the objectives of reference services or by other identifiable factors. In this study, data were collected by means of the following methods: (a) an examination of library records and reports; (b) interview conducted and questionnaires distributed among library directors and reference librarians; and (c) direct observation of reference services. The selected target libraries differed in size, resources, staff, and other pertinent factors. As a result of the case study, support of the institutions instructional and research functions were revealed to be the primary objective of reference services in the two libraries. Reference services of both libraries were found to be similar; the amount of time devoted to these services by employees was also comparable. Direct reference assistance to undergraduate students was found to be largely instructional or directional in nature. Furthermore, more than half of the activities of reference librarians were devoted to efforts that were clearly not of a professional nature. On the basis of this study, it was learned that a reappraisal of reference service was needed to define its actual objectives and to more clearly understand the role of professional personnel providing such services.

Library User Studies

Among the questions that librarians have a distinct obligation to pose and attempt to answer are those relating to library effectiveness, including such factors as the choice and suitability of library materials; the nature of library collections in relation to needs of clientele; the use and nonuse of library materials and services; the degree of awareness about library collections and services among clientele or potential clientele of libraries; the efficiency with which information in libraries is stored, retrieved, and utilized, and user satisfaction or dissatisfaction with libraries. These are all closely related to the role of libraries as social, educational, or informational institution-that is, to the nature and impact of libraries on their communities-whether the community is a university, industry, government agency, school, municipality or some other entity. In other words, librarians should be concerned with the performance of their institutions as well as the influence that libraries and information centers exert on the lives of persons who can contribute to social, political, or economic change or stability. The librarian's interpretation of the utilization of recorded knowledge is based upon the moot question of whether libraries can stimulate or move people to thought, feeling, and action. The question of whether library clientele are actually induced to enter the arena of action, as a result of having made use of libraries, definitely falls within the scope of librarianship's research effort. Therefore, it is not surprising that many of the studies undertaken by librarians have contained heavy overtones of the descriptive sociological inquiry and furthermore, that some investigations in the field have been directed toward socially significant problems. Among these are the following; cultural deprivation, illiteracy, censorship, adult education, rehabilitation of prisoners, and aging.

Studies in the field are often designed to identify and to analyze how various persons or groups use libraries. User studies are similar to audience research in the field of communication. The significance and value of knowing the communication needs and practices of library users and potential library users are being increasingly recognized as librarians find themselves in keep competition for financial resources that can be used to expand information services and resources-particularly new media of communication and innovations such as the electronic digital computer. In underscoring the need for libraries to obtain a better grasp of the process of human communication, Robert Taylor wrote: "The librarian must become a modern generalist, concerned and knowledgeable about print, sound, and image, about automation and computer technology, and about formal and informal communication systems." Therefore, user studies are often instigated as attempts to understand, justify, explain, or expand library usage-and, consequently, to gain more knowledge about the process of communication insofar as libraries and their clientele are concerned.

Accounts about observed library usage are often incorporated into theories that attempt to clarify relationships between library clientele and the information resources, facilities, and services of libraries. Using close and systematic observations of communication and information-gathering habits of people, some librarians have attempted to predict future behavior of their clientele in regard to library usage. Furthermore, the findings of user studies have allowed modifications of clientele behavior with respect to the utilization of certain library resources and services. John Lubans has categorized major types of library use, including the following; browsing in the book stacks, locating useful information borrowing books or other library materials, reading books or other printed materials in the library, seeking assistance from library staff to relate demographic characteristics of populations to library use or nonuse. For example, investigators have commonly endeavored to establish relationships between the benefits of library usage and characteristics of users have been dealt with as independent variables and have been associate with certain dependent variables-particularly with the degree of library use. Writing about research in the field or reading and communication. Alice Lohrer has recognized the need in librarianship for user studies.

What people really want to view or listen to may vary considerably from what they are able to secure in books or through the air or screen. How we can produce better what the consumer of media needs, how we get the product to the consumer in our bookstores, and how we can give better service to the patron in our libraries is of great significance. Knowledge of what research tells use can help us to be more relevant in our programs of service and in producing better books and mass media.

In a similar vein, Helen M. Focke wrote: we do not know enough about our patrons, how their minds operate and what kinds of things they need and ask for, to do a really good job of serving them. We have not gathered objective data continually or been as research conscious as we should be. Although much remains to be accomplished in examining the needs of library clientele, some research in this area has been undertaken. The range of theoretical and practical aspects of the library usage issue has required the employment of various techniques. Among others, these have included such methods as the following: analyses of circulation and reference statistics, interviews with users and nonusers of libraries, mail questionnaire surveys, direct observation, case studies of various programs and services, and various unobtrusive, techniques. Perhaps a brief discussion of several reports of completed inquiries in this research area would be beneficial.

An early user in the field was conducted in the late 1930s by Louis R. Wilson. The study was an attempt to investigate the distribution and status of libraries in the United States. A report of the study. The Geography of Reading. was published by the American Library Association and the University of Chicago Press. Perhaps the most ambitious user study ever undertaken is the Public Library Inquiry, conducted in the late 1940s by the Social Science Research Council with a grant from the Carnegie Corporation of New York. Among the survey's purposes was an examination of the actual and potential role of public libraries in the United states, In addition, the Public Library Inquiry sought to determine the degree to which libraries were achieving their objectives. Based upon nationwide survey research, the study resulted in the publication of several book-length reports, including the following: The Library's Public by Bernard Berelson, The public Library in the Political Process by Oliver Garceau, and The Public Library in the United States by Robert D. Leigh. Recommendations that grew out of the Public Library Inquiry included the following: more emphasis on service to those who make the most use of libraries, an increase in the financial support of libraries to include federal funds, the establishment or larger units of public library service, and the development of better library collections with more emphasis upon materials containing quality information than upon popular and recreational works. Numerous additional user studies pertaining to public libraries have been conducted; however, few of them match the breadth of the public Library Inquiry.

In 1963, findings of the "Access to Public Libraries" study were reported to the ALA Council. The study was conducted in order to examine the extent to which citizens had free and equal access to library services; to develop a framework for the improvement of library services; and to identify the accomplishments of some libraries with respect to free and equal access. As a result of the study, a need was recognized for further attention to library services for cultural and racial minorities for the under-educated, and for persons who speak foreign languages. A list of studies conducted in this area since 1970 is provided at the end of this chapter. The selected studies are examples of attempts to understand various uses made of libraries. A survey was conducted at Purdue University among 6568 respondents to determine whether significant difference existed among uses made of the library by faculty members, graduate and undergraduate students, and other persons. Questionnaires were respect to primary and secondary reasons for using the academic library. Patterns of use were found to be of significant difference among the various categories of clientele.

At Bell Laboratories Library and Information Systems Center, a study was undertaken to evaluate the acceptability and use of microfiche and to measure the effects of microform formats on reading habits. Employees in a division of Bell Laboratories were selected as a test group for this user study. These subjects were issued microfiche rather than hard copies of technical reports during a 9-months period: questionnaires were then distributed to obtain user reactions. The investigator concluded that users were not adversely affected by microfiche formats of reports. Although microfiche reports were found to be generally acceptable, some users complained about an insufficient number of reading machines, as well as the poor quality of some of the machines and microfiche copies of reports.

Government publications and their use by faculty members were examined in another user study at Case Western Reserve University, where documents were housed in a separate collection of the social sciences and humanities faculty. The questionnaire elicited information about the extent and frequency of use of government documents and related bibliographical tools and the degree of user satisfaction with assistance provided by documents librarians. Response rate to the survey was 89%, 65% of the faculty members reported that they used government publications, regardless of where the documents were located within the library. A low correlation was found between use of the general library and that of the document collections. Three-fourths of the respondents reported having consulted documents in the past 10-year period after having found citations for them in professional journals. The majority of the respondents claimed that their use of the document collection was self-sufficient. Professors who needed help with documents indicated satisfaction with library assistance. Investigators concluded that neglect of government publications by some faculty members appeared to be appeared to be associated with a lack of awareness of the library's resources.

Another study was conducted by Cambridge University's Management Research Unit to develop techniques to measure the use and effectiveness of library services. The study was concerned with the failure of readers to locate needed materials in three academic libraries. Specifically, the following information was sought: (a) the proportion varied according to topics of materials and to types of users, (b) titles that were not usually available on bookshelves, and (c) causes of failures to locate books. Two data-collection techniques were employed: (a) records of failures to locate needed books were prepared by library clientele: and (b) randomly selected readers were interviewed as they departed the library during certain periods of selected days. Although results differed somewhat among libraries, investigators conclude that the collected data allowed librarians to establish priorities, to pinpoint problem area and procedures in need of change, and to reassess purchasing policies. This study was viewed by the investigators as an attempt to determine how librarians can better meet demands through an awareness of the information-seeking behavior and problems of readers.

A final example of a user study was conducted at several colleges and universities in California, where investigators attempted by measure faculty awareness of various reference services offered by libraries. The purpose of the study was to determine whether libraries had successfully informed constituencies of the availability of library reference services. A checklist which included selected reference services was distributed to a randomly selected sample of 1967 faculty members at six state-supported institutions. All services on the checklist were offered by the libraries on a regular basis, and respondents were asked whether the services were available in their academic libraries. The survey revealed that the typical faculty member was aware of less than half of the available services and that interlibrary loan was the most widely recognized service. On the whole, faculty members were least familiar with the reference service whereby libraries would provide tailored lists of information sources for specific courses. Academic rank and years of employment were found to be positively related to higher degrees of service awareness among faculty members. As a result of this project, the investigator underscored the value of publicizing and promoting reference services so that more open channels of communication could be maintained between the faculty and librarians.

Evaluation Research

Studies conducted to obtain objective and systematic

evidence of the success or failure of library projects and programs are often categorized as evaluation research. When a program is evaluated its relative effectiveness in terms of standards, goals, and objectives is determined and described.

Typically, evaluation research is an attempt to measure operations in terms of the goals of libraries of library projects or the end results sought. Librarians launch and carry out numerous routine and special projects designed to stimulate the use of services and to improve library operations. Considerable human and financial resources are utilized in these undertakings; thus questions are often posed by trustees, library committee members, sponsors, or librarians themselves concerning the effectiveness of these efforts. Until recent decades, assessments of most library programs and projects. Although earlier evaluations were based primarily upon value judgments of sponsors or project coor-dinators, the current trend is toward more systematic accountability of library activities; thus, the success or failure of various programs is now measured. When financial support is provided for library demonstration or for innovative projects of an experimental nature, the agencies or organizations providing grants often require thorough evaluative research is conducted to describe phenomena, to reveal relationships between variables, and to identify cause-and-effect relationships whenever possible. Evaluative studies are not distinguished so much by their methods as they are by their purposes; thus many research techniques are used to effectively evaluate library programs and projects.

Essentially, the process of conducting evaluation research can be divided into six broad steps as follows:

1. Determine what is to be evaluated and the reasons for the evaluation.
2. Establish the desired level of performance of the object of the evaluation with particular reference to existing standards, goals, and objectives.
3. Select appropriate investigative techniques, and, if necessary, pre-pare a suitable scale or instrument not measure levels of performance.
4. Measure or test subjects to determine actual level(s) of performance.
5. Compare the program's goals with its objectives.
6. Evaluate the project on the basis of analyzed data.

Some evaluative procedures are developed prior to the actual initiation of programs; they are then incorporated into the program's structure. With out a doubt, this approach to evaluation is the most efficient and effective. In other cases, evaluative procedures are developed after a program has been made operational or has even been completed. In the latter case, however, evaluators are somewhat disadvantaged because a project's completion precludes the manipulation of variables and comparisons between before and after conditions. When a program's objectives are unclear or "fuzzy" a meaningful evaluation is also impeded. For example, if the object of a summer reading program was to make young persons " more responsible citizens in a democratic society", the task of transforming this goal into measurable success indicators might be impossible. Of course, this problem is closely related to the need for establishing realistic program goals expressed in terms of measurable operational or behavioral objectives.

One method of evaluation is a simulation of the experimental technique: however, it by no means attains the level of precision normally expected when a true experiment is conducted. Using this technique, a test group is randomly chosen from among persons who participated in or supposedly benefited from the program to be evaluated. A control group is then selected from among persons who are very similar to the experimental group, but who did not "benefit" from or participate in the program.

A measurement index or test is then devised, pretested, and administered to both subject groups in an effort to determine whether they differ with respect to the dependent variable. Because proper pretests and posttests are frequently lacking, this evaluative procedure is not highly reliable; however, in some cases it might render nominal indicators of project effectiveness. It should be apparent that the closer the design of evaluation research approximates that of a controlled experiment, the more revealing the evaluation is likely to be. At times, interviews or questionnaires are used among project beneficiaries to elicit personalized reactions or evaluations. A follow-up study conducted by a graduate library school to obtain evaluations by former students of their completed educational program is a type of evaluative project. These evaluations are also sometimes undertaken by library schools in attempts to measure the professional development of former students, as well as effects of professional education on job performances of graduates. Robert M. Ballard conducted a similar study at the University of Michigan, and the title of the dissertation based upon his inquiry clearly indicates the scope of the research: A Follow-Up Study of the Academic Record and Career Experience of Students Enrolled for the A.M.L.S. Degree at the Department of Library Science, the University of Michigan.

Meaningful research designed to produce evaluations of library programs will require more time and resources than the "off-hand" judgments of administrators and project coordinators which were typical in the past. Formal evaluations are often necessary to reveal whether a program is beneficial and worthy of continuation.

When library projects or programs are complex, evaluation research often is the only means to arrive at intelligent conclusion about their effects and intrinsic values. Penland and Williams have outlined some criteria for evaluations off programs and services. These criteria are grouped under broad categories of interpretation, including question of whether the following were achieved: (a) the individual participant's objectives; (b) the organization's objectives; (c) the objective for program design and communication; (d) community development and coordination; and (e) satisfactory organizational procedures and administration. The following publications by F.W. Lancaster are highly recommended to librarians who plan to conduct evaluation research: The Measurement and Evaluation of Libraries and Information Centers. In addition, Ellen Altman's Data Gathering and Instructional Manual for Performance Measures in Libraries and ALA's Performance Measures for Public Libraries can be useful in certain types of evaluative studies.

Library science evaluation research has been used in several doctoral projects, including the following: an evaluation of information retrieval systems in terms of cost, a study of the effectiveness of a public library's information service, an investigation of library services designated for adults of low educational attainment, an evaluation of the reactions off ethnic minority readers to indigenous ghetto literature, and an investigation of regional resource centers in Pennsylvania in term of their capability to provide social science periodicals. Another example of evaluation research in the field is a study conducted to determine the benefits and level of performance of the Faculty Document Delivery Service (FDDS), initiated in 1969 at the university of Colorado by the university's library. A provision of the service was the delivery of documents to the offices of faculty members. After FDDS had been in operation for an 18-month period, more than 33% of the faculty had requested the delivery of these library materials. In all, 36000 document were provided to faculty members during the first year of the project's operation. To obtain users evaluations of the service, a question-naire was distributed to participants, and 55% of the faculty members responded. Among these, 68% rated FDDS as "excellent," and 28% rated it as "good". Many respondents noted that the delivery of documents had altered faculty library-use patterns and had saved time. Investigators concluded that: (a) FDDS was generally well received: (b) four-fifths of the requested items were delivered; (c) the service could be operated on a cost-effective basis; and (d) and service aided in ameliorating inconvenience sometimes encountered by users of a decentralized library collection.

In another study, the utilization of facsimile communication for reference and interlibrary loan services was evaluated. A 3-month experimental demonstration was conducted by the South Carolina State Library in cooperation with the Charleston Country Library and the Greenville Country Library. The project was supported by funds made available by the Library Services and Construction Act. A triangular facsimile communication network among the state agency and the two participating libraries was established to determine whether the speed and accuracy of reference transactions could thereby be increased. Facsimile devices used in the project were both transmitters and receivers of materials in printed typed, handwritten, photocopied, or graphical formats. A coupling device allowed the transmission of both requests and documents over ordinary telephone lines. Prior to the initiation of the project, the state agency devised an evaluation procedure, based upon the direct observation of operations and the completion of evaluation forms for each facsimile transaction. Investigators at the state agency and the participating public libraries measured the following factors: (a) quality of each facsimile copy (both transmitted requests and responses); (b) speed of each transmission; and (c) quality of the reference and interlibrary loan service in terms of accuracy and patron satisfaction. Investigators concluded that facsimile communication devices are simple and effective means to increase the speed and accuracy to reference and interlibrary loan transactions, and that excellent facsimile copies can be obtained of the following types of materials: printed matter with 8-point type or larger, typed materials, black and white photographs, newspaper clippings, first sheets of carbon copies, printed charts and graphs, printed materials in color with good contrast, handwritten materials in pen and ink or ballpoint, ink sketches, and mimeographed materials. Although the demonstration project was successful in improving the speed and quality of services, the volume of transactions was deemed to be insufficient to warrant continuation of the facsimile network on a cost-benefit basis.

Library Surveys

In the decade of the 1930s, librarians become concerned that they were not "reaching" all potential users and that rental libraries, that radio, and motion pictures were making inroads on citizens use of libraries. Apparently, this alleged competition-coupled with a pervasive desire to described to survey library conditions and services with an aim of improving their overall quality. Between 1930 and 1950, the library survey was among the most frequently used methods to observe, analyze, compare, and describe general conditions in and related to libraries. Many such efforts were status surveys, designed primarily to merely assay library conditions rather than to test hypotheses or to explore specific research questions thoroughly, In this respect, the traditional library survey differs considerably from the kind of survey research discussed in.

In 1940, the American Library Association responded to the need for a manual devoted to techniques of library surveys; thus the organization published The Library Survey by Errett W. McDiarmid. Also Carleton B. Joeckel joined Leon Carnovsky in a survey of the Chicago Public Library. Furthermore, Louis R. Wilson continued to go about conducting library surveys-one for the University of Florida Libraries and another for libraries in the Southeast as part of the Southeastern State Cooperative Survey, 1946-47. In 1958, Ernst W. Erickson described college and university surveys conducted between 1938 and 1952 in a doctoral dissertation prepared at the University of Illinois. In a similar vein, Peter Jonikas compiled a bibliography of public library surveys; it contains a listing of approximately 300 separate studies. School libraries were also the objects of numerous surveys. Frances Henne estimated that between 1927 and 1947 surveys constituted almost 40% of all studies undertaken in the area of school library research.

Therefore, it is apparent that the library survey has been one of the most frequently employed investigative methods in Librarianship, even though its procedures are considered to be among the least exacting and reliable of all investigative techniques. Unfortunately, some library surveys have been rather nominal attempts to observe and describe existing library phenomena. Presumably, most of these studies were undertaken to obtain and analyze information that might allow more intelligent decisions about the development of library systems, collections, services, and other aspects of librarianship. In 1947, when the library survey was still the most popular kind of study in the field, Louis R. Wilson noted that surveys of academic libraries had helped to improve the communication of information abut library support, stimulated library staffs, solved particular problems, and codified library policies.

Other librarians have also questioned the degree of objectivity, reliability, and effectiveness inherent in the library survey approach. In addition, questions have arisen from time to time concerning the extent to which conclusion and findings of library surveys are actually utilized.

Three broad categories of information are normally gathered and reported in library surveys: (a) existing library conditions; (b) comparisons between present conditions and desired standards or goals; and (c) suggestions for the improvement of existing conditions. Thus, the data collected in most library surveys could be placed into the following subject categories: (a) the library environment, including factors such as facilities, buildings, organizational structure, location, space, resources, and so on; (b) the characteristics of library personnel, including features such as educational attainment, experience, sex, age, group memberships, and so on; (c) the nature of users and nonusers, including their age, socioeconomic backgrounds, sex, ethnic origins, communication patterns, recreational activities, reading habits, and so on; (d) the nature of certain library services, including reference and interlibrary loan, audiovisual programs, bibliographic and directional assistance to clientele, programs for children and young people, bookmobile services, adult services, photocopying facilities, extension service, reserve book services, and so on; (e) nature and extent of library resources, including books, periodicals, pamphlets, documents, films, recordings, microforms, reproductions of paintings, and other collections of materials; and (f) degree to which innovations such as data processing and computerized information retrieval technologies have been applied to library operations. Data pertaining to these and other possible categories of information are obtained from numerous sources, including annual reports; government records; direct and indirect observation of services and methods. Maurice Tauber has noted that the methods of library surveys include all the major techniques of research as well as "documentary and statistical analysis, questionnaires, checklist, visits, interview, observation, and the compilation of specialized data for particular conditions.

Typically, library surveys are conducted by persons other than staff members of the library being examined-that is, by outside consultants for agencies, as a general rule. However, sometimes a few of these studies are also undertaken by library staff members, who usually function as a team or self-study group. Therefore, internal surveys of libraries are self-studies conducted by the collective library of by a single designated member or committee from the staff. External surveys are accomplished by a person or persons from outside agencies, that is, state libraries, library associations, library consulting firms. Library schools, etc. The advantages of both of these types of surveys have been described by Maurice F. Tauber. Some noteworthy library surveys conducted since 1965 are listed at the end of this chapter.

In recent decades, use of the library survey technique in the field has appeared to be declining. Perhaps this method of gathering general information about libraries is being replaced by more exacting methods designed to solve specific library problems. Discussing the status of academic library surveys since the mid-1950s, David Kaser has speculated that "increasing professionalization" among resident staff members of libraries has reduced the former need to rely heavily upon outside help for the conduct of library-related studies. Moreover, Kaser noted that the "democratization of knowledge" which results from the placing of more emphasis upon theory in the process of educating librarians may have enabled practicing professionals to find solutions to more of their own problem rather than to rely upon outside experts.

Community Surveys

Closely related to the library survey is another descriptive approach the community survey. Designed to allow careful inspections of the characteristics of communities and to relate the features to library goals and objectives, community surveys are attempts to obtain a detailed working knowledge of various pertinent dimensions, geographic area, or "Publics" served by libraries. Although these dimensions are in a constant state of fluctuation, they are all directly or indirectly related to such factors as local traditions and values, geographical conditions, the nature of the population, the political, climate, economic development, human resources, and the unique features and problems of the community. A purely descriptive community survey is designed to characterize properties and conditions of a group of people living or working together in a district or within an institution. An exploratory community survey devotes attention to interrelationships between these characteristics and the use of various library resources, program, and services. Some community surveys are attempts to accomplish both of these tasks.

Interest in studying relations between libraries and their communities was stimulated by such publications as Joseph Wheeler's The Library and the Community, Leon Carnovsky and Lowell Martin's The Library and the Community, ALA's Studying the Community: A Basis for Planning Adult Education Service, and Roland Warren's Studying Your Community. Community surveys are often conducted by or for public libraries however, they do not appear to be undertaken as frequently within the communities of other types of libraries. The techniques of the community survey can be applicable to all types of libraries and information centers. The surveys can be conducted in academic, professional, industrial, business, and other communities served by libraries and information centers.

A variety of data-collection methods and information sources can be employed effectively in community surveys. We should point out that because the community surveys is a type of nominal research which does not involve collecting data for use in testing hypotheses, this type of study deals with the identification and description of a variety of community features that have a real or assumed relationship to the utilization of library resources and services. The most effective surveys are often conducted as interdisciplinary studies, insofar as both the collection and analysis of data are concerned. Attempts to accurately assess environments of libraries typically focus on social, economic, and political institutions and services, as well as on actual potential clientele of libraries. Complete assessments of communities often consider the resources and information-communication needs of the following agencies, organizations, or entities: (a) educational institutions such as public and private schools, community or junior colleges, vocational and technical education centers, and formal and informal adult education programs; (b) recreational services and clubs such as parks, recreational department, YMCAs, and YWCAs; (c) cultural groups such as arts councils and societies, little theatre groups, music clubs, crafts groups, and book clubs; (d) health facilities and services such as public health departments, community mental health centers, medical clinics, and hospitals; (e) community planning and development agencies such as city and county planning departments and United Way councils; (f) local and government units such as the mayor's office, city manager, fiscal officers, and law-enforcement agencies; (g) citizens groups such as the League of Women Voters, neighborhood development councils, and interracial groups: (h) individual persons such as community leaders or key resource people who possess a thorough knowledge of the service area to be surveyed, as well as selected representatives from various population groups; (i) business and labor organizations such as chambers of commerce, trade associations, and better business bureaus; (j) churches and other religious intuitions and organizations; and (k) communication-information agencies such as newspapers, television, radio, motion picture theatres, bookstores, newsstands, information centers, and public relations representatives of various organizations.

Needed information about may community institutions can often be obtained from the institutions themselves. It is often supplemented with recorded data from local, state and federal government documents; telephone directories; city, business, and industrial directories; annual reports, newspaper articles; published histories; and other relevant sources. Moreover, interviews and questionnaires can often be effective in collecting a considerable amount of contemporary information about the community and its citizens. Surveys of communities can be used to conceptualize libraries as integral parts of their social, political, and economic milieus. An analysis of a library's community can identify groups off actual or potential users so that more meaningful and effective programs can be developed and the usage of library resources and services can be stimulated. Moreover, information collected in the course of these studies can be employed to develop appropriate library personnel, buildings, resources, and facilities. Surveys are often valuable means for collecting information to be used in planning new library buildings and expanding services and systems. In some instance, these surveys can indicate when certain services or programs should be discontinued or deemphasized in favor of other more suitable to an environment. In addition, an analysis is a community can aid librarians in determining the most suitable location for new branches within a city. Thus, the ultimate objective of most of these surveys is to secure an overview of the library's community so that library collections, facilities, and services can be tailored to the general needs of the entire service area, as well as to the unique requirements of special clientele within institutions.

Comparative Librarianship

For many years, comparative studies have been conducted by scholars in disciplines and professions such as economics, law, education, linguistics, and literature. Not until after World War II, however, did interest in international librarianship and comparative library science studies take root in the United State. Since that time, some insightful investigations of a comparative nature have been undertaken. These studies have encompassed comparisons of the practices and study of library science in nations and regions of the world; they have focused on such topics as education for librarianship, political control of libraries, library resources and services, publishing in relation to libraries, patterns of communication, cross-cultural influences in librarianship, and other related topics. Dorothy G. Collings has defined comparative librarianship as "the systematic analysis of library development, practices, or problems as they occur under different circumstances-considered in the context of the relevant historical, geographic, political, economic, social, cultural, and other determinant background factors found in the situations under study. J. Periam Danton, a pioneer in the area of comparative library science studies, has defined comparative librarianship as follows:

> the analysis of libraries, library systems, some aspects of librarianship or library problems in two or more national, cultural, or societal environments, in terms of sociopolitical, economic, cultural, ideological, and historical contexts. This analysis is for the purpose of understanding similarities and difference, and for determining explanations of the differences, with the ultimate aim of trying to arrive at valid generalizations and principles.

According to Louis shores, two research approaches can be taken in comparative librarianship-geographic comparisons and subject comparisons. Shores has also pointed out that, because quantitative comparisons are not likely to produce very reliable results. "the implication of this new research area.... is to investigate parascientifically," He also claimed that comparative librarianship can uncover "neglected approaches to important technical library problems" and furthermore, that it can "suggest a new critical role librarianship". Sources of information for comparative studies in library science include the following: direct observation, historical records, statistical compilations, government documents, library science professional publications, and a variety of other recorded information that can be used to make qualitative and quantitative comparisons. Douglas J. Foskett has written that "comparative librarianship has been noted more for lack of a systematic approach than for its observance." Foremost, comparative Librarianship is a descriptive research approach; thus several methods of investigation can be employed, including case studies, library surveys, survey research, and, in some instance historical studies of recent past developments. In 1974, Danton indicated that relatively few studies of a truly comparative nature had been undertaken in the field. In characterizing a genuine comparative study. Danton noted that it should be cross-societal, compare observed phenomena, explain differences, draw conclusions, and establish principles.

In the mid 1960s interest in international and comparative librarianship at the University of Pittsburgh's Graduate School of Library and Information Sciences led to the establishment of an International Library Information Center. The purpose of the center is to support the study of international and comparative librarianship through the provision of information training, and research opportunities. The International Library and Information Center also serves as a clearinghouse for data about libraries, documentation, and book production in the United States and in numerous foreign countries.

Among the most useful publications containing information and guidelines for the conduct of comparative studies in the field are: John F. Harvey's Comparative and International Library Science, J. Periam Danton's Dimensions of Comparative Librarianship; Miles M. Jackson's Comparative and International Librarianship; Simsova and MacKee's A Handbook of Comparative Librarianship; and articles written by John F. Harvey, Dorothy G. Collings, and Douglas J. Foskett. In addition, Studies in Comparative Librarianship; Three Essays Presented for the Sevensma Prize, 1971, a publication of the Library Association, might be of value to librarians who plan to carry out comparative studies. A bibliography of noteworthy reports of completed studies in the area of comparative and international librarianship is provided at the end of the chapter.

Many library science studies are focused on the users of various media of communication, including books, periodicals, newspapers, films, and government documents. Lees frequently inquiries in the field are concerned with the actual content of media. Among the useful methods in the field of communication that can be employed by librarians to investigate certain internal features of media is content analysis, a procedure designed to facilitate the objective analysis of the appearance of words, phrases, concepts, themes, characters, or even sentences and paragraphs contained in printed or audiovisual materials. Bernard Berelson has described content analysis as "a research technique for the objective, systematic and quantitative description of manifest content of communication. Thus, this technique can be used to describe the contents of communication "messages" -that is, materials such as novels; newspapers; or a variety of additional media and descriptive tasks relating to their content. In analysis of a communication's content, observed data are transformed into sets of symbols such as words, themes, motives, concepts, and so on. The appearance of such symbols in the material under analysis can then be quantified use of the obtained measurements will depend upon the purpose of the research and the study's expressed hypothesis. By breaking down the contents of materials into meaningful and pertinent units of information, librarians attempt to discern certain characteristics of messages. For example, the selection and analysis of information, situations, characters, or other elements in a communication can indicate pertinent features such as comprehensiveness of coverage or the intentions, biases, prejudices, and oversights of authors, publishers, creators, or other persons responsible for the content of materials.

In Content Analysis of Communication, Richard W. Budd and his co-authors wrote: "No content analysis is better than its categories, for a system or set of categories is, in essence, a conceptual scheme." A category has been defined as "either the name given to any class of things, actions, or relationships which recur with sufficient uniformity and frequency as to render the class a useful subject of a prediction of the class itself." Freed N. Kerlinger noted in Foundations of Behavioral Research that: (a) a category is a partition or subpartition set up according to some rule; (b) categories are established regard to the purpose(s) of a unique investigative problem; and (c) categories are exhaustive and mutually exclusive. The "things" placed into categories representing the contents of a document are called units; they are the individual observations or measurements which ordinarily comprise the dependent variable of a content analysis. For example, assume that an investigator is conducting a content analysis of several written policies of metropolitan public libraries regarding the selection of materials. The purpose of the study is to determine the extent of references in the selection policies to written statements of principles adopted by the American Library Association, such as the Library Bill of Rights, Freedom to Read statement. Resolution on Challenged Materials, and other related professional guidelines related to free access to library materials. Each reference to these adopted professional principles in the library selection policies could be counted and placed into a designated category representing one or another of the officially adopted policy statements; thus, references to these statements would comprise the counted units. The number of categories in any single content analysis depends, of course, upon the amplification of factors associated with the research problem to be solved.

Content analysis is aimed at exactness and the elimination of bias in the investigative process; its methods are employed to decrease the degree of subjectivity inherent in procedures designed to analyze or evaluate the contents of materials. Analyses of the contents of messages more explicit. Material may be scrutinized to determine the relative importance or occurrence of textual or graphical elements under analysis. Library and drama critics often evaluate media such as books, plays, and films; however, evaluations by these persons are not based upon rigorous quantification of inherent elements of the object of evaluation. But the procedures used by investigators in a content analysis encompass a care fully prepared and reproducable plan for the collection and quantification of elements of communications. By determining the proportions of a message that fall into clearly defined, conceptually valid, and mutually exclusive categories, the research scholar attempts to increase unit frequency validity.

Although most library science inquires based upon content analysis have been descriptive in nature, this technique can also be engaged to probe hypotheses pertaining to the contents of materials. For example, assume that as test will be made of the theory that themes of most contemporary best-selling novels are based primarily upon sex or violence. By clearly identifying activities that can be characterized as "sex" or "violence," and then by quantitatively analyzing the themes (content) of pertinent novels according to the established categories, the investigator could test the proposition. Furthermore, the hypothesis might be statistically tested, should the study be conducted rigorously. Hypothesis testing is especially facilitated when a comparison is sought in a study between or among elements of various documents.

Typically, the conduct of a content analysis is accomplished in the following general stems: (a) formulation of the research problem (For example, how was the appointment of Daniel Boorstin to the position of Librarian of Congress treated by such professional publications in the field as Library Journal, American Libraries, and Wilson Library Bulletin; how does the appointment relate to problems concerning the image of the "professional" librarian and to the theories of education for librarianship?); (b) definition and establishment of the hypothesis and the categories of analysis that will allow the hypothesis to be tested; (c) identification and selection of the materials to be analyzed (the target documents, message, or media) and, if appropriate, selection of a sample of these; (d) analysis of relevant documents and the measurement of contents according to the predetermined and well-defined categories; (e) quantification and ordering of the categorized units; (f) analysis and comparison of attained data with respect to the independent variable(s); and (g) interpretation of the data insofar as the research question, hypothesis, or theory of the inquiry are concerned.

One problem that is often encountered by librarians in their attempts to analyze communication contents is the mass of cognate materials in many projects that can be subjected to examinations. Sampling procedures can sometimes be used to help solve this problem of having too many materials. Another useful method for reducing materials to a more manageable quantity is to limit the analysis to works published during a specific time period—for example, 6 months, 1 year, or 3 years, depending upon the latitude of an inquiry. Limitations can also be imposed by the selection of a particular media format for analysis (i.e., periodical articles about a topic rather than books and other publications relating to the same subject ares). For example, an analysis of the writings of presidents of the American Library Association since 1940 identify major professional interests of these leaders could be confined to the contents of the subjects' published speeches, rather then to all their journal articles. The selection of speeches as the object of a study might reduce the materials for analysis to a more manageable proportion. In addition, bibliographies that list the best, most significant, outstanding, or prize-winning publications can sometimes be used as selection guides for the research objects to be analyzed, thus limiting the range of pertinent items. The overall purpose of an inquiry and the research question itself must be carefully considered when limitations are placed on the range and quality of analyzed documents.

Techniques that can be reproduced by other investigators are employed in content analysed; thus, the procedures used should be explicitly identified and clearly elucidated in written reports of studies. These procedures should allow the classification of measurable data and the pursuit of concepts being investigated in terms of the frequency of their occurrence, as well as their interrelationships and meanings. No single model is applicable to all content analyses; each of these inquires must be structured according to an analytical scheme directed towered the accomplishment of a specific research task. A unique feature of the content analysis approach is the investigator's reliance upon the quantifiable aspects of communications, rather than upon an expository treatment in the form of explanations.

Although content analysis has been employed in some inquiries in librarianship, an examination of various reports of relevant studies will reveal that this technique has not always been applied correctly. Unless categories of analysis are clearly and accurately defined and the classification and measurement of data are undertaken with objectivity, exactness, and rigor, a so-called content analysis can produce loosely knit or meaningless data. In a criticism of this techniques as applied in librarianship, Jesse Shera has written:

> Though [content analysis] pretends to greater "objectivity" it is no less subjective than those forms of literary criticism against which it is supposed to be a "reaction." One does not achieve objectivity through the quantification of that which is itself subjective.

The following types of content analysis projects are among studies completed by librarians: a comparison of the contents of best-selling novels with those that did not sell well, centering upon themes, readability, settings, and other elements in an attempt to identify the characteristics present in popular books and absent in works having less appeal; comparison of selected novels with the motion pictures based upon them; an analysis of treatments given to the topic of blacks in the United States by four major adult encyclopedias; a study of the roles of priests in contemporary British and American fiction, an exploration of the contents of novels listed in supplements to the Junior High School Library Catalog in an attempt to characterize treatments given to the topic of Catalog in an attempt to characterize treatments given to the topic of adolescent culture; an examination of the published writings of public library directors to determine the impact of the Great Depression on six metropolitan libraries; a study of contemporary realistic fiction for children published since World War II; and an analysis of information provided about educational filmstrips in selected periodicals. At this point, perhaps closer scrutiny of as completed study that employed the content analysis approach would be beneficial. One such study was completed by Joyce Haas. Almost 2000 selected works of fiction included New Jersey school libraries were examined in the analysis to determine the nature of the characters depicted, spoken communications, and settings in novels. Two primary questions were posed: (a) whether the contents of novels in school library collections supported a polarized society, and (b) whether the ethnic contents of fiction collections varied according to ethnic student enrollment of selected schools. The overall purpose of the research was to try to determine the degree to which fiction selected for school libraries prepared children for social change. The study's independent variable was the amount of ethnic enrollment in selected schools; the dependent variable was comprised of the ethnic characteristic of fiction in school library collections. Has accomplished the content analysis by first randomly selecting 30 New Jersey elementary schools libraries from a list of the state's K-6 schools. The selected schools were then classified into five strate according to ethnic minority enrollment. Next, a sample of 1939 books was chosen from libraries in these schools and then analyzed by a group of 51 coders. The group of coders was comprised of persons of both sexes, of various ages, and of various ethnic-minority and ethic-majority backgrounds. The established categories were used by coders to categorize the following facets of books: characters portrayed (e.g., ethnic group, sex, age, etc.); spoken communications included (e.g., ethnic group, sex, age, and responses); and characteristics of settings (e.g., story's time and place). After collecting and analyzing the data produced by coders, Haas concluded that contents of school fiction collections supported the ethnic polarization of American society and the factors elated to patterns of national and regional book publication and distribution appeared to have precluded the development of less polarized library collections. This study relates to the following school library principles: (a) the library-like the classroom—should promote the socialization process of children, as well as their formation of value system; (b) the materials in school libraries should prepare children for social change; and (c) library collections should be developed primarily with the needs of students in mind. The content analysis undertaken by Haas demonstrated that these tenants are sometimes difficult to achieve, especially when certain books are not available or are of such poor quality that they cannot be used in school library collections.

Delphi Method

Comprised of a group f modified survey procedures, the Delphi method is designed for use in refining judgmental data collected from a panel of selected experts. The techniques was developed in the early 1950s by the Rand corporation to predict further developments related to national defense. Olaf Helmer, who was instrumental in helping to devise Delphi, characterized the method as " a carefully designed program of sequential individual interrogations (best conducted by questionnaires) interspersed with information and opinion feedback...." Delphi is a systematic approach to the generation of consensus opinions among a group of carefully selected and anonymous respondents. It is based upon the assumption that majority opinions will have greater credibility and authority than the surmise of only the most articulate spokespersons in a group of participating respondents. Panel participants are often selected because of their knowledge of the subject under investigation; however, the experts need not necessarily be members of the same discipline or possess similar backgrounds.

Most users of Delphi assume that the method prevents the opinions of exerts from being contaminated by: (a) strong personalities of the dominant respondents, (b) the bandwagon effect, and (c) public opinion. The Delphi method is based upon a series of questionnaire interchanges often referred to as "rounds." Participants respond independently to one another's opinions about an assigned attitude object. Typically, consensus opinions are deemed by investigators to be those that fall within the inter-quartile range (e.g., between the first and third quartiles) of the original responses after they have been ranked repeatedly by all participants in the study. In the final statistical analysis of responses, opinions that fall outside the interquartile range (e.g., those that are renked within the first and fourth quartiles) are considered to be aberrant. Four questionnaire interactions, or rounds, may be required to determine consensus opinions; however, three rounds usually suffice for this purpose.

Lending itself to a variety of judgmental tasks, Delphi has been in a process of evolution for almost two decades. That evolution has involved both Delphi's methodology and the range of problems to which it has been applied. Despite the rather widespread employment of the technique since information about it was declassified in the 1960s, the Delphi method does not have a sound theoretical base. Results of Delphi studies are often less than spectacular; however, some studies have yielded very useful data. The method does reduce communication barriers among participants and can be applied to problems that are not amenable to precise analytical techniques. Typically, such problems are "solved" using expert value judgments that were arrived at more or less intuitively. A variety op applications of Delphi are possible. For example, the method can be applied in the following areas: (a) in technological forecasting tasks; (b) in attempts to ascertain values and preferences; (c) in efforts to determine the quality of life or other conditions in future years; (d) in situations that can benefit from a stimulation of the decision-making process; and (e) in efforts to encourage the development of technical inventions ("inventive planning"). The Delphi method has been widely recognized as a means of supplementing information gleaned from past experiences, historical data, or other traditional data sources. One advantage of the technique is its applicability to the collection of information from respondents who possess widely differing views that appear to be irreconciable. The method is also applicable to interrogations of persons who are widely dispersed geographically, and are thus unable to participate in a face-to-face "brainstorming" session or in other types of situations in which ideas are interchanged.

Steps of a Typical Delphi Study

Although the basic Delphi procedure has often been tailored to meet unique needs of a variety of disciplines and purposes, the following list is a somewhat typical series of steps utilized in Delphi studies. Select a panel of experts who are capable of providing insightful opinions concerning the pertinent topic. Explain the rationale of the study to the experts and request their anonymous participation as independent panel members.

Ask each participant to compile a list of value judgments, predictions, or opinions about the assigned issue or topic. (In some cases, participants may be asked to respond to a list of statements preselected by the investigator.) Collect the initial responses and incorporate them into a questionnaire for use in a first-round interaction. Then, request that the same panel members rank the recorded statements according to independently perceived orders of priority or importance.

Upon receipt of all first-round questionnaires from

participants, analyze the data statistically (e.g., determine the median and interquartile range of responses). Subsequently, rearrange the statements according to the new, revised rankings; list them in another questionnaire to be used in the second round; and provide respondents with a statistical summary of the ranked statements.

Submit the second-round instrument to the same panel members, asking them to reconsider their second responses, given the statistical summary of that round. Repeat Step 5 for the third-round questionnaire interaction. Respondents whose opinions still fall outside the interquartile range for the third round are asked to explain why their feelings did not change. At the conclusion of the third round (or, when consensus opinions have been obtained), the investigator prepares a final draft of the ranked statements, revealing how much opinion change has occurred. The consensus opinions are summarized, together with other pertinent comments elicited from participants.

A succinct and critical review of the use of the Delphi method in librarianship is contained in an article by Resell G. Fischer. Sybilla A. Cook has also briefly described some library applications of the Delphi method in a popular articles. An explanation of the use of Delphi in Sweden to decrease uncertainty about future events relating to information and documentation is contained in an article by Ulf Wennerberg. One of the most ambitious Delphi projects in librarianship was undertaken by the Library Research Unit at the University of California, Los Angeles. The study dealt with the future of library education in the United States and was the subject of a report written by Harold Borko. Perhaps the most penetrating and definitive examination of the Delphi method to be published thus far is The Delphi Method; Techniques and Applications, a book of readings edited by Harold A. Linstone and Murray Turoff.

Documentary Research

For lack of a better phases, the generic term documentary research is used here to refer to inquiries into the printed tools of librarianship—books, journals, and indexes. A sample of the broad research questions falling into this category include the following:

1. What are (or should be) the characteristics of a good index? Classification scheme? What kinds of indexes produce optimal retrieval results?
2. How can a computer be programmed to do automatic indexing? Automatic classification? Abstracting?
3. Will an analysis of citation patterns associated with journals in various subject literatures reveal anything useful about the importance of individual journals? Authors? The "hardness" of a subject field?
4. Are there optimal approaches to the design of subject heading lists or thesauri?
5. How does the depth of indexing affect retrieval effectiveness? The exhaustivity of indexing?
6. What effect does indexer/cataloger inconsistency have on subsequent retrieval? How prevalent is inter-indexer inconstancy?
7. How quickly do various classes of literature obsolesce, in the sense of "losing usefulness"? How fast are various subject classes of literature growing?
8. How productive are writers? Journals? What proportion of journals, ranked in order of usefulness, is required to satisfy a given percentage of potential information requests?

Studies designed to shed light on these and related questions frequently include an objective, quantitative analysis of words in the texts of documents, hence the term documentary research. In the paragraphs that follow, a few prototypical, substantive, and seminal studies in documentary research will be cited. Although we shall not attempt to provide a state-of-the-art summary of documentary research, a few examples of early studies in this area will be cited. Perhaps these will provide a flavor of the field.

Bibliometrics involves measurement of several interrelated aspects of writing and publication. "Bradford's law of scattering" relates the proportion of relevant papers in a field to the proportion of journals required to achieve this quantity, when the journals have been ranked according to productivity. The productivity of scientists is the subject of treatment both by Derek Price. and Alfred Lotka. George Zipf looks at the productivity of words in text in much the same way as Bradford and Lotka. There have been several attempts to relate these bibliometrics distributions, notably by Robert Fairthorne.

In the second major thrust of bibliometrics, citation analysis is employed, often with the use of Science Citation Index and Social Science Citation Index. Many hundreds of studies have been performed using the techniques of citation analysis, all of which are based on the assumption that the act of citing an author is meaningful. For example, bibliographic coupling is rooted in the idea that two documents whose bibliographics share one or more citation are more likely to be related to each other than two documents which have no citations in common. Research conducted to test this hypothesis would involve the careful counting of the number of citations common to pairs of documents in a test collection, followed by an independent evaluation of the "relatedness" of document pairs. Citation studies have been used to establish networks of scientific papers, to rank journals importance, to generate additional documents relevant to a search question, and to evaluate a scientist's productivity.

Another body of documentary research deals with automatic indexing, abstracting, and classification. The broad task in this type of research is to define a formal process—a process which is in principle capable of being performed by a computer—to select keywords from the texts of documents likely to be useful as decriptors, to extract key sentences from the texts to serve as abstracts, or to assign documents to subject classes. As with bibliometric research, studies relating to this type of automatic language processing may be based on an experimental design and may borrow such techniques as decision theory from operations research. Sophisticated statistical techniques such as factor analysis may sometimes be utilized. But in the data-gathering and analysis stages of the research the approaches are characterized by a common need to analyze words in the text. For the reason, use of the computer is prevelant in this type of study.

In a splendid opportunity enjoyed by the writer on a British Library Research and Development Department Visiting Fellowship in 1980, the views of researchers and practitioners in the United Kingdom were canvassed on the relationship of research to library practice. The results suggested lack of mutual respect not only between researchers and practitioners but also among researchers, some of whom were at least as antipathetic to the notion of theory as were the practitioners. By its opponents, theory seemed universally to be understood in the narrow context of information retrieval theory. No nation of the theory of human communication or of the behavioral sciences generally seemed to be admitted, let alone was there hospitality to Popper's notion of theory as valuable for "its logical relation to the prevailing problem situation... Its relation to preceding and competing theories, its power to solve existing problems and to suggest new ones."

Attitudes to the relative importance of basic and applied research were consistent with those to theory. A distinguished researcher on the design of information systems complained that the library profession understood basic research as that which was basic to librarianship.

Practitioners influential on the committee which set research policy in the centres funded by the British Library exerted pressure for practical results. Under this pressure, the danger of research effort being co-opted into data compilation exercises could not always be avoided. Individual practitioners tended to criticize academic researchers for their lack of awareness of 'the practical situation', which further inquiry usually discovered to mean the situation', which further inquiry usually discovered to mean the situation prevailing in the speaker's own library. Some of the researchers associated their insistence on being regarded as problem-solvers and not pure researchers, with their wish to stay close to the field or ultimately to return to practice in it. Researchers who told to writer that the support of sponsors was difficult to obtain for long-term projects of which the outcome could not readily be forecast as the outset seemed to have some justification. At this, as at many points, the problems discovered in research in the United Kingdom seem to have parallels in other countries.

This paper argues that researchers in librarianship are isolated from practitioners, from each other and from most of the researchers in related disciplines. In consequence, most research in librarianship is neither nourished by practice nor nourishes practice and neither does it draw nourishment from, nor offer nourishment to, related fields of inquiry. The difficulty of distinguishing causes, effects and symptoms is formidable but it is also asserted here that research, practice and education in librarianship do not constitute a learning system and that this disjunction has hampered both the development of Librarianship as an academic discipline and achievement of excellence in professional practice.

The issues raised in discussing what qualifies as research in Librarianship and complex, and a good deal of ground needs to be cleared. The concepts 'research' and 'Librarianship' need to be probed a little before differing concepts of what properly constitutes research in and out of librarianship are examined. The conclusions will probably be timid and will certainly be temporary, as all such suggestions or remedies must be in a society changing as rapidly as out own.

Research

What 'research' is can from the basic of long debate, though most protagonists will accept as a starting point some such broad definition as Goldhor's, "any conscious premeditated inquiry - any investigation which seems to increase one's conscious premeditated inquiry - any investigation which seems to increase one's knowledge of a given situation". Early in the pursuit of the research debate, protagonists are likely to dived into those who would and would not give the title to all scholarship in all disciplines - to all careful reports of disinterested inquiry even if the data collection does not go beyond the confines of one well-stocked mind. Indeed bibliographers, editors, compilers and other scholars would probably withdraw entirely from debate if 'scholarship' could be re-admitted to the language with a halo as bright as that surrounding research. But, almost certainly for worse, scholarship connotes the leather armchair, solitary tranquil indulgence in esoteric if not whimsical pursuits - in shot, self-indulgence and irrelevance. 'Research' on the other hand, connotes the laboratory, breakthroughs and the dedicated pursuit by brilliant minds of central human concerns - in short, glamour and power. Add to this the fact that research grants are many and scholarship grants almost unknown and it is hardly surprising that most people who pursue intellectual inquiry like their work to be considered as research. Let is also be noted that because science has transformed the world in the century, there is an added cachet for work that can be labeled 'scientific research. Opportunity to combine the pursuits of scholarship and research seems to have contracted rapidly in the last thirty years. Yet Geoffrey Keynes, surgeon bibliographer, has hardly been dead three years and his autobiography, The Gates of Memory, exudes an air of wholeness and sanity as well as indefatigable energy, whether he is describing his research on more humane and effective surgical treatment of breast cancer or his work on the bibliography of John Donne. One benefit from the diversity of concerns of librarianship may be that it remains one of the few callings in which both scholarship and research can be pursued with equal utility and even by one person, though hardly to the Keynesian extremes.

But what is librarianship? Despite the negative answer still applying to one of McLuhan's nervous question, "Is book dead?", there is a doomsday literature which suggests that librarianship is not ling for this world. A British university librarian has chosen to title his recent book The End of Libraries, and it is probably eagerly sought by academic administrators in the hope that the title means what it says. On the other hand, the genuine doomsayers often seem to base their prognostications on the curious assumption that libraries have hitherto enjoyed some sort of monopoly in the supply of information. Heilprin, for example, warns that:

> Unless appropriate and sufficient research is conducted, the library community will not be able to transform itself but will be absorbed by other groups that will tale over the information function in society.

If by contrast, one seeks a definition of librarianship based on the reality of library functions, there are other dangers. Buckland 1983, has drawn attention to "the circular definition of librarianship as that which pertains to the provision of library services". Moreover, with the application of an intelligent methodology, White and Paris have discovered that the perceived needs and preferences of academic and public librarians in the United States in hiring junior librarians suggest need for two different curriculum tracks, while the requirements of special librarians were so diverse as to defy construction of a curriculum track. It can reasonably be assumed that these differences in needs and preferences expressed by librarians refer to differences in the library services provided in their libraries. Such differences could be difficult to codify into a neat definition.

Jesse Shera long since offered warrant for the divorce of librarianship from its institutional ties to buildings and collections with his suggestion that it is "social epistemology" aimed at "maximizing the social utility of the graphic record". But the whole notion of epistemology, of how we know, whether as individuals or societies, has so far proved too cast for effective exploration by researchers in librarianship and too vague and impractical for practitioners.

Other who have sought insight into the nature of librarianship by looking beyond it have found the concept of information science useful. 'The discovery or invention of information science may have owed more to scientists than to librarians and to the arrival of information technology than to any of the traditional concerns of librarianship. But once the concept was in existence, librarianship could be regarded as an applied information science. This definition remains supportive enough, provided one is prepared to adopt a tolerant view of the lack of unifying theory in information science, while admitting to it theory and principles about, the nature and behaviour of men and their interactions with data and machines, drawn from a wide range of disciplines. But many librarians and many of those who practice as 'information scientists' in libraries and other information services will accept no such definition. To them, information science is variously the application of computers and telecommunications technology to the provision of information services, the storage and retrieval of scientific data and the provision of information series to scientists, or some combination of these concepts. In all these variations information science becomes not the basis but an aspect or aspects of the provision of library and information services.

Some diehards, like the writer, will continue to organize their thought round the idea of librarianship as an applied information science, the bases of which are many and diffuse. Such persistence is to be admired as this view has to be maintained in the face of many respected colleagues in research and in practice who do not believe that information science exists or will ever come to exist. More pause is given by Jesse Shera's utterance in possibly has last published work that:

> Twenty years ago. I thought of what is now called information science as providing the intellectual and theoretical foundations of librarianship, but I am now convinced that I was wrong.

Yet in his thoughtful book Library Services in Theory and Context, Buckland bravely launches into what he terms, "the broad and amorphous realm" of information science in order to escape the dominance of the library as institution in the rhetoric of librarianship. He sees the field as being concerned with "representations of knowledge in one way or another" and more specifically with information strange and retrieval. Buckland goes on to offer not a definition of Librarianship but a useful map of its province when he writers:

> In order to see information storage and retrieval in context, we need also to concern ourselves with information science in the broader sense of concern with representations of knowledge, with knowledge itself, and indeed, with people insofar as their needs are related through knowledge and representations of knowledge to information storage and retrieval.

If librarians see themselves as inhabitants of this province, research in librarianship must grapple with the variability and fecundity of information concepts and the lack of a unified perspective on them identified by Levitan in information science research. Indeed the boundaries of concern cannot be drawn at information concepts like representations of knowledge: voyages have to be attempted in the even less well-charted waters of knowledge and wisdom, among all those "intellectual issues with policy implications" discussed by Kochen notion of librarianship as "social epistemology" comes up once more. That the writer, an academic, would take this view of the nature of librarianship, from the deep end so to speak, might have been produced from research by Lynam, Slater and Walker. Their study of 854 library information workers in the United Kingdom revealed that:

> The factor most influencing attitude and receptivity to research was employment sector. Analysis on this dimension revealed the greatest number of significant differences in behaviour and belief. Professional seniority had a real, but lesser impact Qualifications possessed had the least influence. Amongst that factors we examined, where a person worked was found to condition attitudes and expectations most powerfully.

A retreat to situational definition of both librarianship and research in librarianship may be tempting but not useful. The limitations of the definition of librarianship as co-extensive with library service have been discussed already. Furthermore opinion in different employment environments on what constitutes research in librarianship are likely to be contradictory if not self-cancelling.

Research in Librarianship

Lynch chose to describe the research which is associated with librarianship in four categories which she dubbed practical, bibliographical, scientific and scholarly. Practical research she defined as that pursued by "anyone with a problem to be solved who sets out to gather information needed in the solution". Bibliographical research she defined as the "research done in libraries" which is not to be confused with the "research done about librarianship which falls into our third category scientific research". Scientific research in Lynch's terms discovers new knowledge whereas "Practical research and bibliographical research is that typically done by humanists and "Although data are not collected from nature, as is the norm in scientific research, data are collected and organized in an objective way and analyzed according to systematic principles".

Lynch goes on to make clear her belief in the superiority of scientific research and she claims that "librarianship, by whatever name it is called, will need the understanding of information and its uses which only scientific research can provide". The trouble is that many researchers would claim that narrow attempts to apply the hypothetico-deductive method of inquiry, or the `scientific paradigm', preclude rather than enhance possibilities of reaching such understanding. In other words librarianship has to address inquiries into the human behaviour of individuals and organizations which are not necessarily susceptible to scientific investigation.

Here we enter the librarianship sector of the war between 'quantitative' and 'qualitative' or 'positivist' and 'phenomenological' research in the social science generally. In communications research Dervin, saw the emergence of literature "as much typified by profound conceptual discussion as by the evidentiary results of observation" and of "a core of arguments against traditional assumptions about the nature of information and information use". These traditional assumptions that information can exist independent of the observer, and knowledge independent of the knower have been slower to find challenge in librarianship, but awareness is growing.

Stratified has seen "the influence of the positivist legacy" in practice as well as in research in librarianship, and he warns that:

> The concepts of 'information user', 'information use' and 'user studies' should be approached with caution. This necessity arises because of the idiosyncratic definition of the information user by librarians, information workers and teachers of these disciplines almost exclusively in terms of using information systems and services. The information user as one who makes use of information is displaced in favour of that relatively abnormal

> creature, the regular user of the information system and services under review at a given place and time.

This is not to say that information systems and services at a given and time may not offer proper subjects for research but that for such inquiries to qualify as research they should be designed to let in the light shed by comparable studies and to throw new light on problems of all other agents and agencies concerned with the storage and retrieval of information. No doubt there has been ample warrant in many of the inquires carried out by liberations for the acerbic observation by Bundy and Wasserman that:

> The proclivity of a programmatic field, unschooled in and important with theory is to study problems close to what they see as possible practical solutions. The disposition is to deal with the problem as it appears on its surface. And, this forecloses the possibility of deeper analysis more susceptible to deeper insight.

Presumably for similar reasons, Lynch also removed consultancy, demonstrator and development, and in house research from her most desirable category "scientific research". But surely whether the investigation of a problem can be nourished by existing knowledge and offer nourishment to subsequent conceptualization of the problem at hand. Part of this adequacy is the recognition that all problem-solving is based on assumptions, valid or otherwise, recognized or unrecognized. Furthermore, the assumptions, models of reality, even prejudices on which inquiry is besides constitute theories.

It is the writer's experience that students often resist requirements that they should define the problems which they wish to investigate. Perhaps this stems from a natural tendency to believe that finding out what's going on will of itself suggest how to make things work better. And perhaps this naivete is reinforced in library education and practice which both engender respect for the collected records of human inquiry. In contrast to this innocence, neither is it possible to purse research in which the results are pre-ordained by administrative necessity. May be it is the recognition of the 'hired-gun' element in some consultancy which has cast a shadow over this genre of inquiry in librarianship as in many other fields. Research has to connote disinterested inquiry, and perhaps it is because disinterested inquiry into human system is so difficult that the epithet has come to be so widely misused to mean 'uninterested'.

In librarianship there is also a tendency to discount historical scholarship, often because it is not empirical research, or does not rely on observations of behaviour but on the partial records of behaviour in the past. Thus schools of librarianship are sometimes criticized because their student produce a pre-ponderance of historical these. But surely what can be criticized about historical research in Librarianship is not that it is undertaken but that it frequently shares the limitations of other types of inquiry in the field, namely that is chronicle, not focused, nor sufficiently related to causes and effects in the worlds out of which libraries, librarians sand library movements grow and in which they have or fail to have impact. Such writing does not perform history's function of interpreting the past in terms of the needs and knowledge of the present.

There need, however, be no fear that study of libraries by any method is inappropriate to research in librarianship. Buckland nicely expresses the twin ideas that library services offer a proper field for research study and that their proper study will take the researcher into wider fields:

> Library service are almost ideal things to study for all who like challenges. They are long-established, varied, numerous, fraught with non-trivial problems at all kinds of levels, draw on all sorts of disciplines, are rooted in intangible social values, and are important enough to society to warrant the attention of good minds. Yet, if we have any significant insights concerning libraries and if the underlying 'science' characteristic of library services also occurs elsewhere, then it would seem only responsible for those who inquire - and especially academicians - to offer and test their insights in these often, related, non-library contexts as well.

Research out of librarianship

Once in wider fields the researcher who began in librarianship does not necessarily find ready hospitality. To make an impact in another field, a researcher must publish in journals belonging to the field. Such publication can be difficult to achieve and the time an effort expended in sò doing can increase the gap between the researcher and the practitioners in librarianship. Weber has explored this dilemma in relation to inform, action systems research and his commits on the fragility of applied disciplines certainly apply to librarianship.

There is also the danger that in endeavoring to build strong theoretical bases for their work, researchers already embarked on the thin ice of information science may lose all footing in reality. An example is the recent controversy in Social Science Informations, including Roberts, who delivers the following admonition:

> Instead of engaging in the unprofitable exercise of constructing supposedly comprehensive theoretical models which relate to reality through assertion rather than through research experience, out energies should be directed towards the far more difficult, but infinitely more rewarding task of developing

> theories parallel with, based upon and informatively interacting with effective empirical investigation.

The theory proposed by Wersig and Windel has just those characteristics of vastness and vagueness which lead some practitioners of librarianship to use theory in a pejorative sense equivalent to lacking in usefulness. At the same time, for the nourishment of information science, who deserves to win the clashes of minds matters less that such clashes take.

6

Functions of Library

The main function of a library is the collection and preservation of knowledge for its dissemination to all. Its conservation for posterity is also an important duty of a library. The libraries have changed the outmoded concept of preserving a large number of reading materials for the sake of preservation only. Gurudeva Tagore rightly remarked, "the extent to use to which the reading material of a library is put, should determine its importance rather than the staggering number of volumes". He deprecated the idea of putting more emphasis on collecting books alone. He gave an example of a millionaire. "He is judged great in a gathering, not by what he has but what he gives". He illustrated this point by bringing out the difference between a dictionary and literature. The former was a depository of words while the latter was a medium through which the words were used and developed. Gurudeva gave more importance to literature. Similarly, Gurudeva pointedly remarked that constant and increased use of its books gave a library its significance. Library Administration can be studied from theoretical as well as practical angles. To have better results, practical administration must be based on sound theoretical principles. On the other hand, to get sound theoretical principles, these should be based on practical experiences. A library presents almost the same problems as are encountered with in any other social institution-a school, a college, or a commercial or industrial undertaking. It would, therefore, be appropriate to take into account the administrative functions of other social institutions and to apply them to libraries with necessary modifications.

The administrative machinery is responsible for laying down the basic policies of the organisation, for providing a suitable organisational structure to achieve the set aims of the organisation and for appointing the management personnel for translating into reality the desired aims. "That phase of a business enterprise which concerns itself with the overall determination of the major policies and objectives is Administration. For the administrative functions to be effective in operations a `doing' function is required. Similar views have been expressed by other authorities. J. William Schulze considered 'Administra-tion' as "the force which lays down the object for which an organisation and its management are to strike and the broad policies under which they are to operate". According to him, 'Management' is "the force which leads, guides and directs an organisation in the accomplishment of pre-determined object." There is a confusion between the terms 'Administration' and 'Management". Sometimes these are inter-changeable. But at others, one is considered a generic term while the other a specie. "Administration is that function of management which actually executes or carries out the objectives for which the enterprise is organised. This function initiates the work to be performed, sees that personnel is fitted to the task and trained to operate properly, and in general cases for everyday routine necessary to ensure that men, materials and equipments are functioning properly towards the desired end".

"Administration," he said, "regarded in this way must not be confused with government. To govern is to conduct an undertaking towards its objective by seeking to make the best possible use of all the resources at its disposal; it is, in fact, to ensure the smooth working of the six essential functions. Administration is only one of these functions...." Fayol brought out five distinguishing functions of administration, namely, to plan, to organise, to command, to co-ordinate, and to control. The words 'To plan' use for the original word 'prevoyance' means 'to forecast, and 'to plan'. Each of these six functions of administration can be grouped into two groups i.e. process and effect. Accordingly, 'Forecasting, leads to 'planning', 'organisation' is for ensuring 'co-ordination' and 'command' provides 'control'. Fayol's analysis of administrative functions can be implied as under from his list of 'Administrative Duties'.

1. Investigation→Forecasting→Planning.
2. Appropriateness→Organisation→Co-ordination.
3. Order→Command→Control.

Luther Gulick adopted Fayol's ideas and restated the functions under the catchword 'PODSCORB'. It stands for the following seven functions:-

1. Planning.
2. Organising.
3. Staffing.
4. Directing.
5. Co-ordinating.
6. Reporting.
7. Budgeting.

The first function of an administrator is to plan and forecast i.e. determining the goals and ideals of an institution. The ways and means to achieve these objectives are thought out on a plenary basis. These outlines are given concrete shape and a regular framework of authority is established in such a manner that maximum work of best quality is ensured at a minimum cost with minimum efforts. Planning presupposes the stock-taking of the existing conditions and the relevant causes. The solutions are suggested for removing the defects by phased systematic programme. The economic planning is concerned with the production of maximum output with minimum input. In planning, entire wastage is avoided and every constituent factor is made to contribute its own share.. The efforts are made to remove the basic defects and their future implications are taken care of. In library planning, the locality, its make-up as regards its physical features, its linguistic divisions, its cultural diversities a services. The pros and cons are properly studied so that the service is effective and long enduring.

Planning to be fruitful needs a sound organisation, which means that such a structure of authority is established which is capable to achieving the set goals. Through this structure, work subdivisions are arranged, defined and co-ordinated for the set goal. This structure is needed to bring together all the staff members in such a scientific way that the work is done most efficiently and smoothly. In library organisation, the decisions is taken as to what kind of authority is to be provided for an area of service. Should the authority be autonomous or part and parcel of the Local Government machinery? If it is to be autonomous of the Local Government Authority, it is to be found out as to whether this autonomous body would be capable of raising and collecting enough finances for running the library.

An organisation for its efficient working is totally dependent upon proper staffing and recruiting policies. The staff employed should have special aptitudes and capabilities for performing a particular kind of job. For example, the Chief Librarian of a public library should be sympathetic towards readers and should be capable of understanding the varied tastes of the public. Besides advanced learning, he should be able to command respect by his qualities of leadership. He should be a competent person to serve as a Public Relations Office i.e. to serve as a liaison officer between the readers and the books. The common people consider him a guide and the librarian should come up to their expectations.

A University Librarian, in addition, should have an aptitude for research if he wants to become a successful librarian. He must have a sound grounding in research methodology. The other junior staff members should be appointed keeping in view their aptitude for various jobs. The practical experience of various jobs at the credit of applicants for various posts should be taken into consideration at the time of their appointment. 'Staffing' includes the training of staff and the maintenance of favourable conditions of work for them.

The harmony and efficiency of the staff depends upon the personal qualities of the Chief Librarian. He should be capable of performing his duties as a leader. It implies that besides possessing knowledge, he should be able to infuse confidence amongst the staff members. He should be able to boost up their morale. He should be an example to be followed by his subordinates. In other words, he should not be frustrated with his job. Rather, he should do his job with zeal. He should be ready to sacrifice his personal comforts for the sake of library work and library staff. He should prove an ideal leader by dint of his hard work and sincerity for the staff welfare. 'Directing' includes continuous decision making and embodying them in general and specific orders and instructions.

Leadership will be successful only if the leader can

properly inter-relate various parts of an organisation in a harmonious way. This co-ordination can be achieved if the head knows well all the jobs and effects such an automatic administrative machinery that he feels practically no necessity to interfere. It depends upon the kind of organisation which has been brought into being i.e. as to whether he introduces Line Type or Line and Staff Type of structure or Functional Type of organisation. In other words, there should be delegation of powers but staff members in whom the powers are vested should also be made responsible for their jobs. They should be answerable to the Chief. An automatic apparatus should be effected by means of introducing a practice of getting periodical reports from the various Section Heads. He should allow these Heads to use their initiative but whenever there is some difficulty or misunderstanding, the Chief should thrash out the problem in periodical staff meetings.

Reporting' means keeping authorities, to whom the executive head of an organisation is responsible, informed about the progress or regress of his work. To perform this duty efficiently, the executive head has to keep himself and his subordinates informed about their jobs and performances through research, records and inspection. It is a sound principle or organisation that a periodical report is asked from a head of an enterprise. Such a report should be factual one based upon actual and faithful statistical data. The Chief of a library has to submit an annual report to the executive authority concerned. This practice keeps the Chief vigilant about his own activities since he knows that somebody else above him is keeping a watch upon him. Laski, a renowned political philosopher, observed, "vigilance is the price of freedom". The Chief Librarian, in turn, has to ask various Section Heads of his library to maintain proper records and statistics of the work performed by their respective subordinates so that a faithful and factual report is presented to the former.

'Budgeting' includes fiscal planning, accounting and control. No organisation can function properly without adequate finances. But it is difficult to obtain enough funds for all kinds of organisations, especially libraries, which are dependent and spending bodies. Libraries do not earn any revenues in the physical sense. Their services, though essential for the well-being of the individual, the society and the government, are not considered apparently indispensable. Consequently, the legislators and bureaucrats alike reject the demands of libraries on one or the other pretext. The libraries have been given almost the lowest priority in matter of allocation of funds. So the librarian has to muster strength and acquire necessary skill and tact for securing adequate funds. He has to convince the authorities about the usefulness of the service rendered by libraries. This can be achieved only if he advances tangible and plausible reasons for each of his demands. The authorities can be convinced easily by statistical data. So the librarian should maintain proper statistics of income and expenditure of his library. He should ensure proper utilisation of fiscal grants without any avoidable wastage.

In addition to the above-mentioned functions, the following two functions are considered essential for an efficient administration:-

Control

The Chief or the Supervisor will have to be ever vigilant about the rate of progress of the work. He has to ensure best quality and maximum quantity of work from his workers. In order to achieve this the Chief has to control effectively his subordinates. He has to inspect their work personally. He has to keep an eye upon the methods of performing specific jobs assigned to individual workers, the end products and overall costs of production/ services.

Motivation

The Chief can achieve his aim of maximum production only if he instils enthusiasm and team-work amongst his workers. Unless the workers perform their jobs willingly and conscientiously, the aim cannot be achieved. The workers must be motivated by providing congenial service conditions and environments. They must be made to realise that if they work more, they will get rewards for the same.

A library is a social institution. Every constituent of the society wants the library of flourish. On the other hand, the library is a part and parcel of the social framework. It is for the society. Without the society, the library will become extinct. It, in order to flourish, must not lose sight of the principles followed in administering other social institutions both private and public. Miles and Martin state, "The fundamental point is that the librarian is a public administrator. The library is an integral part of vast public service system, a circumstance that is most evident in the field of financial support. And in accomplishing his purpose the librarian performs administrative operations essentially similar to those of other public agencies..Two supplementary assumptions form the basis of the relationship of the library to the general theory of management and to the more specific principles of public administration. The first is that the management of a library involves functions that are essentially similar to those found in any co-operative enterprise..the second assumption is that fundamental tenets of public administration-as to managerial structure and fiscal organisation, for example-apply to such agencies as the school, the police department, and the public library".

The aim of a library is to ensure maximum use of its reading materials by maximum number of persons of its public. This is to be achieved by minimum output at most economical terms. This involves the application of principles of business administration. The purpose of a business organisation is to secure maximum profit. This is achieved by its at the most economical rates with minimum input. So basically, a library and a business organisation are measured in monetary terms while those of a library are judged from the utilisation of library funds for providing maximum reading services to its clientele. It is like other 'service' organisations e.g. Education Services.

Unity of command and management

The first pre-requisite of a good organisation is the Unity of Command-investing one person with all powers so far as his particular sphere of working is concerned. Dispersal of powers and functions to a group of people makes nobody responsible. Joint responsibility is nobody's responsibility. It is essential to have consistency in decisions and their proper implementation otherwise one person may interpret the decisions in one direction whereas the other person may take it in quite an opposite manner. It will create unnecessary confusion both within the group of administrators and their subordinates. The unity of command ensures efficiency and quick decisions. Each worker knows as to from whom he has to take orders and to whom he has to give orders. Ultimately, everybody is responsible to one executive head.

This principle of "unity of command" can be implemented by providing for "unit of management' which implies that the staff members work in a proper set-up and atmosphere which can be possible only if there is unity in planning and its implementation devices. All planning should lead to the fulfillment of the common goal of the library and all the individual ideas should be subordinated to the achievement of the main aim.

Scalar chain

"There must be a clear line of formal authority running from the top to the bottom of every organisation". To get work from other persons is difficult than doing a particular job by oneself, and it is especially so where scores and hundreds of people are engaged in a particular pursuit. For this purpose, a right type of organisational structure is essential. A choice is to be made out of the following structures which have been in constant use in various types of organisations and enterprises. But a proper selection would be possible only if these types of organisational set-ups are discussed at some length.

Line type

When all the workers are responsible direct to the head of the section/institution and to nobody else, the institution is said to have a line type of organisation. In bigger institutions, the control by the Chief himself becomes somewhat physically difficult if not impossible and he delegates certain powers to his deputies/assistants. These deputies/assistants are directly responsible to the head through an intermediary authority. Suppose, one library, besides other junior staff members, has got 5 Assistant Librarians, one Deputy Librarian and Librarian. In a line form of set-up, the Assistant Librarians will be responsible to the Deputy Librarian and not to the Librarian direct. This system implies a hierarchy of officers and it has got its merits and demerits. This rigid type of organisation is found in military organisations. This mechanism can be successful in very small libraries but it is liable to break down in larger institutions.

Line and staff type

'Line' denotes authority whereas 'Staff' stands for advice and counsel. The Staff type of administrative organisation is supplementary to the Line type and it does not serve as an alternative to the later. "A staff officer is one 'who is leaned on' for thinking, seeing, planning, recommending and reporting or co-ordinating, in some special aspect, in contrast to the line officer whose job is to give work instructions and get things done". In order to get sound advice, the work is divided into various departmental divisions and persons with specialised knowledge are made incharge of such divisions. Here, authority and advice are combined, though the executive authority remains with the Line type authorities but the auxiliary services are left to the Staff organisational heads e.g. cataloguing and classification, etc. are given in the charge of divisional heads.

These staff officials, though, do not come into direct contact of the readers, yet, become instrumental in making the library service effective. The theory of organisation has undergone a lot of change. 'Staff and line are co-ordinates, operating not in a hierarchical relation to staff over line, but on a horizontal plans of authority and responsibility under the Chief executives'.

Those tasks which are considered not to be executive are generally delegated to Staff officers. These jobs relate to the provision of information and guidance to library research workers.

But in order to ensure proper functioning of these two kinds of organisations in one set-up, a proper co-ordination is essential. The necessity of co-ordination is felt because the Staff Officers being theoretical in their approach may make certain impracticable suggestions which may not be liked by the Line Officers and they may, on their part, reject these proposals prefunctorily.

Consequently, there is a danger of an unnecessary conflict between the employees of an organisation. Co-ordination is further essential because due to unmanageable size and complex procedures, every section remains engrossed in its own work and does not even try to know the work and workers of the other sections. Consequently, water-tight compartmentalisation results. Co-ordination can be achieved by the Chief Librarian by calling frequent staff meetings and by appointing co-ordinators at various service points such as children, youth and adult departments.

Functional organisation

"Functional planning is found almost universally in nature". The line and Line Staff type of organisations create certain problems like lack of coordination amongst various sections. Even overlapping of duties is reported many times. It is thought advisable to define, once for all, the functions and duties of each person and it is done by dividing the whole library work by the type of jobs involved e.g. acquisition, classification, cataloguing, reference service and circulation etc. In this type of organisation, all the aspects of each particular job are but together under one Section Incharge respectively. For example, all the reading materials are acquired by the Incharge of Acquisition Section irrespective of the fact that the books relate to different subjects and languages. Similarly, the Incharge of Technical Section is responsible for the classification and cataloguing of all books irrespective of the fact that these belong to different subjects and languages. It is claimed that in this way, the functions of each person are clearly defined and overlapping is almost completely eliminated and specialisation in particular jobs is secured.

The Chief Librarian and Deputy/Assistant Librarians are relieved from attending to the routine jobs.

They are able to devote their time in planning future policies for the development of the library and in preparing programmes for closer relations between the staff, the readers and the books. "In most types of administration-and especially in library administration-the basis of planning likely to yield the best results is a functional basis, adopted to the needs of the particular administration.."

But this form of organisation is also not ideal. It becomes instrumental in widening the gulf between various departments and the persons working in each sections tend to forget all other technical jobs except that which comes to their lot. Secondly, under this form of organisation span of control increases. But these defects can be offset by introducing certain modifications. The first defect can be removed by holding frequent staff meetings and by shifting the duties of various assistants in rotation after every two years or so as has been put into practice by the author in the Himachal Pradesh University Library.

Arrangement by materials

Another arrangement followed in very large libraries is by materials. Special divisions are created for handling various kinds of materials. These are Books Division, Maps Division, Periodicals Division, Films Division, Government Publications Division, etc., etc. These division are responsible for acquisition, processing and making available the particular kinds of materials with which they deal. This kind of arrangement has got its own merits and demerits and can be usefully followed in libraries where these materials are received in large numbers. This kind of phenomenon is found in national and depository libraries. This arrangement is useful because each type of material is handled by specialists, proper treatment is ensured and wastage of time and energy of the staff is avoided. This system also avoids overlapping of duties and functions.

Subject arrangement

Since readers' approach is mainly by subject, they are becoming more and more conscious of their specific needs and this awakening on the part of the readers has put a heavy responsibility on the library staff. Unless they organise their collections in accordance with the approach of the readers, the library service may not be effective. In this type of organisational setup, library administrative machinery is geared up in such a manner that all work is divided on the basis of subjects. The general pattern is to divide the whole universe of knowledge into the following main groups:-

1. Humanities.
2. Social Sciences.
3. Biological Sciences.
4. Pure Sciences.

This system implies that one senior staff number is made incharge of each of these branches of knowledge. He is expected to be fully conversant with the subjects of his specialisation. It is better if he at least holds a Master's Degree in the concerned subject/subjects, because such a person should be able to answer many technical questions. It further implies that the Incharge of a Division will be responsible for the acquisition, preparation and servicing of the reading material of a particular subject field. The reference service is also done by the Divisional Head of a particular subject. The latest trend is towards the adoption of subject arrangement pattern and we find that many Universities in the United State of America and other countries of the world have adopted this type of organisation in their libraries. The universities of Cleveland, Los Angeles, Baltimore, and

Rochester have got subject arrangement type of organisation in their libraries. This type of arrangement is very useful for the students and research scholars but it is more expensive than some other types of organisations.

Delegation of authority

In order to secure proper co-ordination and strategic leadership, authority is delegated. It implies that the Chief Executive surrenders some of his powers to his immediate subordinates. Thus he multiplies himself because his authority is manifested in many of his subordinates when they get his orders implemented. In this kind of decentralisation of authority, the Chief Executive rules by the principle of 'Administration by objectives' rather than by that of 'Administration by Authority'. In the former case, the Chief executive brings home the ideals and objectives of the organisation to his subordinates and secures their willing co-operation for fulfilling the set objectives. The responsibility devolves upon the subordinates. In the latter case, the orders are directly issued by the Chief Executive and all the subordinates are directly responsible to him and the work is got done by the show of authority and command.

There are always three jobs for top management:

(i) Managing the business as a whole;

(ii) Managing the managers (Subordinate executives); and

(iii) Managing the workers and the work to be done.

To ensure proper implementation of the above-mentioned objectives the following essential elements must be provided:-

(i) Right type of leadership;

(ii) Clear understanding by every individual of the organisation as a whole, each section of it and the job assigned to every worker;

(iii) The delegation of powers should be commensurate with responsibility;

(iv) Decision making and their execution should be left to the subordinate heads so that they may gain confidence and may take initiative. In this way they would work with zeal;

(v) All the residual authority after defining the respective limits of the Chief Executive and subordinates should be left to the subordinate heads:

(vi) The decisions which are long range, multirelational, qualitative and complex, should generally be referred upward, and

(vii) The Chief Executive should keep a vigil and restraint upon the subordinate heads to ensure that the decisions taken by them are in conformity with the general policies laid down by the top management.

Departmentation

Proper job analysis and assignment of jobs should be planned in such a manner that no overlapping in duties occurs. This can be achieved by establishing various departments. The powers, functions and duties of various departmental heads must be clearly defined. Like jobs should be put under one department and unlike jobs should be isolated from each other. All vagueness or overlapping jurisdictions should be removed by the Chief Executives, Departmentation depends upon the following factors:

(i) Work analysis.

(ii) Division of labour.

(iii) Specialisation.

Work analysis

Work analysis is an attempt to secure a number of close-up views of different operations and breaking down of each task into its component parts.

Work analysis is useful for simplifying the procedures and for ensuring improvement in various processes. It is also helpful for assessing each individual and department's achievement during a particular period. Moreover, the Chief Executive can on this basis plan in a better way.

In work analysis, all the possible jobs are listed and then the following data is secured:

1. How much time is spent by each individual in performing various jobs individually?
2. How much time is spent for each job by the whole staff?
3. How much does it cost in monetary terms?
4. How much amount is spent on various jobs individually?
5. How much amount is spent in providing a particular complete job?

Division of labour

After proper work analysis, each individual worker is assigned a particular job in accordance with his qualifications. The principle of division of labour is based on commonplace experience that every person cannot do every job. In other words, each person has generally more leanings towards one or the other aspect of a job. Some persons are prone to thinking, others are practical-minded and still others are found to be proficient in fine arts etc. To have an economical setup, it is a sound principle to divide the work into various work units and to assign the various identifiable jobs to individuals separately. In a Technical Section of library, classification and cataloguing jobs are assigned to different persons. Still further division is done by assigning various component part jobs of cataloguing to various person e.g. by assigning the work of preparing the main entry cards to one person, of preparing the other added entries to the second and that of alphabetisation of cards to the third and that of filing cards to the fourth and so on and so forth.

Specialisation

Specialisation is another important principle by which a specific job is allowed to a specific person keeping in view his special qualifications and capacities. In a library, we may have competent cataloguers, classifiers and documentalists. So it will be for the benefit of the organisation to avail the services of specialists for doing specialised tasks.

Specialisation will ensure superior, economical, speedy and standards work since the same job done time after again, becomes a routine for the same person. He becomes perfect in doing it and does it speedily. Specialisation is very much desirable in bigger libraries for securing efficient and economical service.

Limited span of control

For efficient administration, there should be as few persons to be controlled directly by each head as is possible. In other words, there should be few sections under the charge of departmental heads to be directly controlled by the Chief Executive. If there are ten to fifteen departments, it is better to have two intermediary Deputy Chiefs so that the Chief Executive will have to deal with two Deputies only and in this way, he will be able to control the organisation easily. Similarly, in the Technical Section of a library where there are about twenty-five persons doing various jobs, it would be better to divide the department's work under two section heads e.g. Head of the Classification and Head of the Cataloguing Section. In this way, each section head will control few assistants and the department head will control the department through two section heads only.

Co-ordination

After establishing various departments, it becomes very essential that proper co-ordination between departments is ensured. In this way, the work is done smoothly without any friction. This can be achieved by the Chief Executive by holding regular meetings of the department heads. He should try to acquaint himself with the problems of various departments and the solution of the problems should be thrashed out in the meetings with the full concurrence of the department heads.

Leadership

The Chief Executive should have the qualities of a leader so that the subordinates derive inspiration from him. The Chief should be a hard worker and intelligent so that his subordinates follow him by example rather than by sermons since empty sermonising instead of having healthy effects lowers the prestige of the Chief. The Chief should be well-qualified, academically and professionally, so that the subordinates when confronted with various problems are able to seek solutions from the Chief. He should arouse amongst his subordinates interest and enthusiasm for the profession and loyalty to the organisation by his own example.

Facilitation

Proper arrangements should be made to secure adequate consultation and contact amongst the subordinates and high officials. In other words, the higher officials should be approachable to the subordinate officials also, so that their genuine difficulties are removed. It should be the objective of the organisation to save the organisation from strict regimentation. This can be achieved by holding general staff meetings on various occasions. The higher officials should utilise such occasions to acquaint themselves with the difficulties of the junior staff members.

Integration

Proper policy decisions must be taken by the Chief Executive so that the department heads are clear in their minds as to the extent of their authority to take certain decisions. For example, it is proposed by the Incharge Technical Section to introduce simplified cataloguing in place of descriptive cataloguing. This decision is going to have many repercussions in many departments. Whether the authority to take such decisions should be left to the department head of the Technical Section or the Chief Executives? Should the Chief decide such important questions by himself or should these be decide in a meeting of senior staff members? Integration is the process by which scattered administrative agencies or activities are combined under central direction or control.

Parity of responsibility and authority

While devolving responsibility upon an official; care should be taken that he is bestowed with corresponding powers. In other words, the extent of authority should correspond to the amount of responsibility.

Library administration, if based on the above-mentioned principles, is bound to be successful. But the success of library administration depends upon the way these principles are practised and the manner in which the decisions are put into force. Expediency and tact are very important for this purpose. In addition to these principles, the basic facts about a library must be taken into account while administering it. A library has got some difficulties and weaknesses. It is, on the whole, a dependent body. "It is likely to be a department of a larger organisation whose central executive usually tends to take advantage of his privileged position and develop a grasping tendency on the one hand and obstructive tactics on the other". Besides, a library is a 'spending body' and a 'growing organism'. Their implications must not be lost sight of.

Scientific management

Administration Vs. Management

Management is "the function...concerned in the execution of policy within the limits set up by Administration and the employment of the organisation for the particular objects before it". On the other hand, Administration is "the function... concerned in the determination of the corporate policy".

There are conflicting and confusing definitions of administration and management. To some 'Manage-ment' is a generic term while 'Administration' is considered only a part of the former. To others, 'Management' is a part of 'Administration". According to them, "that phase of a business enterprise which concerns itself with the overall determination of the major policies and objectives is Administration", while on the other hand, the function which concerns itself with the carrying out of the administrative policy laid down by Administration is 'Management'.

In spite of divergent opinions, 'management' is a very vital part in administration since it is "the art and science of organising and directing human effort applied to control the forces and utilise the materials of nature for the benefit of man'.

Nature of management

"Administration is becoming a science in our life-time.." Management, now-a-days, is a specialised job and it is not within the reach of the common man. It needs proper training and experience. It has a scientific character.

"Scientific management is the application of the principles and methodology of modern science to problems of administration". The motto of the Royal Society of London indicates the nature of modern science. It states, "Nothing on faith. If you want me to accept your view, prove that it's better than mine. I insist on evidence that is measurable". In other words, scientific management requires a complete mental revolution on the part of the workers and the management. Both must pay their whole-hearted attention towards increasing the size of the surplus. The old individual judgment or opinion must be replaced by exact scientific investigation and knowledge. Scientific management, in brief, involves certain combination of the following elements:-

1. Science instead of rule of thumb.
2. Co-operation instead of individualism.
3. Harmony instead of discord.
4. Maximum output instead of restricted output.
5. The development of each person to his greatest efficiency.

Necessity of Scientific Management

Frederick W. Taylor pointed out that the root cause of ills in management was ignorance on part of the management and the workmen. The former did not know as to what could be a fair day's work of a worker. They did not know as to how to convince the workers that they would get a fair reward for their efforts in production. The workers, on the other side, also were ignorant that they could secure a proper output if they were assured that they would get increased reward if the management earned more.

The necessity of following the principles of scientific management was explained by Taylor as follows:

1. That the whole country was suffering a great loss due to inefficiency found in their daily jobs.
2. That the remedy for curing it lay in providing systematic management.
3. That systematic management was a true science based on defined laws, principles and rules.
4. That these principles were applicable to all kinds of human activities.
5. That if and when these principles are applied correctly, the results must be very much encouraging.

He based his principles on Motion Study and Time Study.

Value of scientific management

Scientific management bestows certain important benefits upon those who practise it faithfully and sincerely. These are listed below:-

1. It helps in increasing efficiency and productivity.
2. It provides a scientific basis for fixing the wages of workers from time to time. The basis is the productivity in an enterprise.
3. It provides a valuable information and data about the desirability or otherwise of adopting rationalisation in an enterprise.

Limitations of scientific management

1. Scientific management is not an exact science because it deals with human beings. The human behaviour is variable. Human beings deal among themselves in the form of employers employees, customers and

dealers etc. "Where human beings are concerned, management principles may be so much waste paper".

2. Every organisation has got its own traditions and objectives. Management principles, policies and techniques are applied to specific circumstances in each organisation. They invariably differ in each institution.
3. Science is advancing. So scientific management must change from period to period. Those principles of scientific management which may be good today,. may not be suitable tomorrow.
4. Work methods, work standards and output cannot be measured accurately and easily. Huge cost is involved in making these methods and standards foolproof.
5. The engineering side of the work is given undue emphasis while the human element, a basic factor in scientific management, is ignored to a great extent.
6. From workers' point of view, the scientific management means subjection of their work to their performance. They fear that it will lead to sending many of them out of job.

However, the benefits of scientific management outweigh its so-called demerits. Moreover, the demerits, if any, are remediable by judicious application of principles of scientific management and rationalisation. That is why the scientific management has been popular in almost all the advanced countries of the world. IT has been applied to almost all kinds of human activities.

Levels of management

Generally, there are three tiers of authority or management i.e. top, middle and lower. The top management includes the Chief Executive and other senior executives. In business enterprises these may be represented by the Managing Directors, General Managers or Presidents of the Boards of Management, and Deputy General Managers and Vice-Presidents etc. In Libraries, the Chief Librarians, Head Librarians or Directors of Libraries or Senior Professionals (Grade I) may represent the first type while the Deputy/Assistant Chief Librarians, Deputy/Assistant Librarians or Deputy/Assistant Directors of Libraries or Senior Professional (Grade II) may be the second type. Similarly, the 'middle management' includes those persons through whom the Chief wields his authority and gets the jobs done. They include Heads of Departments and Superintendents. In libraries also they be called as Heads Incharge of particular Sections or Departments of a library. They may also be called as Junior Professionals. The lower management includes those person who directly supervise the work of the workers. In industrial organisations they may be called as General Foremen, Foremen and First-line Supervisors. In libraries, they may be called by various names e.g. Senior Library Assistants, Head Assistants, Office Superintendents and Library Assistants.

Functions

The functions of each of these three types of management may be as under:-

(a) Top management

(i) to take jurisdiction of an issue and to deliberate and decide;

(ii) to confirm the decisions taken by executives at different levels;

(iii) to counsel and guide them in initial stages of policy formulation; and

(iv) to review their acts through reports and inspection.

(b) Middle management

(i) to assist the chief executive;

(ii) to prepare themselves for undertaking broader responsibilities.

(iii) to understand others jobs and problems.

(iv) to serve as leaders for persons below them.

(v) to co-ordinate the activities in three directions i.e. upward, downward and sideward.

(c) Lower management

(i) to supervise the work of the rank and file.

(ii) to serve as administrative link between the workers and authorities.

(iii) to issue orders and directions to the workers to be implemented by them.

Principles of scientific management

Scientific management to be successful must be based on sound principles. Some of these principles may be as under:

1. *Job-analysis.* It is the determination of the jobs and their analysis into more or less independent sub-jobs. These jobs should not overlap each other in any way.

2. *Division of labour.* It is the determination of respective duties of personnel at various levels.

3. *Work methodology.* It means the improvement of methods of work. These should be based upon the tried systems such as time study, motion study and standardisation of tools, equipments etc.

4. *Maximum profits.* The organisation should be run on

the most efficient lines so that there is maximum productivity for the employers and maximum prosperity for the employees.

5. *Incentive wage system.* The wage system must provide incentives to efficient workers so that they are encouraged to further improve their work.

6. *Complete Harmony.* There should be maximum harmony and co-operation between management and workers.

The basic principle of scientific management is the "distribution of responsibility or its decentralisation".

The top management confines itself to the formulation of policies and principles and deciding financial matters. The power of reviewing the execution of the policies etc. is left to the paid executives. The method of random sampling is used for reviewing purposes. The faults are corrected by scientific methods.

The executive officers, on the other hand, undertake full responsibility for carrying out faithfully the policies and principles laid down by the top management. The difficulties experienced by them in their day-to-day work are referred to committees appointed by the top management for necessary amendment or change in policies and principles.

Application of scientific management principles to libraries

The principles of scientific management can be profitably applied to the following library jobs which are amendable to proper analysis.

1. *Frequently performed* jobs such as duplicate checking, typing book orders, classifying, book numbering, reproducing cards, filing cards, book charging and discharging and book shelving.

2. *Repetitive jobs* involving recurrence of same steps

each time a job is performed, such as book charging and discharging.

3. *Jobs requiring frequent movement of people or equipment* such as physical arrangement between acquisition and technical sections, public catalogue, major bibliographical tools, reference, lending and circulation sections.
4. *Jobs with bottlenecks* such as delay caused in labelling or confusion in deciphering call numbers written in ink on the spines of books.
5. *Jobs involving large amounts of money* such as provision of reference service in a large library. Job-costing or cost-accounting is very useful in such a case.

Methodology and procedure of a scientific management study

A scientific management study should be entrusted to that person or body who has enough knowledge of the filed of investigation and the basic principles of scientific management.

Such a study involves the following steps:

1. *Defining the problem.* The scope of the problem should be clearly defined and understood.
2. *Gathering the data.* It is essential to know of what steps a job consists. In other words, the motion study must be made first. It should be followed by the time study i.e. the time required for performing each part of a job. Further, cost data for each item should be gathered.
3. *Analysing the present method.* The present method of analysis made use of should be properly understood in relation to each step of the process as well as the process as a whole. The following six steps can be useful in analysing a particular job:

(i) Why is the job performed?

(ii) What is the purpose of each step in relation to the purpose of the institution? What will it contribute to the overall process?

(iii) Where is the job done? Where else can it be performed?

(iv) When should the job be performed? Can it be performed at some other time with better results?

(v) Who should perform the job? Can it be performed by some other person with less qualification/training at less cost?

(vi How is the job performed? How could it be performed better?

4. *Developing an improved method.* An improved method can be developed in the following ways:

   (i) By eliminating the whole or unnecessary process.

   (ii) By combining various homogeneous process.

   (iii) By changing the sequence or order of the processes.

   (iv) By changing the operator.

   (v) By simplifying the remaining processes.

5. Putting the improved method into operation. The improved method can be put into operation only when it is properly put to the supervisor. The supervisor should be co-operative. The following steps are involved in executing the improved method:-

   (i) Presenting the new plan to the supervisor in writing.

(ii) Overcoming resistance from the supervisor and coworkers. The resistance is generally based on unfounded fear. The workers may feel that the new method may reveal that they were performing their jobs inefficiently; that they may be dismissed; or that their jobs may be considered superfluous and that as a result, they may be retrenched. For example, in India, at present, there is a strong opposition from workers to the introduction of computers in industry and business. The Life Insurance Corporation of India is experiencing such a resistance from its workers. Many people oppose the new methods for mere opposition. whatever the reason of such a fear may be, the innovator must understand the human nature and overcome the resistance with patience, perseverance, courage and wisdom.

6. *Training workers in the new processes.* In order to make the new process a success, the workers must be trained in making use of the new process.

7. *Initiating a trial operation and following it up.* Proper trials should be launched. These must be followed up vigorously. Nobody should be allowed to feel disappointed about the slow progress in the initial stages otherwise the workers would like to revert to their old methods.

Value of scientific management to libraries

Scientific management is not confined to industry and business alone. Rather it can be profitably made use of in public enterprises, may, even in public services also, which do not have a profit motive. The main advantages to libraries which partake the nature of a public service department may be as under:

1. *It helps in developing a factual data and argument.* A library has an onus to satisfy the tax-payer by providing him the maximum return for each rupee paid by him for library purposes. A library is a growing organism.and it needs additional funds year after year. The tax-payer wants to know why the additional amount is required. Not only an ordinary tax-payer but even experienced appropriating committees are impressed by quantitative and factual justification than eulogy of librarianship. Scientific management helps a librarian develop such a quantitative and factual argument in his favour for securing additional funds.

2. *It helps improve routine efficiency.* Majority of library tasks are of repetitive and mechanical nature and are amenable to quantitative analysis. These processes include ordering, cataloguing, card filing, binding, circulation and book shelving. Scientific management can enhance routine efficiency.

3. *It is a useful tool of library personnel management and financial administration.* Scientific management provides us work analysis of a job which is the key to modern job-classification. As a result of this analysis, the executive officer intelligently and precisely knows what he can and should expected from a worker. This provides him a yardstick to measure the work performed by a worker.

Similarly, scientific management helps an admini-strator run his business or organisation on sound financial lines. He knows the cost of each part of a job and thus he intelligently plans and avoids wastage and increases efficiency in service, thereby providing more satisfaction to his clients.

Rationalisation

Besides the rise of scientific management, the concept of

Rationalisation came to prominence in the twentieth century. This can also be useful to libraries.

Rationalisation was taken resort to in Germany after its industries had collapsed after World War I. It is "the employment of all means of technique and ordered plans which serve to elevate the whole industry and to increase production, lower its cost and improve its quality. The main aim of rationalisation is "to raise the general level of prosperity by cheaper, more plentiful and better quality goods". It means the application of rational methods i.e methods based on plausible reasoning and sound judgment. The elements of Rationalisation include the following:-

1. *It is a comprehensive process.* It does not deal with a problem piecemeal. Rather, on the other hand, it treats the problem as a whole. It implies careful planning in all phases of production, distribution and labour problems. Its aim is to improve these, thereby ensuring better quality goods and services at lower costs.
2. *Macro application.* It approaches the problems of an entire organisation rather than any one of its units singally. It implies the elimination of wastage either by winding up uneconomic units or amalgamating the latter with other units with an aim to ensure greater efficiency.
3. *Standardisation.* Rationalisation involves standardisation of products, services and means & processes of production and distribution.
4. *Mechanisation.* Rationalisation achieves its aims by the application of latest discoveries and inventions. It does this by the use of improved mechanical devices.

Advantages

The main advantages of rationalisation may be the following:-

1. It ensures better utilisation of resources/sources of production i.e. men, machines and materials.
2. It results in greater production of better quality goods and services.
3. The cost of production is lowered. Consequently, the prices are lowered. So the ultimate consumers are benefited.
4. The employees secure higher wages or remuneration.
5. As a result of the above, the overall effect is economic stability and industrial cooperation.

Its advantages

Rationalisation is not without some disadvantages. It may suffer from the following:-

1. Danger of over-production and consequent depression.
2. Monopolies may come up.
3. Weak and small units may face elimination.
4. Unemployment may spread.
5. The fruits of rationalisation can be reaped only if huge investment is made by installing latest and costly machines.

Conclusion

These disadvantages can be avoided only if rationalisation programmes are implemented with sincerity and confidence.

In India, though the Government of India and other enterpreneurs are aware of the utility of rationalisation, yet so far it has not been applied much mainly due to the lack of increased finances and skilled labour. The principles of rationalisation can be applied to libraries also with profit.

Library organisation versus library administration

Library organisation and library administration are related to each other so closely that it becomes sometimes difficult to make a clear-cut distinction between the two. Even the well-known librarians, authors and examiners confuse these two important subjects. A newcomer to the profession feels bewildered. This confusion is evident from examination question papers of various universities. Due to their close relation and perhaps due to non-existence of clear-cut distinction between the two, in Library Science courses of various universities, especially of the West, these two subjects are combined into one paper.

But if we go deep into the matter, we shall come to the conclusion that these two subjects are quite different even though the distinction is very subtle. One starts where the other ends. One is concerned with the laying down of theoretical principles whereas the other puts those principles into practice. The distinction between these two topics will become clearer if we define these two terms and find out their elements and functions respectively.

Organisation

Organisation is "the form of every human association for the attainment of a common purpose". "Organisation is the design of the structure, the grouping of positions, which will best carry out the library's planned objectives".

Organisation involves the designing of the structure of authority, defining and classing of posts, their relationship with each other and ensuring proper co-ordination for achieving the objectives of a library. According to Gaus, White and Dimcock "organisation is the arrangement of personnel for facilitating the accomplishment of some agreed purpose through the allocation of functions and responsibilities. It is the relating of efforts and capacities of individuals and groups engaged upon a common task in such a way as to secure the desired objective with the least friction and the most satisfaction to those for whom the task is done and those engaged in the enterprise".

In other words, organisation means that:

1. There should be a common objective of an institution, and
2. All its members must subordinate their individual will to the common will. After the selection of proper staff, the directive function of the leader starts which is the province of administration.

Further, "Organisation implies the process of analysing into component parts and assembling the resultant units into a pattern for the attainment of the object in view".

"Organisation implies a structure of authority which requires a single directing executing authority and many workers. In setting up such an organisation one must

1. Define the objectives of the organisation very clearly;
2. Elect the leaders or directors of the enterprise who lay down the general policy of the enterprise in terms of the objectives;
3. Nominate the Managing Director or Chief Librarian whose task it is to see that the objectives are realised;
4. Determine the nature of the whole organisational framework, the number of specialised work units

into which the task will have to be divided and the number of workers, as well as the various categories of workers required. Sub-division into sections, divisions or departments depends on the nature and extent of the task undertaken;

5. Establish and perfect the structure of authority between the managing director and the various work departments".

Administration

Administration involves the techniques by which the purpose of an organisation is fulfilled at minimum cost with minimum effort. Administration is, in fact, mainly concerned with the directive function through which an administrator unifies the efforts of all individuals engaged in an enterprise and guides their activities in the right direction. The administrator directs the energies of the personnel in the right channels so as to achieve the objectives for which the enterprise is brought into being, "Administration or direction is that function of management which actually executes or carries out the objectives for which the enterprise is organised. This function initiates the work to be performed, sees that personnel is fitted to the task, and trained to operate properly, and in general cases for everyday routine necessary to ensure that men, materials and equipment are functioning properly towards the desired end".

Administration concerns with following functions already explained in the foregoing pages:

1. Planning;
2. Organising;
3. Staffing;
4. Directing;
5. Co-ordinating;

6. Reporting; and
7. Budgeting.

The following devices and methods are used by an administrator for performing the above-mentioned functions:-

1. He provides for unit of management;
2. He divides the whole organisation into various departments;
3. He delegates authority to various units,
4. He finds out ways and means for proper co-ordination between various parts of the organisation;
5. He plans for keeping as limited span of control as is possible;
6. He works as leader of the organisation; and
7. He arranges periodical staff meetings, conducts inspections and issues administrative orders from time to time for smooth working of the organisation.

Distinction between library organisation and library administration

From the foregoing paragraphs, the functions of organisation and administration are crystal clear and their distinction from each other can be stated as under:

1. Organisation provides the structure of authority whereas administration actually uses the devices for achieving the objectives of an enterprise.
2. Organisation is "the machinery of administration, the channels through which the measures and policies of administration are put into effect". Administration, on the other hand, "is concerned with the directive function exercised by the leader of an enterprise".
3. An organisation comes first and administration

follows it. In other words, there can be no efficient administration unless and until there is a sound organisation.

4. Administration starts the moment an organisation is established. A library is planned and established by utilising organising capacities of planners. The administration of the library starts when the day-to-day working of the library is to be undertaken. In other words, by administration is meant the practical techniques used for getting the work done in various departments of the library.

5. Organisation involves the theoretical aspects of ensuring an efficient and sound establishment, whereas the administration applies various principles for attaining the objectives of the organisation.

The difference between organisation and administration is very subtle. In fact, "both administration and organisation are merely the machinery for attaining an aim or objective".

Management by objectives (MBO)

The latest thinking about management is that best results can be achieved through management by objectives and as such it has now been accepted as the best management approach. The principles of this system were propounded in 1954 by Peter Drucker. It is based on two main principles:

(i) Results orientation; and

(ii) Particular view of human behaviour.

This system helps in realisation of an organisation's goals by its members as if those are their personal goals. The mechanism used to achieved the aims is that goal-setting process is made not only an open secret but all the members of the organisation are also made to realise the importance of the goals, thereby resolving the various inconsistencies and misunderstandings before these take firm roots. Any MBO system has four basic components:

1. Setting objectives.
2. Developing action plans.
3. Conducting periodic reviews, and
4. Appraising annual performance.

This system has been based on Maslow's theory of hierarchy of needs, and Herzberg's theory of identification of motivators and hygiene factors in the work environment. The former theory identifies two factors i.e.responsibility, achievement, and recognition while the latter takes into account better salary and other conditions of service. Besides McGregor's theory of management system and Likert's theory of participation fortify MBO theory. The first theory states that if employees are properly motivated to work, they are sure to be achievement-oriented. The second theory provides the mechanism of participative style of leadership and thus fosters commitment to objectives of an organisation.

Merits of system

The MBO system has the following seven benefits.

1. *Improvement in management performance*

It ensures managerial efficiency because manager's commitment to organisation's objectives increases as the members are made responsible for the achievement of their set objectives.

2. *Improvement in planning*

This is possible because each manager's individual goals are made consistent with those of each other and with those of the organisation because these are decided in the presence of their superiors.

3. *Improved co-ordination*
Improved planning and agreement on tapping of resources needed for the purpose result in better co-ordination of the organisation as a whole.

4. *Improved control*
Improved co-ordination results in improved control.

5. *Improved flexibility*
Each manager knows fully well his own objectives and those of the organisation and their priority for them, so improved flexibility is possible.

6. *Improved superior-subordinate relationships*
MBO provides increased opportunities for communication between the superiors and subordinates at various stages, such as at the time of objective-setting and performance appraisal.

7. *Improved personal development*
MBO provides better opportunities for personal development as it fosters personal responsibility.

Demerits of the system

Many writers have challenged MBO theory as enunciated by Maslow and Herzberg.

The main attack against the MBO theory is that it has been oversimplified and that the theory as enunciated by Herzberg is a theory of job satisfaction and not a complete theory of work motivation and improved job performance.

Second plank of attack is that MBO theory does not take into account other variables which affect job performance. For example, Victor Vroom gave three variables i.e. Valence, expectancy and force while according to Porter and Lawler these include efforts, performance, reward and satisfaction. Similarly, Smith and Cranny have proposed a three-pronged approach i.e.

effort, satisfaction and reward. The merits detailed above outweigh demerits because an organisation's inputs, outputs and processes are critically examined through self-analysis. This is the main reason why MBO theory is respected inspite of severe criticism against it.

MBO's relevance to libraries

Libraries can benefit from MBO though in a limited way. MBO is relevant to various technical and procedural operations in Libraries such as acquisition processes and technical services. MBO is beneficial to middle management of library. In other words, it is relevant to Sectional and Departmental Heads. It is useful for libraries because a library can be managed by sharing responsibility among those who are responsible for managing a library. However, those benefits which are likely to accrue from MBO approach should be carefully weighed keeping in view the staff and monetary costs.

7

Online Technical Support Systems

Between the late 1960s and late 1970s, three trends evolved in the development of online library systems. The first consisted of pioneering in-house projects in single institutions. The second centered around the evolution of what came to be known as "bibliographic utilities." The third trend was the emergence of private enterprises developing prepackaged "turnkey" automated library systems.

One of the first online systems was at the Illinois State Library in Springfield, in late 1966, at a time when many other libraries were designing full offline systems. The backbone of the system was an IBM 1620 computer located in the state processing facility. The equipment in the library consisted of IBM 1033 prints and 1031 card readers, which were similar in operation to the 357 Data Collection System, requiring insertion of machine-readable book cards and borrower identification badges. Rather than producing transaction cards or recording transaction data on tape, however, the 1031 at the Illinois State Library transmitted data directly to the computer. By later standard, the online system at the library was primitive. Although transaction information was conveyed directly to the computer as it occurred, it was stored on a separate daily transaction pack and was merged with the main circulation file only on a once-a-day batch processing basis. The system did not include item-specific online query, so that it was still necessary to use offline batch-produced circulation lists to trace circulation information pertaining to a given item. For these purposes, the system was much like wholly offline batch processing systems. What set it apart from those, however, was its ability to perform two important functions online: checking borrower registration numbers for validity and checking each returned item against an online holds file. Each time a borrower identification card was inserted into the designated slot of the 1031, the borrower number was automatically checked against a computer-stored file of valid borrower numbers. If the borrower's number did not have a counterpart in the file, that fact was generated immediately on the 1033 printer. This was a major improvement over completely offline operations. Where such validation, if done at all, could be performed only by manual lookup in a printed directory of borrower numbers. The other important online function of the Illinois State Library system was checking holds, and that had equally important implications. When the book card of a returned item was placed in the 1031 for discharge, the call number was checked against an online list of call numbers of items placed on hold. If the cell number of the returned item matched a call number in the holds file, a message was automatically generated on the 1033 printer showing call number, identification number of the patron who had placed the item on hold, and the data when the hold had been placed. In this manner, greater control over holds was realized than was possible in offline batch processing computerized circulation systems.

Midwestern university system

Another early online circulation system was implemented in late 1967 at Midwestern University in Wichita Falls, Texas. The Midwestern system was unique in that it was, at least insofar as its designers know, the first and perhaps only online circulation system to operate on an

IBM 1401 computer, a decidedly second-generation machine. Like the Illinois State Library system, Midwestern used IBM 1031 input stations and 1033 printers, validated borrower identification numbers, and checked items against an online holds file. But it went further than the Illinois system in several important respects. Not only did the Midwestern systems check borrower numbers during a charging operation for general validation, but it also determined if a borrower had any outstanding overdue items or unpaid fines. If so, the computer generated an immediate list of the charges on the 1033 printer.

The Midwestern system had an online query capability, albeit restricted to searching on a borrower number. The keying in of a number prompted the computer to respond by printing a list on the 1033 containing all items charged to that borrower. But perhaps the fundamental difference in the Midwestern system was that the main circulation file was online in the strict sense of the term, with the file being updated immediately upon completion of each transaction, rather than in a batch mode.

Eastern illinois university system

In September 1968, the Booth Library at Eastern Illinois University in Charleston began to operate its own version of a online circulation system using a third-generation IBM 360/Model 50 computer and the IBM 1031 input stations and 1033 printers. The Booth system had the basic functional characteristic of the Midwestern system, but with an important additional query feature. The Midwestern system had query capability by patron number; the Booth system supplemented this with item query by call number. By entering a particular two-digit code followed by a call number, a terminal operator could retrieve bibliographic information and current circulation data about a specific item. Queries of this nature were made using an IBM Cathode Ray Tube (CRT) terminal located at the circulation desk. A further extension of this search capability was a scanning command that displayed bibliographic entries in call number sequence. Since the Booth Library online file was an inventory file containing an abbreviated bibliographic record for nearly even item in the library—not just items currently charged out—the scanning capability allowed shelflist searching of the entire library collection. The structure and search capabilities of this system suggested possible extension as a public-access tool, and in fact plans were announced to locate a public-access CRT terminal near the card catalog in fall 1971. Still, the known item query capability of the Eastern Illinois system allowed more immediate information about the circulation status of an item—ever if the query had to be generated by a circulation attendant—than was possible in an offline system.

Minicomputer-based hybrids

In the early 1970s, a number of academic libraries began to incorporate minicomputers in their circulation operations. A significant feature of these systems was that at least part of the processing hardware was located in the library itself, although a larger computer, outside the library, still played an integral role. Typically, the minicomputer in the library contained certain files for immediate online access and captured transaction data for later batch transmission to as larger computer located outside the library on which the main circulation file was stored. While some of the operations remained offline, this setup realized the benefits of online processing for certain critical purposes.

One of the most common minicomputers in this type of configuration was the IBM System/7 in use in circulation control in at least six libraries by early 1974. In the system operational at the University of Pennsylvania in Philadelphia, five online files were stored in the minicomputer. Each of these contained critical information against which various types of transactions were checked. There were three item files against which renewal attempts and discharges were checked. A call number file contained the call number of all items placed on hold, the access number file contained a list of all items recalled, and a reserve book file contained all items for which in request had been placed to transfer the item to a reserve book collection upon its return. Another file, against which all patron identification numbers were checked, was the restricted patron file, containing a lost of borrower identification numbers of all users whose further attempts to charge materials were to be blocked for some reason. The fifth online file was the daily transaction file, which recorded the day's activity. Once a day, this file was transmitted to the main computer, an IBM 370/Model 168, located at the university data processing center, for batch updating of the main circulation file. This transmission, usually involving information for about 3,000 transactions, required about 30 minutes.

For the most part, improvements, gained in the Online circulation systems of the late 1960s and early 1070s over what was possible in an offline system were focused on immediate access to information about restricted items, such as holds, and better control of patron privilege. Although improvements regarding access to information about restricted items enhanced public service by allowing more rapid reshelving of returned items and a better system for regulating holds and ensuring identification upon return, these benefits were not always immediately evident to the average library user. The second common capability, immediate access to Online delinquent patron files, could as likely cause ill feelings as goodwill between the library and its users. The lack of reliable backup measures, inexperience in dealing with online systems, and continued reliance on batch-produced circulation lists combined to make early online circulation systems less than revolutionary in terms of public service. At least one facility, the Simon Fraser University Library, had so many problems and so much user discontent with its online system that it abandoned online and reverted to its earlier offline system."

Ohio state university system

Perhaps the outstanding example during the early 1970s of online circulation system that could, in fact, facilitate user services to a degree not possible in an offline system was demonstrated by Ohio State University's Library Control System. The entire philosophy behind the design and application of the system for the Ohio State University libraries was, as described by Hugh Atkinson, "that the system should be one which would speak to the problems of its users rather than simply the problems of the library." These problems included, among others, a decentralized library structure consisting of a main library and more than 20 branches. Only one catalog—the main library's—contained complete information for all items in all 21 libraries.

Similar to several earlier online circulation systems, Ohio State opted for an "inventory" file approach in which the main machine-readable database contained records for all items in the libraries rather than an "absence" file, which would have contained records only for those items in circulation. This principles as fundamental at Ohio State since the system was to be used as a locator file as well as for circulation operations. A massive conversion effort—perhaps the largest of its kind carried out by any library to that date—was contracted to a vendor, which put into machine-readable form records containing call number, unique item number, author, title, date of publication. Library of Congress card number, language code, from of publication code, and holding for each of 1 million distinct titles and 2.5 million items.

The key to the Ohio State system was its items query capability. Searching was possible by call number, title key, and a combination author/title key. When the desired item was retrieved, it was possible to see which library or libraries on campus owned a copy of the item, and whether each copy was charged out. Search terminals were available in the main library and in most of the branches. Thus, the entire union catalog of the libraries' holdings could be assessed from any library in the system. Although this in itself was a fundamental improvement over the single union catalog in the main library. An item not already checked out in one library could be charged on terminals located in any a copy was found to be available in a different branch library, the circulation attendant could issue a command that would generate a charge slip in the branch library that had the copy. The item would be retrieved in that library and placed on a shelf to await later pickup by the patron. The online union catalog, showing location and circulation status of each item throughout the system, combined with the capability of remote charging to remove much of the patron uncertainty that was inherent under prior circumstances.

The Ohio State University library system, like all other online system, was not entirely free of problems, but many of them could eventually be alleviated by design changes and the system was such an improvement over earlier conditions that the problems were of comparatively minor consequence. The impact of this system on library service was probably best exemplified by the fact that, during the first 18 months it was in operation, circulation at the Ohio State University libraries increased by more than 40 percent. The system was an important achievement owing to its scale of implementation, its query capabilities, and its emphasis on public service problem solving. The same system was later taken by Atkinson to the University of Illinois and implemented; today it is the basis of an important networking system in libraries throughout Illinois.

Apart from circulation, the late 1960s and early 1970s saw the development of a number of online technical processing systems. One of the earliest acquisitions systems was designed at the Washington State University Library in Pullman and was implemented in 1968; an online serials control system was up and running at University Level in Quebec the same year. Predating both of these was the beginning of a comprehensive online library system at the Redstone Scientific Information Center in Alabama. Some parts of the system were operational as early as 1966. And by the early 1970s, acquisitions, cataloging, authority control, serials check-in, and circulation were online.

Offline computerization had been an important development in acquisitions, providing for machine-assisted production of purchase orders, improved methods of fiscal control, and more timely updating and generation of status lists. Still, a significant amount of from handling and paper file maintenance remained in many of these systems. The online acquisitions systems developed in the late 1960s and early 1970s represented major improvements by reducing the amount of manual handling and maintenance of paper products, as well as further enhanced those functions that had been performed well in offline computerized system.

Acquisitions

One of the more ambitious projects in the late 1960s was carried out at the Oregon State University Library at Corvallis. Christened LOLITA, this online acquisitions system required nearly seven "staff years" in programming, systems, and clerical labor to develop. It contained three Online files: order/in-process file contained three display screens of information input when an order was placed, and updated as an item passed through the acquisitions and cataloging procedures. The first screen included basic bibliographic data, the second screen contained accounting data, and the third screen allowed for local cataloging information such as call number and location. The amount of time and file maintenance that this system saved the staff, particularly when compared with a manual system, was considerable.

LOLITA generated four paper copies of each order, two going to the vendor, one later used as a cataloging workshop, and one retained as a general hard copy record for the library. The two copies for library use were a reduction over most offline systems, and some libraries went even further. With the online acquisitions systems in use at the University of Massachusetts Library and the Dartmouth College Library, neither library retained any paper copies of the order form in technical processing at all.

One of the greatest contributions made by online systems in general was the expansion of access points, and these early acquisition systems were no exception. It was possible with an offline system to produce lists or maintain paper copies of order forms by more than one point of access, such as by order number, author, and title if desired, but that merely increased the number of lists to be consulted or files to be maintained. As a result, the number of listing parameters was usually minimized in offline systems. In online systems, all files and their indexes could be maintained in the computer, and multiple access points to a single record would not mean an increase in hard copy materials to be consulted or maintained. LOLITA, however, only provided to access points, order number and author, to each record in the system.

The early online acquisitions systems retained some of the capabilities that had been included in their offline predecessors, but the newer systems were much improved in quality, speed, and ease of handling. LOLITA, along with several other early systems, provided for handling of partial shipments and authorization of partial invoice payments, capabilities that were handled, if at all, only with some difficult by offline systems. The fund accounting component of LOLITA was also successful. A year-end encumbrance report could be generated in 20 minutes, and LOLITA was to only much faster, nut also judged more accurate and detailed in a controlled comparison with manual ledgers.

Perhaps the most important characteristic of online acquisitions systems was that, in most cases, it was only one part of a broader integrated technical processing system that brought the acquisitions and cataloging functions closer together. The online order record, upon receipt of an item, became an online cataloging record. This greatly reduced duplication between acquisitions and cataloging and also provided an end product consisting of a machine-readable bibliographic record for each item entering the collection. In LOLITA, the final steps in the online processing after an item had been received were for a cataloger to verify the bibliographic information originally entered by the acquisitions department and the complete the record by adding local cataloging data. The completed record was removed from the online file, but not before it had been copied onto magnetic tape as a permanent machine-readable record. An important feature in the development of online technical processing systems was the incorporation of Library of Congress MARC records. Records on MARC tapes were transferred into the local online systems in various ways. A common feature across systems was that each new order was searched against a locally maintained MARC file, and when a match occurred, the appropriate MARC record entered the local system as the source for bibliographic information for ordering and eventual cataloging.

One of the most comprehensive uses of MARC records evolved in the University of Chicago Library Data Management System. Orders could be searched against the MARC files, and there was a retrospective searching capability whereby incoming MARC records were searched against the local bibliographic file to identify previously created local records as potential candidates for bibliographic upgrading by the new matching MARC record. These features in one from or another could be found in other systems, but an interesting feature of the Chicago systems was its use of MARC tapes as a collection development tool. Subject profiles, defined by Library Congress classification numbers and ranges of numbers, could be maintained online, and each incoming MARC tape was matched against them. The result was an offline list of items falling into each subject profile for use in identifying potential orders for the library. The system also allowed access to these lists online if a bibliographer wished. The system also allowed access to these lists online if a bibliographer wished. Supplementing the LC class number profiles were certain national bibliography online profiles used to identify potential orders from an area studies prospective. In addition to profiles designed to identify items of potential interest for the library, the

University of Chicago system also included a capability designed to assist in better control over blanket orders from publishers. The first four digits of an International Standard Book Number (ISBN), MARC field 020, are unique to each publisher. Each record on the MARC tapes was automatically searched on these first four digits at Chicago. The system could then generate lists of items published by each publisher with whom Chicago had a blanket order arrangement, and these lists could be used to assist in monitoring receipt of blanket order items.

Ballots

Several of the largest research libraries in the United States were interested in the concept of an online integrated technical processing system as early as the mid-1960s, although actual systems could be implemented at these institutions only after several years of planning, design, and experimentation. These of the more well publicized of these large-scale efforts included the Northwestern Online Total Integrated System (NOTIS), the University of Chicago Library Data Management System mentioned earlier, and Standford University's Bibliographic Automation of Large Library Operations using a Time sharing System (BALLOTS). Without minimizing the importance of achievements elsewhere, BALLOTS was perhaps the most sophisticated online technical processing system developed in the early 1970s. Because of its later adoption as the online bibliographic component of the Research Libraries Group (RLG), its impact on American librarianship during the 1970s and early 1980s has been greater than any other system originally designed for use by a single institution. An experimental version of BALLOTS was brought online as early as 1969, but it was not until 1972, after further design and modification, that the system was dully implemented. It ran on the Standford University campus computer, an IBM 360/Model 67, with a Digital

Equipment Corporation PDP 11 minicomputer in the library as a front-end communications processor. The terminals initials selected for accessing the system were programmable Sanders PDS 804s.

The hardware for BALLOTS was in itself an important achievement. The selection of terminals with a programmable capability was based on the design requirements for the terminal display features desired. Two important functional considerations were to allow for protected fields in an online record that could not be modified by a terminal operator, and at the same time to permit line insertion to allow expansion in length of certain nonprotected fields. At the time BALLOTS was being designed, either one of these further could be incorporated by using a nonprogrammable terminal, but not a combination of the two. Only a programmable terminal, such as the Sanders model could allow both protected and expandable fields. In addition, it was possible for several programmable terminals to share a single communications line rather than each requiring its own dedicated line.

BALLOTS was designed around several modules and contained four online files critical to technical processing. One was a MARC file, which held the most recent 6 to 12 months of MARC records from the Library of Congress. A second was an In-Process File (IPF), which contained a record for each item anywhere in the processing stage from initiation of an order to final cataloging. Once received and cataloged, the record was transferred into a third file, the Catalog Data File (CDF), which contained an online record for each item fully processed on BALLOTS. Fourth was a Reference File (REF), which included see references, see also references, and explanatory and history references.

When a request for an order was submitted, a

terminal operator first searched the MARC file to see if as corresponding MARC record was available. If a match was found, the operator requested an online ordering work form, which contained mnemonic fields into which information could be entered. Appropriate bibliographic data were automatically transferred from the MARC record to the work form, requiring the terminal operator to input only the additional information pertaining to the order, such as vendor code and accounting data. An online order record could easily be created for an item where there was no available MARC record, but this naturally required more time since bibliographic information had to be supplied from other sources and typed onto the Online work from. Offline products, such as purchase orders, a cataloging workslip, and a temporary order slip, were printed each evening for all items entered into the In-Process File during the day. Stanford found the traditional 3" x 5" slip too small for its purposes and, as described by Veaner, "because copies of certain forms no longer had to be filed, the forms themselves could be designed around their data requirements rather than a filing cabinet size."

The online order from was updated as its status changed, such as when an item was received. After receipt was indicated, the item was given to the cataloguing department for final processing. One of the helpful features of BALLOTS was its tracing procedure; the location of an item within the processing unit was kept up-to-date online ever to the name of the specific cataloguer handling the final processing. It was the responsibility of the cataloguing department, with item in hand, to verify and, if necessary, modify the information on the online record created in acquisitions and to add any additional pertinent data. Catalog cards and spine labels were then printed offline, with the day's production of all cataloguing cards sorted into filing order sequence. The online record was transferred into the Catalog Data File as the permanent bibliographic and holdings inventory record.

BALLOTS had a number of built-in features that made input and modification of records easy for a terminal operator and at the same time reduced the likelihood of operator error. Fields that were inappropriate for operator input or modification were automatically protected so the operator could not even place the cursor in those positions on the screen display. After entering information into a nonprotected field, the operator could move the cursor to the next nonprotected field simply by depressing the shift and tab keys. Throughout the procedure were default protocols that assumed the operator's next most logical step but these could be overridden by the operator if an item required atypical treatment.

The system also had validation capabilities for certain types of information such as account codes. When an account code was entered by an operator onto the online order work from, the system checked the code validity. This check did not prevent a valid inaccurate code from being assigned to an item, but it did insure that nonexistent accounts could not be charged.

Ordering selected volumes of a multipart set hard always been a problem in acquisitions systems, but BALLOTS handled this in a way that minimized the work of the terminal operator and still allowed flexibility in subsequent processing. If, for example, volumes 1, 2, 3, 8 and 9 were being ordered, the operator merely typed 1-3 and 8-9 in an appropriate field on the order work from, and the system automatically "exploded" the record into five distinct records, one for each volume ordered. These separate records for each volume allows receipt of partial shipments and individualized processing.

One of the strongest features of the BALLOTS system was its search retrieval capabilities. Unlike most other technical processing systems. BALLOTS offered a wide complement of sear fields and allowed searching on truncated words, variant forms of entry, and keywords. A terminal operator could search the MARC file by Library of Congress card number, personal name, corporate or conference name, and title. The Catalog Data File allowed for searching by all these elements, but also by Library of Congress subject headings, call number, and BALLOTS ID number. Searching of the In-Process and Reference files was more restricted than searching of the Catalog Data File, but less restrictive than searching the MARC file.

As an automated technical processing system, BALLOTS was a landmark project far more sophisticated than earlier offline systems and more successful than its online contemporaries of the early 1970s. As might be expected, it had a tremendous impaction Stanford's operation, such as integrating technical processing functions more closely than before. The Acquisitions and Cataloging departments, although remaining under separate supervision were physically consolidated. They had previously been located on different floors of the library. In addition, the number of staff was reduced. One-third of the staff positions in the Order Division were eliminated, as were several positions that previously had been responsible solely for typing unit entry cards, duplicating and typing headings on them, and sorting them into filing order: all functions that were computerized under BALLOTS.

By the mid-1970s, automated efforts in technical; processing were turning to shared systems. BALLOTS remained an exemplary illustration of an in-house system, and itself became the basis of a networking system, first among several libraries in California, then in a wider geographic area in the western United States, and still later among a number of major research libraries across the country.

Although serials control is an integral part of technical processing, development of automated systems for serials handling has usually been carried out somewhat independently of acquisitions and cataloging. This had been the case with unit-record and offline batch processing systems and was equally typical of online development. Offline systems allowed libraries greater control in some aspects of the serials operation, particularly in claiming, and enabled holdings lists to be updated and printed much more frequently and with far less staff effort than in unit-record systems. A considerable amount of manual card and paper handling still was required, however, and the offline lists were a problem in that they tended to be generational, with periodic supplements to other periodic supplements to less frequent master cumulations. Online capabilities offered the potential of reducing the amount of handling and making available up-to-date records of holdings in one place.

In the early 1970s, and on perhaps a somewhat less dramatic scale, the system developed at the UCLA Biomedical Library was to serials what BALLOTS was to acquisitions and cataloging and what the Ohio State University system was to circulation. Although not the first online serials control project to be implemented, the UCLA system was generally considered more sophisticated and flexible than its contemporaries. Design objectives included, among others, the elimination of all card handling and the generation of fewer hard copy lists. By 1972, there were records in the serials control database for about 12,000 titles, slightly more than half the library's current subscriptions. The format of the online records was similar to MARC, but with fewer fields. When an issue of a title was received, the operator retrieved the online record and updated it by keying a simple code. Other codes were defined for updating holdings when back or skipped issues were received.

In additional to the check-in operation, the system had automatic overdue detection and binding status monitoring. Keyword searching of the database could be performed, an especially crucial capability given the complexity and similarity of serials titles. The search component also allowed retrieval of titles by fixed field.

Online systems had many advantages over those based entirely on batch processing. The volume of paperwork and hard copy files was reduced, as well as the amount of staff time required for their maintenance. Although the "up-to-the-second information" characteristic of online was highly touted, many of the earlier systems only partially had this capability, as evidenced by some circulation functions that used minicomputers as front-end communications systems. Nevertheless, even those systems were able to store some of their more critical files in virtually current status.

One of the most important characteristics of online systems was search retrieval capability. Again, some of the early ones are very restricted in inquiry capability, but others were considerable sophisticated, such as at Ohio State University, Stanford, and the UCLA Biomedical Library described earlier. The design, implementation, and continuing operation of the more sophisticated online systems were landmark achievements, but their costs were correspondingly high. In many instances, funding was aided throng grants or heavily subsidized by the host institution's general operating budget; the costs were far out of reach of the vast majority of libraries. It was estimated, for example, that the continuing production and development costs in operating BALLOTS doe a single month in 1974 were $34.225, and this figure pales in comparison to the design and development costs incurred before the system's implementation.

Bibliographic utilities

Left with an alternative of in-house, single-library development projects, only the largest and most well endowed libraries could have used an online system for any technical support systems during the 1970s. As early as 1967, however, a second alternative was being formulated, and the outgrowth of this and similar efforts was the evolution of four system—OCLC, RLG, WLN, and UTLAS—whose use by the early 1980s, extended into several thousand libraries on the North American continent.

OCLC

Although some libraries continued to develop their own in-house systems for certain library functions, it was apparent by the mid- 1970s that automated cataloging in particular was evolving in a different direction. The basis of this transformation was the Ohio College Library Center (OCLC), a system based on the simple premise that, recognizing minor local variations, cataloging data for a given item were essentially similar from library to library. The Library of Congress MARC project had been as major breakthrough in the concept of shared cataloging information in an automated environment, but the general pattern of sharing had been unidirectional and on an institution-by-institution basis. MARC tapes were sent from the Library of Congress to subscribing institutions, each of which then loaded the tapes and manipulated the data on its own computer. The idea that evolved for OCLC was a central file of cataloging records that could be maintained on a single computer system and accessed through terminals sharing dedicated communications line connected to that computer. Not only would this enable libraries to share a MARC file, but it would centralize development costs of the system and virtually eliminated the need for each participating library to use the host institution's computer system.

Because the Library of Congress cataloged only portion of the universe of materials received by libraries, and since the MARC tapes included only the OCLC online system was the capability for allowing original input of records, using the MARC format, by the participating libraries themselves. The impact of this is seen by the fact that even by the end of the decade, less than one-fourth of the master bibliographic records in the OCLC database had been supplied by the Library of Congress.

OCLC was chartered in 1967 and Frederick G. Kilgour named as its executive director. System production first began with offline batch processing in 1970; 54 member academic libraries in Ohio submitted punched IBM cards with Library of Congress card numbers of items for which they wanted catalogue cards produced. The punched cards were searched against a file consisting of the Library of Congress MARC records, and when a match occurred, catalogue cards were generated and sent back to the requesting library within two weeks. In 1971, OCLC went online, installing terminals that allowed each library to search the growing OCLC On-Line Union Catalogue (OLUC), the bibliographic database of the system. The library could order catalog cards merely depressing a couple of command keys on the keyboard attached to the CRT display terminal.

During the first several years of OCLC online operation, a number of far-reaching decisions were made that would enhance-and sometimes plague—the cooperative effort. The display format revolved around the concept of a bibliographic "master record"; in theory there was to be only one record in the database for any given bibliographic entity. When this master record for an item was retrieved by a library, any of the MARC fields could be modified to reflect local practices with respect to subject headings, forms of name entry, local call number, and so on; virtually any element in the record could be modified.

All local changes were reflected on the catalog cards printed offline at OCLC and mailed to the library (and eventually on the library's magnetic tapes of its cataloging activity when this service became available). These modifications, however, were not stored permanently online for the library. Therefore, when a library retrieved a record it had previously used for cataloging, the bibliographic master record was displayed online, without the local modifications that the library had previously made.

The lack of capability to permanently store local information was probably justifiable in OCLC's initial stages. The amount of storage required to maintain this data for each cataloging use of each record by each library would have been enormous, especially since most members of OCLC at that time had a low incidence of adding copies for titles they had already cataloged once. Nevertheless, it was not long after the system went online that some members began to express concern over the lack of a permanent online record containing local modifications for previously cataloged materials.

A characteristic of OCLC during the 1970s was a perpetual gap between announced plans and actual implementation, and the permanent storage and display of local cataloging data—or at least of a scaled-down version of local holdings from selected fields—perhaps provides the most exemplary illustration. In early 1974,

"Definition and Use of the 049 Holding Field," detailing a critical field used to record local data for card production and tape purposes, was published by OCLC partially in anticipation of an impending change, which would allow storage and display of modifications to master records. The actual change proved far less than imminent. Five years later, in 1979, OCLC's development schedule projected the capability of local holdings display for current cataloging records to be available to members in January 1980, with access to local information for previously cataloged materials available sometime later. But less and less discussion of this capability emanated from corporate headquarters and the capability eventually disappeared from all development schedules.

The strategy initially used in creating the online file of bibliographic master records in OCLC revolved around the creation of as large a database as possible in as little time as possible. This may be overgeneralization, but there is little doubt that it was prevalent enough so that a great many of the permanent master records entered into the database by member libraries in the early years suffered in quality and completeness of information. Master records, particularly for retrospective cataloging entered into the database, were frequently created from a description taken solely from the shelflist card of the first member library to convert the title. Thus quality and completeness depended in great part on any given library's past shelflisting practices, on the library's policy for input of new records into the database, and, beyond that, on the accuracy of the terminal operator.

The philosophy of rapid creation of a database at the expense of detail and completeness of record could be seen in OCLC's approach in 1975 to providing records for serials titles, for which a specifically designed MARC format had only recently become available. To greatly increase the number of serials records in a short time, tapes of the Minnesota Union List of Serials (MULS) were loaded into the OCLC database. Although MULS contained accurate information as far as it went, it was primarily a locational tool and provided very abbreviated bibliographic data for cataloguing purposes.

Perhaps the greatest quality control complication in the long run was the extreme difficulty of upgrading master records when a mistake was detected or information found to be incomplete. Written forms had to be completed by a member library and mailed to OCLC; when received, the master record was examined by OCLC staff and modified according to the reported additions or changes. This process was time-consuming and cumbersome for member libraries, and not exactly a foremost staffing priority at OCLC. The result was that a library could easily retrieve a master record containing an obvious typographical error that presumably had been modified locally by any number of other libraries for their own card production, but that remained in the master record due to backlogs at OCLC in record upgrading. Owing to the prominent role of the OCLC database in the Conversion of Serials (CONSER) project, a limited number of libraries were given the capability of making permanent online modifications to OCLC serials master records from their own terminals, thus bypassing the manual error reporting procedure. This proved a tremendous success. The possibility of enabling a small number of libraries a similar online capability for records in other formats was a topic of discussion for several years, and was finally initiated in mid-1984.

The approach used in creating its database and the difficulty in correcting errors in master records earned OCLC a reputation in some quarters as a "dirty database." To be certain, many early records in the database did suffer from lack of quality control. An often overlooked factor by critics, however, was that OCLC was an experiment without direct precedent and included among its membership a segment of the library community that had virtually no previous experience with any type of library automation. OCLC was not the first online system used for collective representation of cataloging data fro a number of independent libraries, but immediate predecessors were based on centralized input and thus centralized control. This was quite different from the structure of OCLC, in which any member library could input an original bibliographic master record for an item. Given this degree of autonomy and decentralization, combined with the lack of previous experience with library automation on the part of most of its members, and a lack of precedence to gauge the implications of shared databases, the early 1970s were an individual and cooperative learning experience for OCLC members which served to demonstrate both the strong points and the problem areas of cooperative ventures in library automation.

During its first year of online operation. OCLC remained a cooperative venture of Ohio academic libraries. During 1972, membership was extended to Ohio nonacademic libraries, and in 1973 to libraries outside the state. Although the major computer facilities were to remain centralized at OCLC headquarters, a decentralized approach to the provision of general support services emerged by the mid-1970s. OCLC and various independent state and regional agencies entered into contracts for the brokering of OCLC services and for provision of training and ongoing assistance. Some of these networks had predated OCLC; others were formed in direct response to the need for an agency to provide OCLC services in a particular area. Two exceptions to the general pattern of independent brokering were the formation of OCLC Western (referred to as PACNET-the OCLC Pacific Network), consisting of several branch offices on the Pacific Coast, and OCLC Europe, both being service agencies under the direct administration of OCLC. The independent affiliate networks, which have usually numbered about 20, have remained administratively separate from OCLC a relationship that has at times worked to the benefit of OCLC and at other times served as a source of conflict.

Within four years after OCLC's decision in 1973 to expand its base of participation beyond Ohio, the number of libraries using the system had increased to more than 800. Increasing numbers of public and special libraries were joining, but the majority of new members continued to be academic libraries. These included many members of the Association of Research Libraries as well as medium-sized university libraries, but an influx of new participants continued from among the ranks of four-year colleges, a pattern that underscored OCLCs role in introducing automation into smaller institutions. A major factor in the opportunity for these smaller academic libraries to join OCLC during these years was the availability of implementation grants from the Kellogg Foundation.

By 1977, it had become apparent that OCLC governing structure had not kept pace with the growth of the system. General "membership" and positions on the board of trustees were still restricted to libraries in the state of Ohio, with libraries in other state defined as "participants" and having no elective say in the governing body. The Arthur D. Little firm in Cambridge, Massachusetts, was commissioned to study OCLC's governing structure and to suggest alternatives. With recommendations based on a report submitted in June 1977, the Ohio OCLC membership later that year voted to adopt a new governing structure to reflect its national character. During the same year, OCLC changed its official name to the acronym by which it had become known, and in 1981 it adopted the name of OCLC Online Computer Library Center.

RLIN

The concept of resource sharing was the basis for the formation of a number of formal cooperative ventures during the 1970s. One such, begun in 1974, was the Research Libraries Group (RLG), comprised of Harvard, Yale, Columbia, and the New York Public Library. Its board goals focused on the sharing of resources, collection development, and preservation and conservation of library materials. RLG felt that a common automated bibliographic system would enhance cooperative efforts among member libraries. By early 1978, the four systems under final consideration for adoption included OCLC, Standford's BALLOTS, the University of Chicago Library Data Management System, and the New York Public Library bibliographic control system.

In spring 1978, RLG announced agreement with Stanford for the use of BALLOTS as the group's automated bibliographic component. Although RLG may merely have chosen what it considered to be the best available system, the choice drew strong reactions from within and outside the group. In June of the year, Harvard announced withdrawal from RLG, although Director of Libraries Douglas Bryant indicated that the choice of BALLOTS was not the motivating factor. A wide spectrum of emotions was expressed throughout the library community concerning RLG's decision not to go with OCLC, which many saw as the emerging national bibliographic network.

In comparing the online features of BALLOTS and OCLC, there is no question that BALLOTS was the far more sophisticated and flexible technical processing system. Unlike OCLC, it also provided for online storage and display of an individual library's cataloging data in a network environment, as well as other features such as searching by title keyword and subject, not available on OCLC. Although on a smaller scale than OCLC, BALLETS had also proved capable of serving as a shared system as early as 1975 when seven public libraries in California entered into a networking arrangement with Stanford, and the number of libraries using it has increased since then.

The greatest source of resentment among OCLC libraries about RLG's selection of BALLOTS was probably not so much the choice itself as it was the accompanying implicit, and sometimes explicit, attitude that OCLC and its "dirty database" were unacceptable, and that the needs of RLG members were somehow quite apart from those of the rest of the library community—including those of many prestigious research libraries that remained ardent supporters of OCLC. Equally crucial in the reaction, OCLC had come to be recognized by then as much more than a shared cataloging database. Because of library identifier symbols attached to each bibliographic record, OCLC had grown into a tremendous tool for facilitating interlibrary lending and, to many, was the most current and reliable source of occasional information available in the United States. The selection of another system by RLG virtually cut off those libraries and their collections from this source of information and ejected a major obstacle to their participation in resource sharing on a broader scale. To many OCLC libraries and even to those using neither system, this detachment seemed a conscious and motivated effort to minimize the role of RLG members in the broader context of American library cooperation.

The reaction to RLG did little at that time or later to discourage the image of elitism. Full membership in RLG, in essence, required a library to be a member of the Association of Research Libraries (ARL), and this restricted potential membership in RLG to a pool of early 100 libraries. RLG permitted other libraries to apply for participant status, meaning a library could use and contribute cataloging data, but the feeling was that this did little to soften the image of elitism.

BALLOTS, which in the RLG environment became the Research Libraries Information Network (RLIN), may have been functionally superior to OCLC as a technical processing system, but not all of its distinctions were carried over into the new network. At Stanford, the system had been, and remained, a full technical processing system, which traced an item and built on its online record from the initial point of ordering to its final point of cataloging. Crucial in this progression was the In-process File (IPF), described earlier in this chapter. Although any RLIN member library had searching access to Stanford's IPF, there was no capability for other members to build a similar file for their own institutions. Thus, one of the strongest features of the original BALLOTS, which provided the continuity for its realization a more complete technical processing system, did not exist under RLIN in its earliest manifestation for any library other than Stanford.

WLN

During the 1970s, work was also being conducted at the Washington State Library on the design of an online bibliographic system. Supported by a $1.2 million start-up grant from the state legislature, the system went online in 1978, the Washington Library Network (WLN) was being used in 12 public and 9 academic libraries in the state, along with 2 libraries in Alaska. Later that year,

3 libraries in Idaho and 1 in Oregon joined WLN. From the start, it was apparent that WLN was a well-designed and highly sophisticated system. It included retrieval of local information, subject access, and, not long thereafter, authority control. WLN took a cautious approach to building its bibliographic database. As in RLIN and OCLC, Library of Congress MARC tapes were loaded, but unlike the other two utilities, WLN established a standing policy to centrally review all records input by member libraries.

In January 1979, the library press reported that the National Library of Australia had signed for membership in WLN had sold its system software to the National Library. The distinction was significant. All three of the major utilities—OCLC, RLIN, and WLN—were based on a centralized computer system linked through telecommunications lines to terminals in member libraries; none of the utilities up until that time had attempted to transfer any part of its system for use in another computer.

In 1978, it was not entirely clear to American library community what role WLN would assume in national bibliographic networking. Although WLN was focusing on regional cooperation in the Pacific Northwest, OCLC had also been a geographically limited system at one time, and BALLOTS had been implemented in a single library. It seemed possible that a third nationally competing system may have been emerging in the form of WLN. In 1979, however, the network reaffirmed its regional emphasis, adopting a policy that expansion outside the Pacific Northwest would-be restricted to sale of the WLN software in a manner similar to what had taken place with the National Library of Australia. In the years immediately following, a number of such transactions occurred, including sales to the Southeastern Library Network (SOLINET), the University of

Illinois, and the University of Missouri. Membership in the WLN network in the Pacific Northwest had increased to 60 members by 1980 and, as OCLC had done slightly more than two years before, WLN modified its government structure to reflect the expansion of its membership base beyond a single state.

UTLAS

Although its impact in the United State has been limited, the University of Toronto library Automated System (UTLAS) was a fourth major online bibliographic networking system to have emerged on the North American continent during the 1970s. Implemented in an online networking mode during the mid-1070s, UTLAS had increased its membership to more than 200 libraries by the end of the decade.

UTLAS membership was limited primarily to Canadian libraries, with some important exceptions. In 1980, the network signed its first member in the United States, the Rochester, New York, Institute of Technology. The following year, UTLAS signed a million-dollar agreement with a Japanese firm to broker UTLAS in Japan. The system did not make concerted efforts to expand into the United States, but it is noteworthy that in 1981, in a comprehensive comparison of the four major utilities, the University of California at Berkeley ranked UTLAS first in overall technical capability. The University did not, however, opt for UTLAS. In 1984, UTLAS opened a U.S. branch office in New York, and it will be interesting to see what impact this will have on its position in the nation.

Over the years, each of the four bibliographic utilities has strived to become more than simply a shared cataloguing database. Development efforts by one or more have gone into acquisitions subsystems, serials check-in capabilities, circulation systems, interlibrary loan communications, online union lists, provision of Computer Output Microform (COM) catalogs, and terminal compatibility for searching other databases.

WLN, OCLC, and RLIN made a tremendous impact on librarianship in the United States during the 1970s in terms of providing online cataloging capabilities, but their impact in circulation control, acquisitions, and serials check-in was negligible. Some libraries continued to develop their own in-house systems to handle these functions. However, another alternative emerged, particularly in the area of online circulation, in the form of commercial vendors of automated library systems.

Commercial online systems

Commercial enterprise played a pivotal role in library automation long before the advent of online systems. Automation via unit-record equipment had been almost the exclusive domain of IBM. Remington Rand offered unit-record equipment comparable to IBMs, but its impact on the library market was negligible. IBM continued its domination into the early 1960s, when offline computer processing came into use in some libraries. As the decade progressed, however, computers manufactured by other firms began to appear in universities, corporations, and municipal facilities. By the end of the decade, IBM was still the predominant name in computers for library applications, but it no linger maintained the exclusively it had once enjoyed.

During its years of dominance, IBM had been responsible in devoting time and effort to assist in applying its equipment to the library environment. Libraries certainly did not receive an undue share of attention, but IBM representative were often assigned to help libraries with implementing applications, and the corporation published descriptions of and guides for use of its equipment in library applications. The company also sponsored seminars, the most notable being a symposium held in Endicott, New York, in 1964.

Although IBM and its new competitors expressed at least nominal interest in library applications during the 1960s, it was evident that this was an infinitesimal share of the total computer market. According to estimates in the early 1970s, less than one-tenth of one percent of the computers in the United States were being using by libraries in the way. To make these facilities still less conductive as a market, even those with computers were inevitably using equipment purchased by host institutions for a variety of applications, the foremost usually not being those of the library. Libraries had little control in either the selection of equipment or in the decision to replace one manufacturer or model with another. As long as large-scale, multipurpose mainframes were the only available computers, libraries were essentially at the mercy of their host institutions. Although some libraries established excellent relations with their computer centers and did play a role in automation decisions, procurement was an unpredictable and uncontrollable environment for many.

The advent of minicomputers radically altered the computer field for libraries, enabling at least the large ones to perhaps purchase their own equipment and create a more predictable environment. A number of libraries did purchase their own equipment and designed applications software in-house in the 1970s, but another alternative began to emerge in that decade—the library-specific commercial vendor of automated library systems. In terms of the total computer market as viewed by larger corporations, libraries were too few to attract a great deal of attention, but the potential volume demonstrated a suitable market for smaller and specifically library-oriented commercial ventures.

CLSI and circulation

One early commercial venture came from Computer Library Systems, Inc., later shortened to CL Systems. Inc., and later again simply to CLSI. The company's first automation efforts involved acquisitions systems, and one of its first installations, in 1972, was at the Cleveland Public Library, which had been using a batch processing system on IBM equipment for eight years. In a description of the CLSI system at Cleveland Public, Richard Palmer observed that, over a five-year period, the cost of the new online system was expected to be less than one-half the cost of the IBM batch processing system, had it been continued. In addition, the new system offered broader and more library-specific features.

CLSI soon turned its attention toward circulation control. Its LIBS 100 system and other vendor-supplied systems introduced subsequently come to be known as "turnkey," a reference to the premise that, upon delivery and installation, virtually all that was required to make the system work was to plug it in and turn it on. Although in practice this has not always exactly proved to be the case, the idea was essentially sound and formed the basis on which these systems would become cost-effective alternatives to in-house development. As so many libraries had learned in implementing their own online or even batch processing systems, the cost of design and development were considerable. With a mass-marketed system, such up-front development costs could be distributed among many customers and hence would be far less for each library then independent design and development. With a turnkey system, programming expertise was not required of the library staff or even at the host institution. Perhaps most importantly, the library's minicomputer could be operated and maintained within the library itself, and the software was marketed by vendors whose entire business was specifically library applications. Other vendors joined CLSI in the online circulation control market during the early and mid-1970s, nut for several years the field was fairly unstable. Various companies entered and left the market, were purchased by other companies, and radically redesigned their systems. By 1975, five commercial vendors were offering turnkey automated circulation systems with varying degrees of online and offline capacity. Two years later, three of them had cased marketing efforts in the United States and another had been sold and its system totally redesigned. CLSI provided the only continuity in this short span of time.

The year 1977 was pivotal, however, in that several new vendors of circulation control systems entered the market and would prove more stable than most of their predecessors. Among these were Data Phase, Geac, and Universal Library Systems. Entering the 1980s, CLSI was still the leading force in the commercial market, with 177 installations and more than 300 other libraries remotely accessing computers located at one of the installation sites. The fastest growing computer was Data Phase with 50 installations, followed by Geac with 22. Gaylord, active since 1978, had 11 installations by 1981. Although not actively marketing in the United State since about 1977, the Plessey online circulation system popular in Great Britain had 9 users in the United States and Canada.

Acquisitions, serials control, and cataloguing

With the exception of early CLSI efforts, commercial activity in online acquisitions and serials control has lagged behind circulation control and did not really begin to make an impact until the late 1970s and early 1980s. The primary source of commercial developments also differed between the two areas. For the most part, vendor-supplied online circulation control systems have resulted from new commercial ventures into the library marketplace. In acquisitions and serials control, in contrast, many of the earliest efforts came from long-established library vendors; book jobbers for acquisitions and subscription agents in serials control.

Baker and Taylor's offline BATAB system was available to libraries since the 1960s, and by the late 1970s the system had been redesigned, enhanced, and offered online as LIBRIS. Around the same time, Brodart also announced availability of an online acquisitions system. By the early 1980s, book jobbers had been joined by other vendors, such as Ringgold and Innovative Interfaces, in offering online acquisitions, as well as by each of the four bibliographic utilities. In addition, several vendors of circulation systems were in the process of testing acquisitions modules, promising even more competition.

Commercially available online serials control systems have appeared comparatively recently. Two major subscription agencies, Ebsco and Faxon, each announced plans for an online system in 1981, capable not simply of ordering, but encompassing functions such as check-in and claiming, and not limited to titles ordered through the respective agency. Ebsco eventually abandoned development of its own online check-in component, while Faxon did incorporate one into its online system. Also in 1981, the MetaMicro Corporation of San Antonio, Texas, announced a serials control software package for minicomputer application, although active marketing of this system eventually ceased. Activity in the not-for-profit sector also showed signs of life in the early 1980s, exemplified by marketing of the CHECKMATE serials control system by the California Library Authority for Systems and Services (CLASS) and by OCLC planning efforts to make its rather dormant serials check-in subsystem more attractive. Changes in the OCLC sub-system were made in 1983, but had a negligible impact in attracting new users. An interesting activity occurred with CHECKMATE, as Ebsco began to market that system when it abandoned development of its own online check-in module.

Although the bibliographic utilities emerges during the 1970s as the clearly predominant supplier of automated cataloguing systems, there were a few commercial attempts to penetrate the cataloging market. One of these was the BIBNET system, announced by Information Dynamics Corporation in 1974. BIBNET was to operate similarly to OCLC in a number of ways: it was principally intended to be a shared cataloging database; it was to contain member input master records as well as LC MARC records; the master database was to be stored on centralized computers; and library identifier symbols were to be affixed to each bibliographic record as an aid to interlibrary loan.

Several features of BIBNET were planned conspicuously different from OCLC and attempted to answer some of OCLCs more pressing problem areas. Keyword-in-title search capability was to be available, along with plans for the eventual introduction of subject searching of the database. BIBNET users would be encouraged to access the system though a minicomputer housed in the library to facilitate local production of offline products and to reduce telecommunications cost. By using a minicomputer, libraries could retrieve records from the master database, copy them onto a cassette tape, and then break the telecommunications link. Master records copied onto the cassette would then be displayed on a CRT terminal connected to the minicomputer, modifications made to the records, and the revised records copied into a second cassette. Catalog cards and other offline products could be printed locally, based on the modified records on the second cassette. Although access to BIBNET could be gained through means other than a minicomputer, the front-end interface was strongly promoted as the most useful for allowing flexibility.

Information Dynamics had ambitious intentions for BIBNET. Not only was it to contain post-1968 LC MARC records, but there was a plan to centrally input access points into the online system for more than 3.5 million Library of Congress manual cataloging records created between 1953 and 1968. When a library retrieved such an index entry, it could notify Information Dynamics through the system that it would like a full record in the database for that title. Information Dynamics would then create a record in MARC format for the title requested and load it into BIBNET within four days.

BIBNET'S entry into the marketplace coincided with the rapid and successful expansion of OCLC. The system simply never established a firm position. A more successful venture was launched several years later by Informatics, Inc., with the introduction of MINIMARC. It was minicomputer-based, but with no pretense as a networking system. The entire LC MARC database was supplied on floppy diskettes. The library retrieved these records locally on its minicomputer and modified them according to need. For titles not found on the LC MARC database, the library could create and input records into its own working file. Catalog cards and other offline products could be locally produced.

Since a premise of MINIMARC was local processing, the system did not incur the telecommunications charges as did use of a bibliographic utility, and the overall cost were not as per-unit-dependent. On the other hand the initial investment could be as tenfold that of joining a bibliographic utility, and monthly maintenance and other costs were substantial enough to make participation in a utility more economical for smaller libraries. A limiting feature of MINIMARC was that, as a nonnetworking system, its core database was restricted to LC MARC records and was therefore smaller than those of the bibliographic utilities. Since its emphasis was so much on being a local system, it did not serve in any capacity as an interlibrary loan locational tool. In 1981, however, Informatics, RLG, and the California Library Authority for Systems and Services (CLASS) announced availability of an interface whereby MINIMARC users would be able to search the RLIN database through their MINIMARC system equipment, an arrangement that would enhance MINIMARC as a local system with access to a broader utility. By 1981, more than 30 libraries had installed MINIMARC, and the number had increased steadily since then.

Another successful commercial venture into automated cataloging was the Carrollton Press REMARC project. In 1980, Carrollton announced a five-year project in which it would convert more than 5 million Library of Congress cataloging records, not included on MARC, to machine-readable from. Libraries could submit brief data to Carrollton, in either machine-readable or nonmachine-readable form, to match against both the LC MARC database and the REMARC database being created by Carrollton. For items for which a record could be found, Carrollton would supply machine-readable bibliographic records containing relatively complete LC cataloguing data.

In addition to MINIMARC and REMARC as alternatives to the bibliographic utilities, a number of commercial book jobbers and COM vendors were maintaining machine-readable cataloguing databases for their customers. These were really a quite different matter, since initially with these stored databases, a customer did not have direct online access to its own database. This circumstance has been changing, as some of these vendors now provide online access.

In the late 1960s, the only choice for libraries implementing an online system was to design and develop it in-house and use a large mainframe computer housed in central facilities at their host institution. During the 1970s, additional alternatives emerged: systems designed and developed be bibliographic utilities and commercial vendors; systems that could be operated on library-owned minicomputers and, more recently, on microcomputers. What was once a very restricted environment has broadened into a increasing range of options. As with unit-record equipment and batch processing computerized systems, the use of Online has been a learning experience for those libraries implementing their own systems, for the bibliographic utilities, and for the commercial vendors. Libraries implementing online systems in the late 1960s and throughout the 1070s provided a valuable basis of experience upon which other institutions could draw. This building on experience has helped to create a more solid foundation of general principles and specific tenets for automation of technical processing operations, but changes in technology and increasing competition in the marketplace certainly give assurances that the options available to a library are not likely to become stagnant or mundane.

8

Online Cataloguing Systems

The earliest on-line cataloguing systems used routinely for production of catalogue cards began in 1970 at the Shawnee Mission Public School system in suburban Kansas City. IBM 2740 and 2741 type-writer terminals were used to input bibliographic data, and an IBM 360 Model 40 computer to do the processing and print catalogue cards. A generalized package of programs called FASTER was obtained from IBM, thus avoiding much of the programming effort (and expense) such a system normally requires. Unit costs to create and key data, print cards and labels, and prepare items for delivery were estimate at $2. 50 per item, based on an estimated 100,000 items to be processed in 1971. In 1972 the cost of cards and labels was calculated at $2.25 per item, or $2.53 if the various listings, reports and other printed products were included. The development of the system write that " the librarians are satisfied that direct access to master library disk files is an efficient, accurate, and economical method of creating and updating bibliographic can holdings information. The public schools of Oregon were also early user of an on-line system using the same terminals. A large, generalized computer system located in Eugene was already available. This systems, called OTIS (for Oregon Total Information System), utilized an IBM 360 Model 50 computer with 77 keyboard terminals located in various buildings around the state. Three of these terminals were placed in the Springfield School District's Library Processing Center, and approximately 43, 000 titles, representing the complete holding of the district's libraries, were then entered and edited on-line. 4 By 1971 catalogue cards were being supplied for several other libraries. University systems also began to be implemented in 1971. At Northwestern University, 2470s were connected to a small IBM 370 Model 135 computer in the Administrative Data Processing Center. The system as implemented is a "total " system in what it provides information or titles in process as well as those cataloged, plus bibliographic and holdings information for approximately 35,000 serial titles.

The machine-readable files were originally on a data cell (a large and relatively inexpensive form of computer storage), but when this became operationally inconvenient the records were transferred to portable disk packs. Lack of tape drives in the Data Processing Center created another inconvenience, necessitating; tape drives were later added for this reason. The most serious equipment limitation, however, was the "display" rate of the typewriter terminals which is only 14 characters per second, "far from ideal when long bibliographic records are involved." This difficulty in communication has been the chief reason for the use in later on-line systems of cathode-ray tube terminals with their much faster and often almost instantaneous response. Georgia Tech, whose work on other methods of catalogue card and book catalogue production was noted in earlier chapters, began inputting data in 1971 with Model 33ASR teletype terminals on line to their Univac 1108, 8 and the University of Toronto began the same Year, using Model 1 KSR37 teletype terminals on line to a Xerox Sigma 7 computer. The toronto teletypes were modified to include a large number of characters—seven more, in fact, than the MARC character set. The toronto system also uses a

Xerox Graphic Printer which provides upper and lower case type fonts and various type sizes, thus allowing more characters to be placed on a single card and reducing the number of second (continuation) cards needed. Several hundred thousand records have been input at Toronto using the on-line system, and another 700,000 by a separate keypunch activity. Commendably, the university offers the services of the system to other libraries in the area.

OCLC

The largest best know and most influential cataloguing system the Ohio College Library Center in Columbus, Ohio, know universally as OCLC—also began its on-line operations in 1971. Perhaps no other system has had as much effect on library practice in this country; indeed, if the development of MARC is the most significant accomplishment to date library automation the development and operation of the Ohio College Library Center is probably the second most significant. This is not primarily because of the technological expertise employed in the development of the system (although that is great) but because it is the largest and most efficient shared cataloguing system yet implemented. OCLC produces catalogue cards economically, as do many of the other systems already described, but its important lies in the fact that it provides a common cataloguing data base for searching and consolation by almost 350 libraries. The margin of savings achievable by any system of catalogue card production is small in relation to the total budget of most libraries, but the cost of performing the intellectual task of original cataloguing is much larger; the OCLC system provides significant savings because both MARC records and the cataloguing records prepared by all member libraries can be displayed of the terminal screens in any one member's library, thus obviating the need for any library but the first to catalogue it. Catalogue cards can then be ordered from Columbus and arrive in a few days, formatted to a member library's specifications and arranged in rough filing sequence.

The Center was founded by the Ohio College Association in 1967 with over fifty members "to operate a computerized, regional library center to serve the academic libraries of Ohio". 10 From the beginning, it was agreed that records compatible with the MARC II format would be used in the Center's cataloguing system so that the Center could play a part in any future national systems. By 1970, the first OCLC operation, an off-line card production system was functioning. Members submitted IBM punched cards containing the LC card umbers of books for which they wished catalogue cards, along with their own call numbers if they were unwilling to accept LC's and OCLC then ran these requests against the MARC II data base. If the titles were in MARC, catalogue cards were then produced on computers at Ohio State University using programs modified from the Yale project described earlier.

Two technical developments associated with this effort should be noted in particular. Visual display terminals were abundantly available by 1971, but most of them were unsatisfactory for library use; typically only uppercase characters could be displayed, and the number of characters that could be displayed at any one time on the screen was far too low. After beginning with Spiras LTE terminals the Center contracted for production of a visual display terminals specifically designed for the OCLC application, manufactured by Beehive Medical Electronics, Inc.. Called the "OCLC 100" the terminal has been enthusiastically received in those libraries employing it. The second development of interest is the designs of an efficient searching mechanism. OCLC files could be accessed from the beginning by a Library of

Congress card umber, but a method was also needed to allow searching by authors and titles. After some interesting experiments at OCLC and elsewhere, a search "key" technique was devised which requires the terminal operator to input only six characters: either the first three characters of the author and the first three letters of the first word of the title not an article and the first letter of the next three words. This technique and the programs written to accommodate it reportedly retrieve five or fewer titles 99 percent of the time or 80 percent of the member libraries; additional standardized procedures reduce the number of replies in the remaining one percent to less than eighteen with very few exceptions.

For many of these customer as for Ohio members, the economic justification for a participation in the system is more than the saving on cataloguing costs. As the price of library materials has risen, the need to share regional library resources has become increasingly urgent, and the OCLC system provides a convenient and effective means of doing so; precise statistics are difficult to come by, but it is clear that more and more participating libraries are using the OCLC system to find and request a copy of a book owned by another library, rather that to catalogue a copy already owned. Indeed, the implications of the system for resource sharing have often been felt to be as significant as the implications for savings in cataloguing costs.

One problem that plagued the old system may still be a problem with the new, although the library appears to be taking steps to avoid it. In the old system, the computer used was changed from a 360 Model 30 to a 40, then to a Model 50, then to a Model 65, and somewhat later to the present 370 Model 168, all with inevitable delays.

Significantly the new system is also designed so that

eventually it can support other user, whereas the old system supported only the University of Chicago library. Perhaps ironically, the part of the system that makes it accessible to multiple user is called CHASM, 28 symbolizing the wide gap between a single-library system and a cooperative one. Whether Chicago will bridge this chasm in time to attract users away from such established and growing cooperative projects as OCLC remains an important question.

Perhaps the most sophisticate technical processing system presently in operation is the system at Stanford University. Development of the system began in 1967, but its first portion operations did not occur until 1972, when the capability of searching the MARC data base and using it to produce catalogue cards become operational. A large IBM 360 Model 67 computer is used with a small PDP 11 computer as an intermediary and a number of Sanders 804 programmable display terminals. The searching capabilities of the system, developed for the most part under another program called SPIRES (for Stanford Physics Information Retrieval System) are its most impressive feature with many files and indexes on - line and numerous automatic promptings and suggestions from the computer to the terminal user as a search proceeds.

For cataloguing, the user consults one of eleven terminals located in a single area shared by Acquisitions and Cataloging, and following the instructions displayed progressively on the screen calls up the bibliographic information generate in the acquisition process, makes any necessary changes, and adds copy numbers and shelving locations symbols. The end of this process signals production of cataloguing products, including not only catalogue cards and necessary cross-references sequence, but also two kinds of labels, produced on an IBM 2741 terminal with a Se-Lin labeling device attached.

One label is for the spine, the other for the inside of the book in connection with circulation use.

If the record used in acquisitions was not derived from marc, the cataloguing department may also search the on-line BALLOTS/MARC files to see if a MARC record is now available. If so, the user may substitute the MARC record for the preliminary acquisition record and add information as needed. If no MARC record is available, original cataloguing does not necessarily have to be performed at this point, because the system is designed to continue searching for MARC records automatically, at least in categories for which MARC data are expected. If the system later finds a MARC record, the library is notified automatically; in one is found within a specified period of time (up to eight months), the search is terminated and original cataloguing is then performed.

In the event that no MARC record is found either on receipt of the item or after the automatic search period, the terminal presents a pretagged from to facilitate input. Editing of the input may be done directly on the terminal or a "catalog data sheet" which the cataloguing personnel use for making handwritten changes that clerical staff the enter via the terminals. The catalogue data sheet may appear redundant, but it has the advantages of providing a portable version of the proposed catalogue or other sources of information for checking. In this respect, the BALLOTS system has overcome a disadvantage noted for the OCLC system: the physical problem of checking information retrieved on a visual display terminal against information located elsewhere.

Foundation support for the project has been used solely for development and Stanford has paid the operating costs, so when the grant funds eventually disappear the operation of the systems presumably can continue. Nevertheless, certain operational aspects of the system are expensive, and Stanford shares with Chicago the danger of having a glorious white elephant on its hand unless these costs can be spread over a broader base—presumable by supporting the technical processing activities of other libraries as well. In Stanford's case, work along this line is well advanced. With a new grant from the Council on Library Resources of almost $350,000 an-nounced in early 1975. Stanford will alter the system's software to develop BALLOTS as a California library automation network, and in-cidentally enable it to handle all of the diacritics in the MARC character set. The California State Library has also arranged with Stanford to make BALLOTS available to seven public libraries as the first step toward a California Public Library Automation Network (PLAN). If these trials are successful, a West Coast net work of the OCLC type may emerge, with interesting and important consequences.

Commercial cataloguing systems

Commercial firms have also become interested in the possibilities of on-line systems. The System Development Corporation began development of a project called LISTS (for Library Information System Time-Sharing), which would allow libraries con-nected to the system to perform a variety of technical processing tasks, including not only production of catalogue cards but also printing of orders and acquisition reports, maintaining outstanding order and in-process files, and even circulation control. The system began in 1968 with seven libraries (two public and four academic, plus the SDC library) connected by ASR33 teletype terminals to a 360 Model 67 located at SDC headquarters in Santa Monica, California, but it has never been seriously marketed.

The Information Dynamics Corporation announced a service called BIBNET, which uses Datapoint 2200 or Hazeltine 2000 terminal connected via regular telephone lines (though Tymshare's TymNet service) to a computer owned by System Development Corporation. The Datapoint terminals have not only a keyboard and a cathode-ray tube but also a small computer memory and provision for insertion of two magnetic tape cassettes containing programs or data; in effect, therefore, they are minicomputers themselves. When a desired record or information is located by searching. It can be stored on one of the cassettes and them called up on the screen at a later time and edited without tying up expensive telephone lines. GE Terminet printer terminals are also available, with rated speeds of either 30 or 120 characters per second. The printers can be used for production of catalogue cards, or printing of proof sheets to be checked against an existing card catalogue.

Searching may be done by the LC card number the International Standard Book Number, by author, by title, or by use of a "Ruecking algorithm" (a code made up of several characters from the author and title, as in the OCLC system). In early 1975, company was still in the process of leading MARC record into the system, but brief "index" entries for many records were already available, providing the full author, titles and imprint, as well as LC card number and ISBN. If the full bibliographic record is desired, a key on the terminal can be depressed to ask personnel at IDC headquarters to search manually for the full record, convert it to machine-readable form, and send it back, several days later.

The New Mexico State Library has used the systems and a Hazeltine terminal to add holding codes for eighteen libraries in the state, and then search for locations on request from interlibrary loan librarians around the state. SDC's ORBIT program is used for the searching operation. The costs, in addition to the cost of the terminal and its installation, are $45 per hour, plus 20 cents per location added and 90 cents per location retrieved. All of the systems described above use on-line input and searching techniques in connection with the production of catalogue cards; one other large on-line system, however, has book catalogs as its final product instead. This is the New York Public Library system, perhaps the best and certainly the biggest book catalogue system, in existence at this time. NYPL is really two libraries in one-a large research library, and public library with eighty six branches—so two book catalogs are produce, each containing records added since February 1927. The catalogs are produced on a schedule of so-called "continuous re-accumulation". This means that in order to locate a particular tiles the user must consult only the cumulation for that portion of the alphabet, plus the cumulative supplement, plus the old card catalogue for entries prior to February 1972. 36 To reduce printing costs, all added entries are condensed, omitting "title page extension", publisher and bibliographic notes, "the assumption being that the user who is interested in such data will take the trouble to refer to the main entry."

Input to the system is off-line but three 2740 terminals are used for inquiry. An IBM 370 Model 145 computer is used for processing, and production of the book catalogue pages in done by an RCA Videocomp photocomposer. In 1972, the cost of production was about $100, 000 per year for 550 to 600 copies of the branch libraries catalog, and about $90,000 per year for 200 copies of the Research Libraries, catalog, of which about forty are sold. The costs of development for the system have been estimated at anywhere from $2 million to $4 million, and the annual computer bill is around $360,000; of this latter amount however approximately $200,000 is paid of by renting out time to private industry.

The project traces its origins to the work of a Columbia University doctoral candidate who found that at NYPL approximately 20 percent of its nine million cards showed substantial deterioration. This study led to a fuller report, which recommended that the library cease adding to the card catalogue cards for new titles using automated techniques. By 1968, plan had been developed for new card catalogs which would grow for five years and then be converted to book form; by 1969 however, the idea of using catalogue cards had been dropped, and a decision was reached to use book catalogues exclusively. The largest program in the system and its strong feature is its authority file control; a single machine-readable file includes all subjects, series titles, and names used in the system, and every new record is checked against this file before being entered in the system. This provides valuable assistance to the catalogers and avoids the problem of variant forms of entry, a problem that has plagued other similar systems, notably OCLC. This feature also makes it possible to change outdated terminology for new, readily and efficiently, both in catalogue headings and in the cross-reference structure.

Other products of the system include processing information lists, cataloguing work sheets and two shelflist cards for each book which are sent to the branches or divisions. Several other book catalogs, including one of the Dance Collection of the Research Library of the Performing Arts, have also been published.

At least two systems have been designed to produce both catalogue cards and book catalogs fro on-line input. The Western Kentucky University library in Bowling Green originally began its project as a means of reclassifying from Dewey to the Library of Congress classification. Ten IBM ATS (2741) terminals were installed in 1971 on-line to an IBM 360 Model 40 computer and temporary workers were used to enter data. The computer printed out proofsheets of the data daily, and these were then proofread and edited by catalogers, reinforced as needed by librarians from other parts of the library. Labels, pockets and book cards were produced of reprocessing of some 250,000 items, and both catalogue cards for a divided card catalogue and book catalogs were then printed. Since the reclassification project, catalogue cards and book catalogs continue to be produced on a regular basis.

The UCLA Biomedical Library's cataloguing application differs from most other in that it makes no attempt to use MARC records, and is designed to accommodate only "original" cataloging. The majority of the records acquired by the Biomedical Library are not available on MARC in any case, since the Library of Congress by policy avoids adding works in clinical medicine or other areas covered by its sister institution the National Library of Medicine. The cataloger for the Biomedical Library types information on a "cataloging coding sheet" which a clerk then rekeys on a terminal, the redundant keyboarding action apparently necessitated by the objection of the cataloger to using the terminal. The terminal itself is a Delta Data Systems device with a cassette section added; the information is recorded on the cassette, and periodically the computer reads the information from the cassette into disk storage. A prooflisting is printed periodically, and is used by the cataloger to make editing changes. Corrections are then input by the typist. Catalogue cards are produced once a week on a 360 Model 20, prearranged in filing sequence, and a list of new accessions is produced once a month. The same programs that arrange the cards are also used for the book catalogue, which is produced primarily or regional interlibrary loan purpose. A three years, $40,000 grant provided funds for development of the system, and operating costs are estimated at $1,000 per month.

A few libraries have taken what some regard as the ultimate step and devised systems that use on-line terminals not only for input and searching but also for regular conciliations of the catalogue file, thereby eliminating the use of catalogue cards and book catalogs altogether. Perhaps the first such system was the Experimental Library Management System (ELMS) at the IBM Advanced System development Division Library in Los Gatos, California, parts of which have been in operation since 1965. Catalogue information is input via IBM 2741 terminals and is consulted by both library staff and patrons using IBM 2260 display terminals. There are four of these—two in the processing area, one at the reference desk, and one in a carrel. Public use appears to be successful but since this is a small, specialized library it is difficult to estimate the problems that might result if the same techniques were used in a large research library. Before the on-line reference function was implemented, the system produced nine separate book catalogs or listings, and apparently this capability is still used. Spine labels and book pocket labels are produced.

On-line reference to machine-readable catalogue files was also the subject of much intensive study during Project Intrex at the Massachusetts Institute of Technology. Intrex was a multimillion dollar research project, which began in 1965 and was finally terminated in 1973. On idea that received much experimental study during the lie of the project was the concept an "augmented catalog", which would be consulted on-line and would contain not only the usual bibliographical information, but such additional data as the "author's purpose", the "level of approach", excerpts from the text, all except the author being what the project staff referred to as "content-indicating" fields. Main entry and publisher were deemed helpful only 9 percent of the time, and such fields as edition, place of publication, and physical dimension were ignored completely by the users. A variety of terminals was used, some of them designed by the project and some commercially available. Not surprisingly, those terminals with full screen displays were preferred to those that had only a typewriter for communication from the computer to the user. The other major effort of Project Intrex that is pertinent here was the attempt to store and retrieve, via on-line terminals, the full text of documents. Storage of the text was in microform, scanned and transmitted electrically, on demand, to the same terminals used for searching and other purposes.

9

Online Catalogues

The development of online catalogues, on the other hand, has not reached a comparable stage of maturity. There is no common agreement even about the major features or basic approach that should be provided, much less about how the major functions should be performed in relation to one another or how much and what types of information should be provided to the system user. Some OPACs stress simplicity of operation above all else, even if the resulting product is little more than an electronic card catalog. Others are highly sophisticated retrieval systems that allow the user and greater flexibility than is available through other from of the library catalog. This level of sophistication, however, is often achieved at expense of simplicity of operation. The sophisticated system may require catalogue users to master techniques to which they have had little or no previous exposure, either in the library or elsewhere. Most OPACs attempt to draw a balance between extremes, striving for simplicity of operation and, at the same time, attempting to provide benefits that are lacking in other forms of the library catalog. This compromise may be the prevailing philosophy in the design of OPACs, but there is a great deal of room for interpretation as to what constitutes the limits of "simplicity" of operation or "sophisticated" retrieval capabilities. Compounding this problem are very basis differences of opinion as to what library users need in a catalogue, and how sophisticated a system most people can handle effectively or even want to use. In mid-1983, Hildreth reported that OPACs were in use in more than 100 libraries in the United States. These and subsequent systems have evolved from several different directions and variety of sources. For example, of 34 OPACs described by Matthews in 1982, about half had been developed by libraries; the other half were developed commercially. OPACs developed by libraries generally are in use only at the originating institution, although an increasing number of libraries gave sold or leased their software to other libraries. Commercially developed systems are already in use in a substantial number of libraries.

Some OPACs in use today emerged from online circulation systems. Probably the best example of a long-standing library-developed OPAC with origins in an online circulation system is LCS at the Ohio State University. In the commercial area, all of the largest-and longest-established online circulation system vendors have developed OPAC modules, including such firms as CLSI, Data Phase, Geac and Universal Library Systems.

The evolution from circulation system into a system that incorporates a public-access component has been fairly common in the commercial area, but a number of OPACs developed by libraries were designed first and foremost as online catalogues, independent of circulation functions. The University of California's MELVYL system and the catalogue Access system of the Minnesota State University System Project for Automated Library Systems (MSUS/PALS) are two examples. Whichever component of a large-scale, in-house automated system is developed —circulation or OPAC—development of the other may follow. Some of the systems developed by libraries, such as VI designed by Virginia Polytechnic Institute, also incorporate function in addition to circulation and public access; acquisition capabilities are the most common, and some provide serials control capabilities. Locally designed OPACs are found in many types of libraries, although the most widespread development has occurred in the academic library. Some of the better known include systems developed by Ohio State, the University of California, Northwestern University, the Minnesota State University System, Virginia Polytechnic Institute. Dartmouth College, the Claremont Colleges, Washington State University and Pennsylvania State University OPACs have also been developed in medical libraries, such as systems at the National Library of Medicine (NLM), the Washington University School of Medicine in St. Louis, and the Beth Israel Hospital in Philadelphia. OPACs developed by public libraries have not been as numerous, although the Pikes Peak Library District in Colorado and the Dallas Public Library are examples of public libraries that have developed and currently use the own online catalogue systems. In addition to academic, medical, and public libraries, some smaller special libraries, especially in corporations, use locally developed online catalogues.

In the commercial field, the almost universal tendency has been to offer OPAC capabilities as only one of several system components, Earlier we noted various vendors initially offering online circulation systems; large-scale multipurpose systems with public-access modules are also available from a number of other commercial vendors, such as Advanced Library Concepts. Biblio-Techniques. Data Research Associates, Dynix, Easy Data, Electronic Memory, Inc., and OCLC. Carlyle, Inc., founded by some of the individuals involved with the development of the University of California's MELVYL system, was for a long time unique in the commercial sector in offering a large-scale system that is exclusively an OPAC, without capabilities for circulation or other applications. As more libraries can afford online catalogues, activity in the commercial marketplace it likely to density. New vendors will appear, and some of the existing ones will undoubtedly go out of business.

Online catalogues can be looked at from several perspectives. Many issues pertain to their design and use in libraries, ranging from the number of terminals required to service a given number of users, to the ergonomics of terminal placement, to the types and amount of information to be included in a catalog, as well as its arrangement on a screen display. But in examining any from of library catalog, online or other, the distinction between its implications for the internal operations of the library and its implications for library users must be kept in mind. Even though these two perspectives do act on one another in the creation and use of the final product, the distinction is important. The internal-operations perspective has to do primarily with the production and maintenance of a catalog; the library-user perspective has to do with the presentation and use of it.

The introduction of offline, computer-produced book and Computer Output Microform (COM) catalogues was a significant step in the evolution of the library catalog, but almost exclusively in terms of production and maintenance. Computer-produced, offline catalogues addressed many of the problems inherent in card catalogue production and maintenance, and many labor-intensive tasks that were fundamental to card catalogues were eliminated with the use of computers and machine-readable records. With offline computerized catalogues, only one unit entry record had to be created for each item; the computer expanded this record into as many individual catalogue entries as necessary and performed all alphabetization and filing tasks to maintain the catalog. It was also much easier, at least in theory, to change a major catalogue heading; the change could be made once and applied to all effected entries by the computer-quite a difference from manually typing a new heading onto each which a change applied.

However, as far ass the library user was concerned, the benefits of computer-generated offline catalogues were far less pronounced. The actual format of the catalogue certainly changed in some instances, but the basis content, and the basis avenues through which records in the catalogue could be found, rally did not. The principles used for access to entries in computer-generated book and COM catalogues mirrored those of the card catalog, and the information was often identical and sometimes even less in amount. From the users standpoint, computer-produced book catalogues were little more than card catalogues in bound volumes, and COM catalogues little more than card catalogues in a box. Given such frustrations as dealing with multiple parts of a catalogue issues in editions and supplements, and equipment breakdowns with COM catalogues, more advantages of computer-produced offline catalogues were not noticeable to the user and, at any rate, could often be overshadowed by the logistical difficulties in using them.

In contrast, many OPACs, represent a radical departure both from card catalogues and from offline computerized catalogues in their implications for the user. As describe later in this chapter, access to records can be enormously broadened in an online catalogue over what had typically been provided in other forms, but these benefits are accompanied by a new set of requirements and demands on the catalogue user. The relationship between user and online catalogue is fundamentally different from that in use of other catalogue forms. The online catalogue is interactive, not passive, and requires the user to engage in a dialogue quite uncharacteristic of card, book and COM catalogues.

Just to look into the catalogue requires new procedures on the part of the user. A search must be physically, not just mentally, initiated by typing onto a keyboard issuing a command through some other means. The system will respond according to the very specific action initiated by the user. In many instances, the user will then have to initiate further action based on the system's response, and so on back and forth until the user. arrives at the desired end of the search or otherwise terminates the dialogue. This interaction and the nature of system responses represent a significant departure for the user from simply thumbing through catalogue cards or pressing a button, turning a knob, or sliding a handle on a microfilm or microfiche reader.

The design of an online catalogue must take into account a quite different set of circumstances. Considerable diversity exists among users in their level of knowledge about library catalogues and in the extent to which they are familiar with the use of computerized systems. The library will usually have little or opportunity to balance its diversity though a planned program of controlled instruction and monitoring. Most people will not use the OPAC as part of everyday routine, and hence their knowledge and skills will not be constantly reinforced. An example of the well-placed emphasis in discussions of OPACs on users and their interaction with the catalogue is the series of studies sponsored by the Council on Library Resources (CLR) during the early 1980s, aimed at gaining a better understanding of what users want and need in online catalogues, their likes and dislikes, and the dynamics of their interaction with catalogues. Despite the vast array of differences among existing OPACs and lack of specific guidelines for development, at the base of these differences is a common goal: to design online catalogues that will allow the user maximum flexibility and yet will be easy to use. Investigations like those sponsored by CLR should help to establish a stronger foundation for realizing such a goal. Phrases such as "user friendly" have become almost meaningless because of their sometimes indiscriminate use to describe systems or features that commonsense observation show are 'anything but.' Yet the overuse, and ever misuse, of well-worn phrases does not negate the relevance of the concepts they represent. The degree to which OPACs are willingly accepted by library users will indeed depend in large part on just how user friendly these systems are.

Access to bibliographic records

The usefulness of different forms of library catalogues can be compared in a variety of ways. One of the most important criteria is simply the extent to which a catalogue fulfills its basic purposes. Although the purposes of the library catalogue are not case in stone and depend on one's perspective, one set of standards by which library catalogue functions have been measured throughout the twentieth century is the principles of Charles Ammi Cutter as noted in his Rules for a Dictionary Catalogue.

> Cutter enumerated three major "objects" of a library catalogue.
>
> A catalogue should allow someone to find book if its author, title, or topic is known.
>
> A catalogue should fulfill a gathering function, showing what a library owns by a given author, on a given subject or in a given type of literature.
>
> A catalogue should provide assistance in the change of a book, either as to its edition or its literary or topical character.

A fourth commonly recognized catalogue function, although not explicitly noted by Cutter, is collection, having to do with the arrangement and relationship of headings within the catalogue. Underlying most of these functions is the fundamental matter of access top bibliographic records in the catalog: the points of entry through which a record for an item may be found. Cutter's first object—the finding function—is the essential basis for access, nut the gathering and collocation functions also have to do with accessibility to records. The function least directly related to access is assistance in the choice of material, which has more to do with content of a bibliographic record than access to it. Whether Cutter's objects still provide the most viable criteria for defining the purposes of a library catalogue in an online era is debatable, and some have questioned the degree of completeness to which these objects have ever actually been realized in libraries. Cutter's principles stem from a time quite different from the 1980s. New factors—including but not limited to those of a technological nature—should not be disregarded in defining the purposes of a library catalog. Nevertheless, Cutter's principles serve as a point of departure in many decisions of online catalogues, and concerning access to bibliographic records they still provide a convenient framework for comparing online catalogues with one another and with other forms of the library catalog.

Access to bibliographic records in library catalogues has traditionally been marked by a high degree of rigidity, requiring considerable knowledge and exactitude on the part of the user. Generally, access is gained through four types of bibliographic elements: author, title, series, and subject. Multiple author and subject headings are assigned to an item as rules or judgment dictates, but the number is usually kept to a minimum. The terminology selected for headings is also tightly controlled, with the library usually trying to establish a one-to-one correspondence between headings and the persons, corporate bodies, or concepts they represent. These practices may be understandable from a practical point of view, but they do impose certain limits on accessibility to records. The user can indeed locate an item in the collection for which the author, title, or subject is known, but only under some rather inflexible conditions. To find a record under the title, the user must know the full and exact wording of the title—not some or most of the words, but all of the words, and in their correct order. For access by author, because of the pre-AACR practice of establishing full and singularly valid forms of names, it has not always been enough to know the from of an author's name as it appears on publications or by which the person is popularly known. It has been necessary for the user somehow to know the exact from of a person's or corporation's name as it has been established by the library, often on the basis of considerable research. Where there are discrepancies in name form, it has been up to the user to figure out the form selected by the library. Access by subject is even more problematic.

Singularly valid forms of headings are selected from among all possible equivalents, but because of the greater conceptual complexity involved, there is even greater likelihood in subject searching that discrepancies will arise between the terminology selected by the library and the vocabulary chosen by the user. The problem is further compounded by the general conservatism in libraries toward changing the vocabulary used in headings and by complicated subject heading formation and filling sequences.

Such practices, which result in a lack of flexibility, are all but dictated by necessity in card catalogues; however, they were also carried over generally intact to offline versions of computerized catalogues as well.

Given the capabilities of computers and the elimination of the need for manual filing, there is no strictly technological reason for some of these practices to have been retained so uniformly. Additional access points, such as by keywords appearing anywhere in titles or assigned subject headings, could have been provided with little or no appreciable increase in human labor. Similarly, duplicate listings under variant forms of names could have been supplied in the catalogue. These expansions would have required greater sophistication in indexing and would have resulted in a far greater number of entries, and thus larger catalogues, but whether for economic reasons, ties to tradition, or something else, expansions of this type were never characteristic of offline computerized catalogues. Only with the introduction of online catalogues have such expansions taken firm hold, and they are changing the very concept of access to records in the library catalogue.

Some OPACs adhere quite closely to other forms of the catalogue in the ways in which access to records may be gained, requiring just as much exactitude and exhibiting just as little flexibility. These are essentially electronic card catalogues. Other OPACs significantly broaden, and even fundamentally change, the traditional concept of access. An over few of several techniques by which this is accomplished is presented in the following pages.

Keywords searching

One technique that many OPACs use to allow greater flexibility of access to records in the catalogue is keyword, or term, searching. This feature enables a user to retrieve records on the basis of single terms or combinations of terms appearing anywhere within specified fields of a bibliographic record, such as author, title or subject heading. In finding an item by title, for example, a user can retrieve a record simply by entering one or more words in the title, regardless of sequence or position. A user can find a record for The Peoples of the Soviet Far East, for instance, by entering the title-search terms "Soviet," "East," and "Peoples." The record can also be retrieved simply by entering the term "People," or any other single term or combination of terms in the title. A number of OPACs also allow keyword searching on author fields and on fields containing assigned subject headings, and some permit retrieval on the basis of terms appearing within a variety of other bibliographic fields.

Keyword searching has certain advantages over the exact order full-phrase searching required in other forms of the library catalogue. In corporate author searches, the keyword capability means that the user does not have to know the exact hierarchy and order in which a corporate author name appears in the records. For title searches, the user does not have to know the full and exact wording of the title to be able to find it in the catalogue. A key work search capability expands, and actually alters, the traditional concept of locating an item for which, in Cutter's terms, "the author or title is known." In searches for single title or single names, although the entry of selected keyword is certainly less precise than a full title or authors, name and can rest in retrieving extraneous records, among those retrieved will be the desired items.

Keyword capabilities are particularly useful in subject searching. When a catalogue permits retrieval of terms appearing anywhere within assigned subject headings, the user does not have to know the full and precise working and filing sequences of assigned subject headings and subdivisions as they appear in the records themselves. Many OPACs allow a broadened view of the subject elements in a bibliographic record; for instance, by allowing keyword searching on title fields. Given the usually high level of correlation between the subject content of works and the terms appearing in their titles, a keyword title search composed of one or two terms can be a viable from of subject searching in online catalogues. Some OPACs, in fact, automatically retrieve from title fields when subject searches are initiated. When the user carries out a subject search, records are retrieved for items in which the search terms appear either in assigned subject headings or in the title field of a record. Whether or not this combination is provided automatically by the system, the ability to search assigned subject headings by keyword, supplemented with term searching on other fields of the bibliographic record, makes subject access generally far more expensive in and OPAC than in other forms of the library catalogue.

Some OPACs allow a use to truncate, or abbreviate, search terms. For example, many online catalogues allow retrieval of records with an author's surname and first initial. Even though the full forename may be stored on the bibliographic records, the use of an initial is sufficient for retrieval.

In addition to truncation or even omission of forenames and middle names, some OPACs permit retrieval on truncated forms of surnames. Others allow truncation of keywords in titles and assigned subject headings. Entry of the term "prehist" in a title search, for example, will retrieve records containing the terms "prehist" in a title search, for example, will retrieve records containing the terms "prehistoric," "prehistory," or any other derivative in the title. This facility often applies to phrase as well, especially in the case of searching on assigned subject heading fields. Entry of the phrase "Moving Pictures," for example, will retrieve records assigned subject headings "Moving Pictures, Talking," or "Moving Picture—History," and so on.

In a search on assigned subject headings, truncation on most OPACs requires an explicit expression by the user. A special character must be keyed to indicated that a term or phrase is being entered in truncated rather than in complete form. In title searches, some OPACs require the user to supply a special truncation designator; others provide an implicit form of truncation whereby the system automatically truncates a search term or phrase for retrieval according to an internally prescribed number of characters or words, regardless of how many the user has entered. By either means, the net effect of truncation is to broaden the set of records retrieved over what a possible in a search requiring complete and exact terms or phrases.

Boolean operators

Most OPACs allow the user to combine two or more search terms through the use of Boolean operators, such as "and," "or," and "not." In most OPACs, a Boolean "and" is assumed when two or more terms are entered in a search statement, especially if the search is conducted of a single field or type of information such as author, title, or subject. Only records containing all specified search terms will be returned. In the earlier example of entering the terms "Soviet," "East," and "Peoples" in a title search, one records for works containing all three works in the title would be retrieved.

Some OPACs allow the combination of terms from different fields or serving different functions, such as an author's surname and a title word, in which case the user is generally required to enter a economic code preceding each term indicating the field or function to which it applies and then linking the terms with an explicitly stated "and." OPACs with fuller Boolean capabilities allow the user to construct search statements with other operators as well as the most common being "or" and "not." Depending on which operator is used, the result of Boolean search capabilities is to allow a user to other broaden or narrow the set of records retrieved.

Capabilities such as keyword searching expand access to records through traditional avenues like author, title, and subject. Some OPACs index other fields of bibliographic description as well. In a few OPACs, virtually every tern in every field of a bibliographic record are replaced by an all-encompassing concept of access by "bibliographic description" the more specific elements of author, title, and subject headings become simply qualifiers for refining the scope of a search. OPACs generally have not taken quite this broad an approach, although some have indexed certain additional elements, such as names of publishers, for retrieval on tern searches that act upon several different fields simultaneously.

A number of OPACs offer a more restricted idea of nontraditional access points in the from of bibliographic qualifiers that the user can employ to limit the results of a search. The two most common are language and data of publication. By including a language code or publication data or range of dates in a specified manner as part of a search statement, a user can block the retrieval of records for items that would otherwise qualify but are considered too old or too new to be useful or are in languages that the user does not read.

Other bibliographic elements could be incorporated into OPACs for purposes of qualifying search statements. The possibilities depend largely on the types of information discretely identified and consistently entered into records in the bibliographic database. For libraries with records in the MARC format, one likely source of qualifiers is from the elements constituting the fixed fields. Based on these elements, an OPAC could provide the ability to limit retrieval according to government publication, conference publication, fiction, juvenile literature, and a host of other categories. Few existing OPACs, however, currently offer a range of qualifiers beyond the elements of language ad data of publication.

In a somewhat different but not unrelated category, OPACs have attempted to address traditional limitations of access in library catalogues in the treatment of alternative forms of name headings and subject terminology. The most frequent method used by card and offline catalogues has been to provide cross-references guiding the user from variants in the form of a name or subject term to the authorized, library-established, heading under which full bibliographic entries are listed. As noted earlier, this technique is not altogether service-effective, since cross-reference cards can be "buried" within long lists of entries or complex headings.

Online catalogues generally fall into two categories in attempting to deal with likely alternatives in the terminology through which users might seek access. One technique essentially mirrors the approach commonly used in card catalogues, namely, by cross-references guiding the user to the authorized terminology. When an online cross-reference is displayed in response to a search, the user must then key in or otherwise instruct the system to search under the authorised term or phrase. Although this approach is similar to that used in most other forms of the library catalog, the presentation is usually more distinctive because the cross-reference message will be displayed prominently on a single screen instead of being buried among other information.

Other OPACs have taken a different approach with respect to cross-references by essentially dispensing with them from the user's point of view, using instead a recognition of equivalent terms as valid for retrieval. If the library has assigned "Women" and "Females" as equivalent subject terms in an online authority file, for example, the user will retrieve the same full listing of records in a search on assigned subject headings regardless of which of these two terms is entered in the search statement. This approach still requires the creation and use of an authority file, but the linking of terms is strictly internal and visible to the user.

Other features, such as the use of word proximity in term searching, have been incorporated into some OPACs father expand the accessibility to records in the catalog, but those described here are the most common, and they significantly broaden the ways in which library users can approach catalog. Now of these features is new to online information retrieval systems used in the library environment in general; they have been standard in such systems as DIALOG and BRS for many years. What is new is their incorporation into the public catalogue librarians have long assumed that systems such as DIALOG and BRS require special expertise and training for effective use. What is most challenging about OPACs is that at least some of these same sophisticated features are intended for people without formal training and with only limited need to use them. Taking these factors into account is perhaps the most crucial element in the successful design of online public-access catalogues and their implementation in the library environment.

Because they are interactive and can offer far broader approaches to access, OPACs are a fundamentally different from of catalogue than their predecessors. The overall difference can result in greater value for the library user, but not without costs in human terms. Interaction with computerized systems and the use of such techniques as keyword searching, truncation, Boolean combinations, and so on, involve skills that many users do not have, especially within the context of application in a library catalog. For many, lack of familiarity with computers and retrieval techniques extends well beyond use in an Online library catalog. There are still many library users for whom interaction with a compute for any purpose remains an alien experience. This situation is changing rapidly as more and more of the population become educated in computer use, but for some time to come, unfamiliarity is a condition that must be taken into account in the design of online catalogues.

User/System/Catalog Interaction

Using an OPAC requires the interaction of three primary participants: a library user, a computerized system, and a library catalog. With an OPAC as both a system and a catalog, the rules governing behavior can be fairly mechanically and consistently structured, even if at times they are complex. As an online computerized system, an OPAC incorporates certain rules that dictate how a user must enter commands and how the system will react to them. In the library catalogue function, certain aspects of interaction will be governed primarily by rules and conventions adopted by the library regarding descriptive cataloging, summation of subject content, and so on.

Rather than distinguishing between on OPAC as a library catalogue and as the mechanical means of conveyance, some discussions blend the two functions together. However, it is important to recognize such a distinction on at least a conceptual level, for each purpose has characteristics that can independently contribute to success or failure in using an OPAC. Some patrons may be well versed in the use of computerized systems and their retrieval techniques, but may be almost totally unfamiliar with the library's cataloguing and other bibliographic practices that do, in fact, influence the degree of success in using the system. Other patrons may have a fairly comprehensive understanding of the structure and organization of library catalogues, even in online form, but may be unskilled in the mechanics of using computerized systems and unfamiliar with retrieval techniques. Any advantages gained by introducing clarity, case of use, and greater flexibility at one of these levels can be offset by undue complexity or lack of clarity at the other. By taking advantage of the power of the computer, an OPAC can be more flexible than conventional catalogue forms, but it must be so in a way that allows these new methods to be easily learned and understood.

Although the rules that govern the behavior of an OPAC as a system and as a catalogue can be fairly mechanical and consistent, the rules that govern the behavior of the library user are not. First and always, "the library user" is an elusive entity. Human factors that influence online catalogue use, such as levels of knowledge, skill, and motivation, vary widely from one user to another, and even within the same user at different times. Complicating matters is the user's perception of how an OPAC works. It is one thing to say that an online system performs a certain way or that certain rules govern the structure and organization of a library catalog, but the more important consideration is the user's own perception about how the system works or how the catalogue is structured and organised.

The design features of an OPAC can either facilitate or inhibit interaction between user and system. As noted earlier libraries are not always able to provide the desired level of guidance and assistance when making as significant a change as introducing a sophisticated online public-access catalog. Therefore, an OPAC must be designed to minimize the need for offline guidance, taking on some of the instructional responsibilities and burden of assistance itself. An OPAC must be easy to use and its features easy to learn, and it must be a free as possible from retype language, confusing conventions, and complex rules that are meaningful only to the system. The term "user friendly" may be ambiguous and trite, but the concepts it represents are perhaps the most crucial criteria for evaluating systems designed to handle the interaction between a computer, a library catalogue, and a diverse group of library users.

OPACs vary in the extent to which each stage in this general sequence is explicitly necessary, especially in the earliest and latest steps—the begin-session, file-selection, and terminate-session procedures. Many OPACs do not require the user to instruct the system that a new search session is about to begin or to explicitly select the catalogue file. Instead, the OPAC is constantly set for a bibliographic search, enabling the user to begin searching immediately on arrival at the terminal. Similarly, many OPACs do not require the user to explicitly information system when a session is completed. The user terminates the session simply by walking away from the terminal, and the display remains on the screen until a new search statement is entered. Even when specific begin-session or end-session procedures are required or available, their execution is normally simple and straight forward. The real substance of interaction occurs between the time a user enters as search statement and the time at which he or she feels the search is completed. The end of a search may be the display of a single bibliographic record for an item, a list of abbreviated bibliographic records containing one or more of the desired items, or a response or display that leads the user to conclude that the item or items are not in the catalog.

The dialogue from entry of a search statement through final resolution may require any number of user-initiated actions and system responses. The more specific manner in which various OPACs handle the stages outlined above is examined in the next chapter. But in terms of the general nature of the user interface, it is important here to moment on two of the stages in particular. The first involves entry of a valid search statement and the initial system retrieval of appropriate records. In some OPACs, this stage consists of a single step by the user and a single response by the system. In other, there are two or more interactive steps involved. For example, the use may first be required to indicate the type of search being conducted—author, title, subject, whatever—to which the system responds by acknowledging the type and issuing instructions to enter search terms. The user then keys in the appropriate term or terms, and the system responds by providing first-level retrieval of all records in the database matching the two-step search statement. Some OPACs, depending on the complexity of the search statement, require even more that two interactive steps before the statement is complete and records are retrieved.

The second major stage of interaction involves the manipulation and refinement of the search results provided by the system at the first level of retrieval. If the search is satisfied at the first level, this will be unnecessary. In many cases, however, the search is not satisfied at first stage, and final resolution may require several steps in manipulating and refining the initial results. For example, a user may seek full bibliographic detail about a specific work, but can remember only one or two words in the title. If the words are very general, for example, "History" or "Education," a keyword title search will retrieve a large number of records at the first level. To identify the specific work and arrive at a full bibliographic display, the user may have to wade through a rather lengthy discourse worth the system.

These two crucial stages of interaction—entry of a search statement and manipulation and refinement of first-level results—are in fact, part of a continuum in interaction worth an online catalog. The distinction between them is made partly on the basis of convenience for purpose of discussion, but also partly on the basis of the crucial role that first-level retrieval plays in establishing the content for subsequent interaction.

These examples underscore the diversity among OPACs at this crucial stage of interaction. Whatever method is employed, the first level of retrieval is the starting point from which interaction between user and online catalogue will progress. For any of the stage of dialogue outlined previously, there are specific issues that have a direct bearing on the degree to which an OPAC can clarify and assist interaction between a user and the catalog. Some of these are examined in the next chapter. But underlying the specific issues are more general concerns that are pertinent to the user/system/catalog interactive process regardless of the stage at which interaction is occurring. Among the more important of these general concerns are the explicit features designed to assist the user in conducting dialogue with the system, the language and related conventions employed in OPACs, the nature of the progression of dialogue, and the extent to which a system accommodates different levels of users.

Earlier we divided the sequence of dialogue between a user and an OPAC into general stages. The length and complexity of dialogue can vary from one OPAC to another and from one search session to another on the same system, but a requirement of any OPAC is that the dialogue must be carried out according to a specific set of rules and within the range of options designed into the system itself. At least at this time, conversation with any OPAC is not entirely free-form. An OPAC will understand only certain instruction expressed in a prescribed way, and often only at certain points within the course of the dialogue. A command that is valid at one step in the dialogue may not be valid at another. Thus, the range of commands available, the manner in which they must be expressed, and the timing with which they may be used are all strictly defined by the system, For meaningful dialogue to occur, the burden of adjusting to all those limits is on the user. It is the user who must learn, understand, and confirm to the syntax and semantics of the system, not the other way around.

Despite occasional protests to the contrary by some OPAC designers, the rules of operation and conventions of dialogue are not self-evident in most OPACs. A user does not simply intuit the available commands or how and when they are to be entered. They must either be learned obviously presented to the user on a step-by-step basis during each search session. In response to these needs, OPAC designers have tried to build in various online mechanisms to assist a use in carrying out his or her portion of the dialogue. Some of these address short-term and very specific needs, informing the user at any particular moment in a dialogue about the options available at that point and how they mat be exercised. Others are more general or long term. The form in which, and the extent to which, such features are provided very tremendously among OPACs, but they can be grouped into six general catalogues :

1. General explanatory messages.
2. Search history: messages indicating what has been done at a previous step or steps during a search.
3. Options and prompts: messages indicating what options are available for the user's next action and how they may be exercised.
4. Error detection: messages displayed in response to an invalid command entered by the user.

5. HELP screens.

6. Online tutorials.

User assistance features do not always fall distinctly into one and only one of these categories. For example, a message explaining a user error might also outline the options available for the user's next action; a message in response to a valid command that outlines the options available at that point might also explain what was just done. More often than not, however, these different types of messages and the user-assistance features they signify are independently identifiable, even when two or more are represented on a single screen display.

Most OPACs provide messages outlining the general limits of using the system. Frequently, these messages are concentrated on an introductory screen displayed at the beginning of a search session. They commonly carry the following types of information:

Generally library data: name of library, hours the system is available and so on.

Files available on he system (library catalog, community calendar, and the like).

Scope of coverage of the bibliographic database.

List of commands or features that may be used during a search session.

Options available for searching (author, title, subject, etc.).

How to enter a search statement.

How to retrieve detailed online HELP screens.

Where to obtain offline assistance.

No existing OPAC can provide all of these types of information on a single screen display, and some types are less commonly included than others. A list of files available on the system, for example, is necessary only on multipurpose system in which the user must select the library catalogue file as opposed to some other. Although general explanatory messages are usually emphasised on introductory displays or outline in fuller detail on separate HELP screens, some may be included on displays at stages of the dialogue as well. This is most often in the form of message reminding the user of the major options available for searching, the procedures required to enter a new search statement, or the command required to retrieve a HELP screen either general in content or specific to the step that has been reached in the dialogue. An example of this type is shown in. Search history. Some OPACs can keep track and inform the user of dialogue that has occurred up through any given point in a search. Few, however, have this capability beyond repeating, as part of a system response, the single most recent command entered by the user; for an example,

A number of OPACs, in fact, do not even go so far as to repeat the most recent command; instead, they simply display a response without repeating the command or terms that led to that response. Not surprisingly this can lead to confusion, especially if the user has made an error in entering a search term. If the search term was not repeated as part of the system response, the user would probably surmise either that he or she misspelled the term or that the library did not own any materials by an author whose surname was Commoner. One cannot assume that the user would conclude the former over the latter. Even in OPACs that so repeat the user's previous command as part of the response, there is always the possibility that the user will not read the screen thoroughly enough to realise that a term was misspelled or that a command was entered inappropriately, nut such a feature at least attempts to give clearer explanations of system response to user commands.

Along with each response to a valid user command, some OPACs display messages that can assist in selecting and executing the next step in the dialogue. In some cases, these messages only inform the user of which options may be exercised at that point. In others, the actual procedures required to exercise each option are also explicitly stated. The types of messages that provide either or both levels of assistance generally fall into one of three major categories.

1. Questions prompting the user to answer yes or no.
2. Lists of alternative actions that can be taken at that point. Sometimes including how to exercise each.
3. Textual or other prompts that indicate where a command is to be entered.

Error detection. When unfamiliarity with computerized systems in general, and online catalogues in particular, is combined with the stringency of rules and conventions required for dialogue with an OPAC, one result is that there is bound to be a certain amount of miscommunication and misunderstanding between the user and the system. The ways in which a user contributes to a breakdown in dialogue vary in degree and kind. So do the ways in which the system responds.

In terms of system response, the primary distinction is whether the system can detect that the user has made a mistake. If not, the request will be processed as though correct; for instance, when a user simply misspells a search term. If the command itself was structured correctly, an OPAC cannot tell tat the search term was misspelled, and it will attempt to retrieve records and display a response oh the basis of the misspelled term.

For certain types of mistakes, however, the system may be able to recognize that the user has made an error. This usually occurs when a user has misspelled the command name itself (as opposed to just the search term), has tried to use a particular command at a point in the dialogue where it is not allowed, or has entered more search terms than are permitted in a single statement. These and other possibilities have common source: The user has made a request that the system recognizes as contradictory to the basis set of rules and conventions required for dialogue. The system does not full understand what the user is trying to do. It cannot process the request into normal fashion, but it can detect the fact that miscommunication has occurred.

The exact forms of system response under such circumstances vary, but they generally fall somewhere within the following four levels. The system

1. recognises that an error has been made and responds in a prescribed manner;
2. responds by including an explicit acknowledgment that an error had been detected;
3. attempts to explain why it considers the user's request to have been an error;
4. suggests what corrective action should be taken.

The relationship amount these levels is usually hierarchical. It would be possible, of course, for an OPAC to respond to an error only by suggesting corrective action, without explicitly stating that an error had been made and without any attempt to explain why the user's action was considered an error, but this is unusual. In practice, a response at one of the four levels almost always includes action or explanation pertinent not only to that level but also to each level preceding.

In general, assistance to online users in response to errors is not well developed in OPACs. A number of OPACs do not interact at even the second level of response. One OPAC, for example, merely displays the "begin-session" screen when an error is detected, regardless of the point to which the search has progressed, and without any explicit statement that an error has been made. Others respond simply by redisplaying whatever was on the screen at the time that the erroneous command was entered, again without explicit statement that an error has been made. Others respond simply by redisplaying whatever was on the screen at the time that the erroneous command was entered, again without explicit acknowledgment of an error or statement explaining why the system responded in that manner.

Most OPACs, however, do respond at least at the second level of error detection, displaying a new screen that includes an explicit statement noting an input error. Some stop at this level, with no further elaboration about why the command was in error or how it could be corrected, thus giving the user only minimal assistance. The language in which the acknowledgment is stated is often cryptic if not downright unsettling for an inexperienced user. Messages such as "Error Type 23" or "You have entered an Illegal Command" are likely to be discouraging two the novice, whose level of confidence in approaching the catalogue may not have been very high in the first place.

More and more, efforts are being made in OPAC design to provide error messages that are meaningful in content and positive in tone, explaining the nature of an error or indicating why the system is unable to process a command, and in some cases even suggesting what corrective action should be taken.

You have attempted to change the TYPRUN OPTION, whose value is fixed for your terminal and cannot be changed. The value of the TYPRUN OPTION for the terminals is "$TYPRUN."

The format requested was unclear. The command should be entered:

Format: D Set #/Format/Display Option

Example: D 1/LTTL/ABST

The first example does in a way attempt to explain why the system considers the user's command to be in error, but its content is about as comforting, and as useful, as an "Illegal Command" message. The second example has detected the nature of an error and has even shown the user how to format the command properly, nut the corrective action is still offered in summary OPAC language rather than being explained in easily understandable language. Regardless of the clarity and comprehensiveness with which OPAC massages explain errors detected by the system, there is still the question of miscommunication that is not automatically detectable. A user may enter a command or terms in a search statement that are perfectly valid from the system's point of view, but that do not really represent the action the user wishes to take. Because a system cannot provide information about, or suggest corrective action to, mistakes that it cannot detect, these sorts of errors are potentially the most damaging to a dialogue. Some techniques, such as repeating the user's command as part of the system response, can provide some help, but they still really solely on the user not the system to recognize the mistake.

A rather exceptional feature has been incorporated into the OPAC at the Washington University School of Medicine Library, which attempts to provide at least some level of error detection beyond the fundamental rules and convention required for dialogue. In the event that no records are retrieved on a search term, the system systematically modifies the user's term by omitting vowels, double consonants, and final's, and then searches the modified term against index terms that have been created similarly. The result is that, under certain conditions, appropriate records can be received even when a search term has been misspelled. This feature, while certainly not foolproof, goes one step further than most OPACs in attempting to incorporate greater tolerance of user errors into the system. No matter that sophisticated features are included, OPACs will not automatically detect all types of user mistakes, but this problem is certainly not unique to online forms of library catalogues. And, in fact, OPACs have a far greater capacity for recognizing user errors than do any other forms of the library catalogue.

Most POACs provided some degree of online assistance in the form of special HELP screen, which contain information describing various aspects of using the system. Their function is not unlike that sometimes provided on general "begin-session" displays or in informative error messages, but these screens are usually displayed in response to a specific, user-initiated request for aid.

The available number of HELP screen ranges from only one or a few on some OPACs, to 30 to 40 on others, to more than 150 on the University of California's MELVYL system. On OPACs that provide comparatively few, the instructional data are usually quite general and related to major stages of a dialogue. On POACs with a greater number of HELP screen, explanation is usually offered on several levels ranging from the very general to the more specific. The more specific levels of detail may provide guidance related to the use of particular commands, access points, or system features such as Boolean searching or truncation, and they sometimes pertain to specific points that have been reached in a dialogue. The HELP screen repeats the entered subject term and suggests possible reasons why no records were retrieved. If the user concludes that the first reason was the source of the problem, he or she might take the OPAC's advice and enter the command "s" to see a more complete explanation about subject searching for materials in the main library.

Of all existing OPACs, the MELVYL system on the University of California campuses has the most extensive array of HELP screens. Many pertain to specific circumstances and are most relevant after certain prints of progress in a dialogue. When requested in reaction to a system-supplied error message, the data on some HELP screens are somewhat diagnostic.

It is extremely important that, after display of either a user-requested HELP screen or a system-initiated error message, the point of progress in a dialogue is not lost. The user should be able either to return immediately to the point in the dialogue reached before a HELP screen or error message was displayed, or even to proceed from the HELP or error display directly to the next logical step. Although this capability is fairly common to OPACs, in some a request for HELP or a system-detected error will mean that the user has to begin the search all over again.

Probably the most elaborate from of online assistance that OPAC can offer is programmed tutorial instruction. Rather than begin problem-or situation-specific, an online tutorial is more a teaching facility than a "moment-of-need" reminder. Few existing OPACs currently provide a fully developed online instructional package. Although such a feature might be useful, it does presume two conditions. First, it implies that the rules and conventions required for dialogue are too complex, or at least not self-evident enough, for effective communication without formal instruction. Second, its value would ultimately depend on the inclination of users to take advantage of it. Both of those condition run counter to trends detected in most OPAC-use studies. Users generally prefer to be led through a dialogue on a step-by-step basis, getting point-of-progress assistance only when necessary. They do not want to spend a great deal of time and energy reading about how to use the system and memorizing rules and conventions. Some users might indeed welcome such features and would be glad to use them, but OPAC designers should never view online tutorials as a substitute for clarity and completeness provided as part of routine system response during interactive dialogue. Such a shifting of priories would ultimately detract from the overall suitability of an online catalog. An online tutorial can be of value, but only if intended as additional to, not in lieu of, other types of online user assistance.

Each of the system features already described can play a crucial role in determining the ease with which a user can carry out a dialogue with an online catalog. But merely incorporating any or all of these features into an OPAC does not ensure their usefulness. The manner in which they are presented in equally important, and one of the most critical elements in this is language; the terminology used to convey message, to prompt commands, to explain options, and so on. The difference between a feature itself and its mode of expression can be illustrated by an example cited earlier. An error message was displayed informing the user that he or she had attempted to change the TYPRUN OPTION, whose value was fixed and could not altered. The user probably had not the faintest idea of what a TYPRUN OPTION was, much less wanting to change it. From the message displayed, the user may have been able to surmise that the intended command had been entered incorrectly, but that conclusion was not part of the actual language used in the error message. That example may be extreme, but in fact most OPACs so use a great deal of specialized system and other jargon. Generally the language carries a certain degree of ambivalence in basis approach. There is a commitment to employ "natural-language" vocabulary, both expressed by the OPAC and required of the user, that as closely as possible resembles everyday conversational language. At the same time, there is also a strong and visible reliance on language that is not natural in any common conversational sense. It is, rather, "inside" language, specific either to the OPAC itself or in some cases to computerised systems or library catalogues in general. To understand inside language, the user must be familiar with it or clever enough to figure it out. In either case, at some point the user must learn new vocabulary that may have little or no application outside the specific context of the OPAC itself.

The specialised meanings of natural-language terminology in OPACs apply not only to "system" vocabulary, but also to the vocabulary of librarianship. Phrases such as "main entry," "copy number," "full bibliographic record," "Library of Congress Subject Heading," and many others displayed on OPACs all use fairly common terminology, but the way in which the words are combined probably not obvious to most users. Even such an innocuous term as "author" can cause confusion under some circumstances. In OPACs with the traditional distinctions of author, title, and subject for searching, for example, a user who wishes to see a list of books about rather than by an author must treat the author's name as a subject term rather than as the as the name of an author. This may be an easy distinction for librarians, but it may not be self-evident to all OPCA users. In judging the appropriateness of terminology for presentation in OPACs, librarians should not only be wary of vocabulary that seems somewhat "computers," but should take into account the effects of using their own jargon as well.

The language used in some OPACs draws appreciably on non alphabetic characters, both in the presentation of information and in the command structure used in dialogue. In searching an online catalogue users may have to treat certain characters differently from the method that is usual in searching other forms of library catalogues. Most online systems, for example, recognize some nonalphabetic characters, particularly numerals, as valid in themselves. Thus, in searching of the title 50 Houses of Charleston, South Carolina, users of some OPACs may have to enter the first word as 50, not fifty. This runs exactly counter to the standard procedure in searching in card catalogues.

Punctuation within search terms can be another problem, and some OPACs have strict rules governing its use. In dealing with words, phrases, or abbreviations such as O'Hara, Al-Hardalo, I/O, or I. W. W. as search terms, some OPACs retrieve records only when the punctuation within the term has been entered in the search statement exactly as it appears in the appropriate field of the machine-stored bibliographic record or records. This places something of a burden on the user; he or she may not know the exact punctuation, and is certainly unlikely to know how it appears in the record until the record is actually retrieved. In contrast, some OPACs do not allow any punctuation within search terms, even though the punctuation will be displayed on the retrieved records. Still others are flexible, retrieving records whether the user includes or omits the appropriate punctuation within search terms.

Some OPACs rely heavily on the use of punctuation to separate major elements of information in search statements and bibliographic displays. Users frequently must separate elements of a search statement—for example, the command name or functional qualified from the actual search terms—by some form of punctuation, most commonly a diagonal slash (/) or equals sign (=). In OPACs that permit Boolean searching, special provisions —sometimes in the form of punctuation—must be made for the user to differentiate between the function of certain words as Boolean operators and as normal search term, he or she must place quotation marks around the world in the search statement.

In some OPACs, forms of punctuation are used to separate elements in bibliographic displays. In one OPAC, for example, imprint data are enclosed between a less-than sign (<) and a greater-than sign (>), and subject heading are separated by a diagonal slash followed by a number sign (/#). Although this practice tends to clutter the display with nondescriptive characters when used in excess, this use of punctuation does separate desecrate pieces of information and is not really a problem unless the user infers that the characters signify something more than simply demarcation.

Most OPACs attempt to use natural, easy-to-understand language in explanatory messages, descriptions of options, bibliographic displays, and so on, but they have not broken entirely free of cryptic codes, computers and technical library jargon. In fact, it is doubtful that they could, or should even try to, free themselves entirely of specialized language. Terms such as enter, entry, exit, record, index, and so on, will always have different meaning in that context asks no more of catalogue users than might be required when applying the terms in other contexts. Clear and understandable language should be part of the pursuit of user-friendly

OPACs, but individuals will always have to learn certain precise meanings to carry on dialogue with an OPAC. This is not to say that OPAC languages should not be refined; on the contrary, there is still a great deal of room for improvement. The language used in OPACs must be balanced between the need for precision in a specialized context on the one hand, and the case with which it can be learned, understood, and applied on the other.

Many of the features already described relate to the clarity with which an OPAC can assist a user in progressing from one point in a dialogue to another. A related but some what broader question concerns the ease and speed with which a user may move around among various points or change the direction of a dialogue.

In general, OPACs impose fairly stringent limitations on the number of directions that a dialogue may take from a given point. At any juncture, the user will usually have two or more immediate options, but these will not necessarily include all the options that a user might see as the next logical step for his or her own purposes. The user will always be able to move the dialogue to a point where that desired option may be exercised, but it may require several separate steps to do so. For instance, an OPAC may contain the holdings of several different libraries. A user may complete an author search in one library's catalog, but find no records under the author's name. If the user wishes to search the same author in one of the library's catalogues, several steps might be required just to get to the point where the same name can be searched in the other catalogue.

The speed and case with which an OPAC allows a user to mover in various directions during a dialogue are dictated by design. In the example just given, greater complexity in progression is caused in part by the fact that the OPAC is multi-institutional, containing the catalogues of several different libraries. In a multi-institutional, containing the catalogues of several different libraries. In a multi-institutional OPAC in which so many steps are required to execute the same search in different libraries' catalogues, design assumption would have to had been made that a user was much more likely on want to search a single library's catalogue for different items than different libraries' catalogues for the same item.

But even in OPACs where dialogue does not have to take into account such factors as switching from one library's catalogue to another's, the progression through which dialogue must occur is usually rather inflexible and often requires several steps if the user wishes to change directions or otherwise exercise an option that is not immediately available at a given point of progress. One of the more common circumstances is when a user has begun or completed one search and decides to begin a new one. In a number of OPACs, three separate steps are required to enter the new search statement under these circumstances. First, the user must return to the main menu. He or she must then select the type of search desired: author, title, subject, and so on. When the OPAC acknowledges this second step, the user enters the search term or terms, the third step.

The limitation of options at any given juncture in a dialogue and the segmenting of dialogue into separate and distinct steps can actually be quite helpful for novice OPAC users, minimising ambiguity and reducing the risk of a user's becoming overwhelmed and confused by a plethora of alternatives and different rules and conventions. Such actions emphasize simple and logical progression, proceeding one step at a time. For users who have little or no experience with computerized retrieval systems, who are unfamiliar with library catalogues, or who have very straightforward needs, such an approach can help them understand what is happening and gain greater confidence and skill in the use of an OPAC.

For the user who has greater experience or more complex needs in using an online catalog, the degree to which an OPAC tends to segment the progression of a dialogue can be something of a nuisance. The necessity of carrying out two or three or even more interactive step to get to a logical nearby point in a dialogue can come to be seen as overly rigid, simplistic, and time consuming, leading to impatience and frustration on the part of the user.

Thus, OPAC design is faced with the formidable task of attempting to accommodate both novice and experienced users, and both simple and sophisticated needs. Some OPACs have tried to minimize this problem by building in at least a few optional capabilities that allow dialogue to be expedited, or more sophisticated features to be used, without compromising the availability of the simpler actions for those who are less experiences or who have less complex searching needs.

Among some of the features designed to expedite dialogue, one is allow the user to "stack" commands, that is, to enter two or more commands in a single statement. For example, in an OPAC that normally requires two separate steps to enter search terms in a combined author/title search—one to enter an author's name and the other to enter the title—there might also be an optional procedure that enables the user to construct a single search statement containing both elements.

Another example of stacking commands, this one pertaining to commands for displaying bibliographic records, van be drawn from the MSUS/PALS online catalog. Like many OPACs, MSUS/PALS can display individual records in several deferent formats, each containing a different amount and arrangement of information about the same item. Although there is a "default" from that normally displays, a user also has the option of requesting a longer, more detailed version. When a search statement has retrieved several records, the user can select any one of them to display in the default format by entering the command DI 3 for the third record in the set. When the default format display, the user can then enter another command to display the long version of the record. But there is also on option for these two steps to be combined in a single statement, DI 3 L, which will immediately display the third record in a set in its longer format.

Although stacking commands enables a user to expedite dialogue by combining two or more steps that may otherwise be carried out separately, there are other, usually less powerful features available in many OPACs that can also reduce the amount of time and effort required of the user. The most common is simply to allow a user to abbreviate some of the language required in entering commands. For example, one OPAC allows the command name FIND to be entered in either its complete from or abbreviated as F. A number of OPACs offer similar options; they do not really affect the course of progression, but they do give a user the opportunity to reduce the amount of keying effort required.

The realised and potential ways in which OPACs can accommodate both novice and experienced users, frequent and infrequent users, and simple and complex needs all at the same time are important, but greatly complicated by two additional factors. First, the user population does not include simply novice and experienced users, or simply frequent and infrequent users. The overwhelming majority of OPAC users are occasional users who defy the simplistic dichotomy of novice versus experienced in any matter pertaining to

OPAC use whether it is familiarity with computerized systems, knowledge about library catalogues, or the complexity of their needs. A second and related factor is that these limits cannot always be stated even with respect to a single user. Each user will have his or her own mix of expertise and levels of retention when it comes to specific features and rules and conventions, and one person's strengths can be another's weaknesses.

The complexity and nonuniformity of the library-user population pose a tremendous challenge in the development and refinement of online catalogues. It not a condition, however, that is unique of new to online versions of the library catalog. The same diversity influences catalogue uses whether one is dealing with card, COM, or online catalog. The latter certainly brings in new elements in the form of computer terminals, interactive dialogue, and the possibility of more flexible retrieval techniques, but it also provides the opportunity to introduce mechanisms that can at least begin to address the question of diversity by enabling a single catalogue to accommodate different levels of expertise, knowledge and need without prejudice award one group of users. Other forms of the library catalogue have never been about to make this claim. OPACs have only just begun to address this issue, and there is no way of knowing how far it will be possible or desirable to go in developing hierarchically structured features tat accommodate different levels of user need and even tale into account such matter as increasing familiarity on the part of individual users.

Assisting patrons and conducting formal instruction in the use of library catalogues are recognized functions of public service libraries. If carefully designed, the library catalogue in its online form can assume some of these responsibilities, but it is unlikely that online user-assistance features will ever altogether obviate the librarians' role in providing aid and instruction in the use of the catalog. As Anne Lipow has noted with regard to online catalogue use, "If there is a way to make a mistake, to misinterpret instructions, there will be a large number of users who find that way."

There is a growing and already sizable oral history of miscommunication between OPACs and their users. The range of incidents is itself staggering, nut two examples can illustrate a common type of misinterpretation and miscommunication. In describing online catalogue use in four different libraries, Carole Weiss Moore noted that a common experience was for users, realizing that they had made a spelling or other error before transmitting a command, to try to delete the command from the screen by depressing seemingly logical keys marked "Clear," "Erase," "Rub Out," and so on—the results were never those desired, and such attempts often threw a search into near total collapse. Lipow relates another experience at the University of California at Berkeley, also having to do with the use of the terminal keyboard: "I found a man the other day typing `return' because my catalogue instructs you to press return after keying your side of the transaction. He was indeed pressing R-E-T-U-R-N; he didn't realize there was a return key." Some such problem could perhaps be at least partially alleviated through better system design and more user-friendly equipment or instructions. Especially in the first case, it is difficult to fault novice users for depressing inappropriate keys when the language on them seems to express exactly the action that they want at their point. But there is only so far that care in design can be expected to go in solving the multitude of problems that some users experience with online catalogues. In the second example, the misinterpretation might have been avoided if an instruction had elaborately informed the user to "depress the blue RETURN" key located on the right-hand side of the keyboard" or some such statement. For each situation for which the more detailed message would add clarity, however, it would probably lead to confusion in another.

Especially given the contemporary environment into which online catalogues are being introduced, there will always be users, inexperienced with computerized retrieval systems or library catalogues or both, whose problems would not be avoided regardless of the clarity of instructions, the explicitness of error messages, or the number of HELP screens available. Explicitness and clarity of explanation should be guiding principles in the design of OPACs, but they are still not likely to eliminate the need for offline guidance materials and human assistance. If anything, the present state of OPAC design and the current environment in which online catalogues are being introduced argue for more, not less, offline assistance and formal instruction in the use of the library catalogue.

Index